Soviet dissent in historical perspective

SOVIET DISSENT IN HISTORICAL PERSPECTIVE

MARSHALL S. SHATZ

Associate Professor, Department of History,
University of Massachusetts, Boston

CAMBRIDGE UNIVERSITY PRESS

Cambridge
London   New York   New Rochelle
Melbourne   Sydney

Published by the Press Syndicate of the University of Cambridge
The Pitt Building, Trumpington Street, Cambridge CB2 1RP
32 East 57th Street, New York, NY 10022, USA
296 Beaconsfield Parade, Middle Park, Melbourne 3206, Australia

First published 1980

Printed in the United States of America

Library of Congress Cataloging in Publication Data
Shatz, Marshall.
Soviet dissent in historical perspective.
Bibliography: p.
1. Russia – Politics and government – 1953–
2. Dissidents – Russia.
3. Intellectuals – Russia.
I. Title.
DK274.S393   947.085   80–13318
ISBN 0 521 23172 8

To the memory of my mother

Contents

Preface

This book is intended primarily for the nonspecialist reader and for the student new to the study of Russian and Soviet affairs, although it is hoped that specialists will also find it useful. Therefore I have tried to keep the footnotes to a minimum, restricting them for the most part to works directly quoted, and I have limited the bibliography to those books most likely to be of value to the general reader. Where a work is available in English I have cited the translation. Whenever possible, however, I have gone back to the Russian text to check quotations, revising the translation as indicated.

In transliterating Russian names from the Cyrillic alphabet I have used a modified version of the Library of Congress system. When citing translations and quoting from them, however, I have preserved the transliteration they use. Prerevolutionary spelling has been modernized.

Whether, and to what degree, Russian first names should be Anglicized is largely a matter of taste. In general, I have Anglicized those names that have close English equivalents, as well as the names of rulers. Exceptions have been made in cases where an individual has become known in the West by a particular variant of his name (e.g., Leon rather than Leo or Lev Trotsky, Evgeny rather than Eugene Evtushenko).

The present work is the product of several years of research and teaching, and a number of people contributed to it in different ways and at different times. My debt to Professor Marc Raeff of Columbia University is large and of long standing. He was my guide as I first set out to explore the vast spaces of Russian history, and it was he who introduced me to the use of memoir literature as an historical source, which plays an important role in this book. As though that were not enough, he read the manuscript and suggested ways of improving it. Jean Highland of New York City contributed the warm support and the sound judgment of the expert editor that she is, and her advice was valuable.

It is one of the pleasures of the academic profession to be able to call on knowledgeable friends to read manuscripts that they have no time to read, and to be treated with more consideration than one deserves. Professor Jay Bergman of the University of Miami and Professor Rudolf Tökés of the University of Connecticut both responded generously to my request, and I benefited greatly from their special competence in the area of Soviet dissent.

Finally, I wish to thank my students, first at Brandeis University and then at the University of Massachusetts at Boston, to whom I have sounded out many of the themes contained in this book. Their responses and questions forced me to clarify many thoughts I had foolishly believed to be clear already, and their enthusiasm kept the subject constantly fresh and alive for me.

M. S. S.

Cambridge, Mass.

1

Introduction

[The peasants'] duty is to obey and to serve us by paying the quitrent levied upon them in proportion to their capabilities; ours is to defend them from every harm and, while serving Sovereign and fatherland, to fight for them in battle and die for their tranquillity.

A noble landowner in a Russian comic opera of 1777.[1]

In the years following the death of Stalin in 1953, the West began to witness a phenomenon long grown unfamiliar: Soviet citizens publicly expressing disagreement with the policies of their government. The rebirth of dissent in Russia astonished many observers.[2] Some believed that a hermetically sealed "totalitarianism," enforced by unrelenting terror, had eliminated for all time the expression of independent views. Others believed that the Soviet population had been intellectually lobotomized by decades of "thought control" and was no longer even capable of formulating independent views. As so often in the past, Russian history had confounded the expectations of outsiders.

This development has elicited not only surprise but a certain sense of historical déjà vu, for the forms in which contemporary dissent is cast often bear a close resemblance to the forms antitsarist protest assumed in the nineteenth century. Once again, an embattled little minority of intellectuals is determinedly resisting the power of a mighty state; the hallowed tradition of literature as an instrument of dissent has been resurrected; lives are being shattered by prison, exile, and emigration. Even such specific government responses as the detention of dissidents in lunatic asylums have their historical precedents, for this approach to nonconformist thought was foreshadowed as far back as the 1830s by Nicholas I's treatment of Peter Chaadaev. With justification, many parallels have been

1

drawn between dissent in tsarist times and in the post-Stalin period. Yet, no detailed investigation of those parallels has been undertaken, and no systematic attempt has been made to place contemporary dissent in the larger context of modern Russian history as a whole. Several narrative accounts of the dissidents' activities are now available in English, and it is not my intention to repeat them. The major purpose of this book is, first of all, to reveal the underlying dynamics of those activities by viewing them in the light of historical perspective. Soviet dissent is a product not only of the immediate pressures of contemporary circumstances but of long-term historical forces, and only by tracing its roots deep into the Russian past can we fully understand its genesis and development.

Historical perspective can be particularly illuminating in regard to events that are still going on around us. With Soviet dissent the subject of newspaper headlines almost every day, we find ourselves too close to events, too much a part of them, to evaluate them properly. We cannot always tell which individuals or ideas or instances of behavior are of lasting significance and which will prove to be ephemeral. We cannot know whether a particular event is a crucial turning point or a passing occurrence. Enterprising journalists can keep us abreast of day-to-day developments, but they are unable to probe deeply enough into their underlying sources. We see only the tip of the iceberg; its true contours and dimensions remain hidden and its future course unclear.

What can help is the unique time perspective that the historian can supply. While the story of contemporary dissent remains unfinished and its literature fragmentary, the origins and development of dissent in tsarist Russia have been well studied. The literature it produced is ample, and the generous segment of time it occupied enables us to see what was significant, typical, or recurrent in its history. If we can show that post-Stalin dissent has closely similar origins, then we can profitably bring the findings of the past to bear on the present, using the patterns historical research has uncovered to help explain what is happening today. Obviously, the parallels will not be exact, and we must be as sensitive to the changes in historical circumstances that have conditioned contemporary dissent as to the continuities with the past. It is not the function of the historian to demonstrate that there is nothing new under the sun – our source of heat and light may be fixed and unchanging, but the world itself is constantly in motion as it traces its path around it. But the historian is equipped to pick out long-term configurations of human behavior in a changing society, and thus to add an historical dimension to our understanding of contemporary events.

The second major purpose of this book is to trace the psychological and sociological origins of dissent in Russia, as revealed in the historical perspective described above. I have not attempted a comprehensive survey of dissent in Russian history, nor have I focused primarily on its political or intellectual development. The question I have asked is why particular individuals have become dissidents: what kinds of people are they, what sort of background do they come from, what impels them along such a stony path? For this purpose the most important and revealing kinds of material are not programmatic or philosophical statements but more personal sources, particularly memoirs and fiction. It is in these works that Russia's dissidents have most directly revealed their feelings, motivations, and aspirations. The book undertakes a fresh examination of a number of significant and representative works of this sort, some of them familiar, others less so, in order to uncover recurrent patterns of individual and group experience in past and present alike. Obviously, because Russian dissidents have translated their experiences into ideas and programs these must be discussed, but I have treated them in relatively broad, general terms. Close analysis of those ideas and programs has been the traditional approach to the history of Russian dissent, and the ground has been well tilled. The emphasis here is on the personal sources rather than the ideological or political manifestations.

History is often compared to a vast colorful tapestry, a dense texture of interwoven elements that have formed the past and continue to shape the present. But if we stand too close to a tapestry all we can see are the separate threads of which it is woven. To distinguish the patterns in its composition, the way its lines and shapes and colors come together to form a coherent design, we have to step back and view it from a broader vantage point. Only then does the picture as a whole as well as the role of its individual elements become clear. That is what I hope to accomplish here by viewing the rise of Soviet dissent in historical perspective.

Most Western readers would agree that the outstanding characteristic of Russian writings critical of the tsarist regime, particularly fictional writings, is their burning moral intensity. The best of them still seem to glow with an incandescent moral anguish and sincerity that time has not extinguished. Who could fail to be moved by such heartfelt outcries against oppression and injustice, voiced in such a vivid and compelling manner? Yet, the message most of these writings convey is that all of Russia's afflictions stemmed solely from selfishness, ignorance, stupidity, or a repellent mixture of all three. If only the wicked oppressors were chased out, the wrongs they had inflicted on the Russian people could be righted. To be sure, the Russian political and social system has never been lacking in self-ishness, ignorance, or stupidity, not to mention instances of outright bar-barism. But the system's critics, precisely because of their passionate moral engagement, usually failed to take up the concrete historical conditions that had given rise to Russia's institutions – that, after all, was not their pur-pose. Brutal and inefficient as they have often been, the country's political and social practices developed over the centuries in response to specific historical circumstances in which Russia found itself. Only if we under-stand how and why those practices arose can we fully evaluate the criticism of them that began to appear in the late eighteenth century and the gov-ernment's response to the critics.

For more than two centuries, the twin pillars of the Russian institutional structure were autocracy and serfdom. Until the emancipation of the serfs in 1861 these institutions made Russia unique among the major countries of Europe. Other states in central and eastern Europe displayed elements of one or both of these institutions, but only in Russia were they so fully developed and virtually unchecked.

Autocracy means literally "self-rule." Originally, the term autocrat in Russian usage seems to have referred to a fully independent ruler, one who was sovereign in his own right and not someone else's subordinate or vassal. Soon, however, the term acquired the more familiar connotation of a ruler with unlimited power over his own subjects. In this sense, Russian rulers of the eighteenth century were autocrats in full measure. No legal or institu-tional forces restricted their powers: there were no estates or parliament vested with traditional rights; there was no tradition of law as something above the person of the sovereign, nor was there an independent judiciary to interpret the laws that existed; even the Orthodox Church was fully subser-vient to the monarchy. The tsar, or emperor as he was now called, was the sole law-making authority and could change or violate his own laws at will.[3]

The only effective curbs on autocracy – aside from assassination, which removed several Russian rulers in the eighteenth century – were of a purely practical nature. For one thing, the mechanism of government was very cumbersome and many of its officials corrupt or incompetent. As a result, the monarch's orders could be impeded, improperly executed, or not carried out at all, sinking quietly beneath the sea of bureaucratic paper. Through-out the eighteenth and nineteenth centuries, Russian monarchs made numerous attempts to reform the government apparatus, not for the purpose of limiting the prerogatives of autocracy or sharing its powers but in order to make autocracy more effective by streamlining its operations. A second factor that diluted the autocrat's power was geography, the vast distances over which the Russian government operated, or aspired to operate. In the days before the telegraph, telephone, or airplane it might take weeks for a government courier to bring the tsar's orders from the capital to the outlying provinces of the empire. With the transfer of Russia's capital from Moscow to St. Petersburg at the beginning of the eighteenth century, the seat of government was now some 7,000 or 8,000 miles from the most distant corners of the realm. As a result, officials in remote areas were often able to assert an independent authority that the central government found difficult to control or supervise. Except for these practical restraints, however, the autocracy held a monopoly on political and legal power.

Many of the distinctive features of autocracy replicated themselves in the institution of serfdom. The serf estate was in many ways a microcosmic version of the autocracy. In theory and in law, the serf was attached to the land he tilled and was not the personal property of the landowner. In practice, however, it was fairly easy to evade this restriction and to treat the serf as a slave. Serfs could be removed from the land and turned into house servants of their master; they could be bought and sold as merchandise, without their land; and their persons and property were at the full disposal of their owner. Aside from murder or flight, the serf had little recourse against mistreatment. As long as the serf population paid its taxes and delivered its quota of recruits to the army – and the master was in charge of collecting both items – the state and the law generally refrained from interfering in master–serf relations and the landowner's authority went virtually unchallenged. Again, as was the case with autocracy, practical considerations often tempered the exercise of that authority: most landlords had little interest in ruining the serfs who provided their income or in seriously disrupting their work and way of life. In addition, bonds of personal loyalty and affection often mitigated the harsher aspects of master–serf-relations. The chief problem with both serfdom and autocracy was not that they invariably ground the individual down with daily acts of oppression and injustice, but that the two institutions were inherently arbitrary. They had the power to disrupt an individual's life unpredictably, at any moment. They did not always choose to do so, but when they did the individual had no reliable means of defense against them.

Russia's autocratic system of government was the product of a number of historical pressures. One of the most important was the Mongol (or Tatar) conquest and domination of Russia from the thirteenth to the fifteenth centuries. After the initial invasion, the rule of the Golden Horde, as the western branch of the Mongol Empire was called, was in fact relatively benign. On the whole, the Mongols interfered little in the Russians' life and gave them a considerable degree of social and cultural autonomy in return for the payment of tribute. Nonetheless, the Russians resented and feared the rule of an overlord alien to them by race, culture, and religion (the Golden Horde adopted Islam soon after the conquest of Russia), and always ready to send a punitive expedition to suppress any sign of independence. A centralized monarchy with the military strength to check the Mongols and ward off other predators seemed the best guarantee of Russia's security. Not only the people but the Orthodox Church, which had inherited the Byzantine tradition of support for a strong monarchy, looked to autocracy as the guardian of Russia's religious and cultural integrity. The Mongols themselves, while permitting Russia's native princes to continue ruling as vassals of the Golden Horde, found it convenient to promote the authority of the Grand Prince of Moscow over the local Russian princes. In doing so, they unwittingly contributed to the rise of a Russian state that would ultimately prove capable, in the latter fifteenth century, of overthrowing the domination of the Mongols themselves.

Thus the conditions of Mongol rule created a political and psychological climate favorable to the development of autocracy. The socioeconomic effects of the Mongol conquest led in the same direction. When the Mongols invaded Russia they leveled most of the towns, killing their artisans and craftsmen or drafting them for work in Mongol territories. At the same time, Mongol rule isolated most of Russia from the West and severely restricted its trade with Western Europe. More than ever before, Russia became an agricultural society whose social and economic life centered on the self-sufficient manorial estate. Russia never fully recovered from these circumstances, and as a result it never generated a strong, vigorous urban middle class comparable to the bourgeoisie that played such an important role in shaping the life of modern Western Europe. Russia's merchants remained culturally backward and politically and socially insignificant. Only on the eve of 1917 did a substantial business and professional middle class begin to emerge, only to be shattered by the Revolution and civil war.

Besides the invasion and long rule of the Mongols, a second set of conditions contributed to the rise of autocracy. These were the circumstances created by Russia's geography. The Russian population had settled in the western reaches of the vast flat plain that stretches virtually unbroken across Eurasia. Except for the limited protection that thick forests and a harsh climate could offer in the north, this exposed terrain presented no serious obstacles to a determined invader. Russia had no Alps, no English Channel, no Atlantic and Pacific oceans to guarantee its security. The Mongols were only one of the many external forces surrounding it to the east, west, and south, menacing its independence and its autonomous cultural development. Even after the power of the Golden Horde was broken, the several Tatar successor states (which were Moslem by religion) on Russia's eastern and southern borders continued to raid its settlements in search of booty and slaves; to the northwest were the Swedes and the Baltic Germans, two formidable military powers with whom Russia had a long series of encounters; and on the western frontier were the Poles and Lithuanians, contending with the Russians for control of the borderlands between them, and threatening Orthodox Russia with the possibility of Catholic domination.

The constant necessity of warding off all these threats (which were, of course, by no means always unprovoked, as Russia's own rulers, like those of its neighbors, nursed expansionist ambitions) induced something of a siege mentality in the Russians. The task of maintaining national self-preservation under these difficult geopolitical conditions reinforced the tendency to rely on a strong monarch capable of mustering effective military forces. A weaker, more limited ruler was a luxury most Russians would have felt they could not afford.

Geography had yet another effect. The Eurasian plain, devoid of effective natural barriers, invited not only external invasion but internal colonization. With little to impede their movement, the Russians spread out over the immense distances the Russian Empire was eventually to encompass. They colonized vast areas of wilderness or sparsely inhabited territory in much the same way that North America or Australia were colonized, the difference being that in this case the colonized areas were contiguous to the mother country rather than overseas. One of the consequences of this expansion was that Russia, by the sixteenth century, had become a multinational empire, as areas inhabited by diverse peoples and tribes were incorporated into the Russian state by colonization as well as by conquest. More relevant to our concerns was a second consequence: the population of the country, though large in absolute terms, remained thinly spread over a huge territory, and, in this harsh climate, was unable to produce much of an economic surplus. To mobilize and organize such a country's human and economic resources was a formidable task – yet it was an essential one if military security was to be assured. The result was that the state to a considerable degree resorted to coercion as the way to organize a society that seemed incapable of organizing itself but faced the threat of extinction otherwise. In this way, yet another set of circumstances reinforced the trend toward autocracy: the need for a strong, centralized political force capable of mobilizing the resources geography had scattered so widely, in order to ward off the dangers and potential dangers which that same geography invited.

Serfdom had its origins in the same conditions that generated autocracy. Serfdom was not a natural, spontaneous product of Russian social and economic development, although it had strong roots therein; as an institution, it had been legally established by the Russian government specifically to serve the state's military and financial needs. A series of decrees issued in the late sixteenth and early seventeenth centuries had the cumulative effect of binding the Russian peasants to the land they currently worked and abrogating the right they had hitherto enjoyed to move elsewhere at will. The state acted as it did in order to protect its military resources. Lacking the funds to support a standing army, the state paid its military men with landed estates from which they could draw their subsistence. Peasants formed the labor force of these estates, and if they abandoned them in search of greener pastures, the state's military servitors – especially the poorer ones – would be unable to support themselves in time of peace or to equip themselves when summoned to military duty. Therefore the state set out to fix the peasants to the land in order to secure the economic position of the military class. In the eighteenth century the relationship between state, nobility, and serfs altered considerably and removed much of the original justification for serfdom. In its origins, however, serfdom was a byproduct of the Russian state's persistent effort to place the country's sparse resources at its disposal for military purposes.

The dominant position of the autocratic monarchy remained one of the permanent features of modern Russia's historical development. To regard the autocracy merely as a source of repression and exploitation of its subjects, as its critics so often did, is to ignore its historical role and, indeed, the main reason for its persistence. For all its negative features, and these should not be minimized, it was also a dynamic and progressive force that took the initiative in promoting Russia's defense, expansion, and economic development. The Westernizing reforms of Peter the Great in the early eighteenth century; the emancipation of the serfs in 1861 (like their enserfment more than two centuries earlier); the rapid industrial expansion of the late nineteenth century – all were deliberate state policies designed to meet national needs as the state defined them. Stalin's decisions to collectivize Russian agriculture and embark on the prodigious industrial expansion of the 1930s must be viewed in the same light. These programs were despotic in their implementation and profligate of both men and materials, but they were also recognizably products of the Russian political tradition of state initiative, the origins of which stretched back to the fifteenth and sixteenth centuries. Hence such actions by the state had a considerable degree of legitimacy in the eyes of the Russian people, and this was doubtless part of the reason why, for all their cruelty, they ultimately prevailed.

Such a political tradition is fundamentally paternalistic. It is based on two assumptions: that the society is not capable of meeting the country's basic needs on its own initiative, so that the responsibility for determining and fulfilling those needs must be assumed by the state; and that the individuals who make up the society must be at the full disposal of the state in order for it to carry out its responsibilities. To some extent, this became a self-perpetuating relationship. The state took the lead because no group within society seemed strong enough or competent enough to provide the impetus for progress; then the state, jealous of the powers and prerogatives it had acquired, stifled the development of any social group that might have attempted to assume a share of the state's burden. Such groups were slow to arise, however, for society itself had grown accustomed to looking to the state for leadership. By and large, this arrangement worked effectively until the latter eighteenth century. It was only then that Russian society began to produce a small but growing number of individuals prepared psychologically and intellectually to question the autocratic system.

These individuals came from the Western-educated nobility. They began to challenge the paternalistic relationship between state and society on two grounds. First, they wished more of a voice for society itself, or at least its educated stratum, in discussing public issues and setting national priorities. Second, they began to insist that the state treat its individual subjects as ends in themselves and not merely as servants of state interests. These were the new attitudes at the root of the criticisms of autocracy and serfdom that began to be heard in Russia toward the end of Catherine the Great's reign.

Recognition of the changing nature and role of the educated elite in Russia is crucial to an understanding of the origins of dissent, because this is the segment of Russian society that has issued the most persistent challenges to the state's monopoly on political power since the late eighteenth century. Peasant revolts and workers' strikes, though they sometimes attained ominous proportions, were usually local and sporadic, flaring up unpredictably and unable to sustain themselves. Even the mass rebellion of 1917 could not have succeeded in destroying the old regime so quickly and effectively without the contribution of the educated members of the revolutionary parties. But this educated elite was in fact a product of the state's own handiwork. To accomplish the tasks of defending, modernizing, and developing the country, tasks to which the Russian state was consistently committed, an up-to-date educated elite, possessing the intellectual training and technical skills appropriate for modern life, was required. Because Russian society, culturally backward and traditionalistic, was incapable of generating such an elite spontaneously, the state set out to create one. Here we encounter yet another example of the tradition of state initiative: from the time of Peter the Great (and to some degree even earlier) to the present, the impetus for modern education in Russia has come from the state. It was the state that began to send Russians abroad for training in technical skills, and it was the state that subsequently built an extensive network of educational institutions as well as educational incentives in order to nurture an elite group capable of carrying out the tasks the state set for it.

This modern educated elite has presented its creator with one of its most intractable dilemmas. The dilemma arose when the state discovered that it could not keep the educated elite within the narrow intellectual boundaries it had set for it. First of all, even strictly technical training requires a certain amount of broad intellectual preparation and intellectural curiosity. Inevitably, some of the more thoughtful and sensitive educated individuals, newly equipped with the tools of inquiry, began delving into matters of public concern that the government insisted on reserving for its own judgment. Second, even professional and technical specialists require a certain amount of creative autonomy and self-expression in their work in order to carry it out properly. This in itself can bring them into conflict with a government which, through censorship, attempts to supervise and control intellectual activity along with all other aspects of national life. Third, and perhaps most important, the educated elite has to be given a certain degree of social and economic privilege. If their skills are in short supply, yet are essential for the country's development, educated individuals must be given both material incentives and social prestige in order to induce them to apply their talents. These very privileges, however, breed a sense of pride and self-esteem that leads them to resent the restrictions and arbitrary treatment they must sooner or later encounter at the hands of a paternalistic government.

From these circumstances comes the state's dilemma. It cannot simply take advantage of its monopoly on political power and crush the educated elite by brute force when it steps out of line without jeopardizing its own goals of modernization and material progress. Outspoken dissidents are usually only a small minority, but they must be handled carefully in order to avoid alienating, or panicking, the educated elite as a whole. At the same time, the state cannot grant too much intellectual autonomy and freedom of self-expression to the educated elite without eroding its own monopoly on political decision making – a monopoly which, from its paternalistic perspective, it regards as essential for the welfare of a backward and dependent society.

This is the dilemma that has confronted every Russian government from the eighteenth century to the present. It manifested itself, among other ways, in the curious pattern of reform and reaction that the imperial regime traced over and over in the latter eighteenth, nineteenth, and early twentieth centuries. Time and again, from Catherine the Great to Nicholas II, the Russian government embarked on a policy of liberalization designed to release the pent-up creative and productive energies of the nation; time and again it reversed course and withdrew or curtailed many of its own reforms when they showed signs of undermining the powers of the autocracy. The same cycle of reform and retrenchment marks the period since Stalin's death, when the criticism of the past unleashed by Khrushchev seemed to his successors to be calling into question the very foundations of the Soviet system.

It is the contention of this book that contemporary Soviet dissent, though it has its own unique characteristics, is the product of a pattern of development Russia has been following since the eighteenth century. The dynamics of dissent are generated by the evolving relationship between a paternalistic state imposing modernization on its subjects from above, and the educated elite on which it must rely to carry out the modernization process. While great differences distinguish the Soviet state and society of today from those of imperial times, the emergence of dissent since the death of Stalin must be viewed as the latest cycle in a recurrent pattern that has helped to shape Russian history since the age of Peter the Great. For a full understanding of this most recent cycle, we must go back to the very origins of the relationship between the state and the educated elite in modern Russia.

2

The genesis of the Russian intelligentsia

You kindled in our hearts the holy spark of love for truth, you instilled in us a feeling of proud dignity and freedom . . . Then, when we had ceased to be children, you grew estranged from us, as though you had become frightened of what you had done.

Letter of Michael Bakunin to his father, 1836.[1]

In a recent account of Soviet life in the 1970s, an American journalist drew attention to the lack of individual self-assertiveness he observed among Soviet citizens: "We sometimes speak of a person's 'sense of self.' This concept does not exist in the Russian language."[2] Historically, however, if not strictly speaking, linguistically, Russian life did contain just such a concept: the intelligentsia. The history of this unique Russian social phenomenon extended from the late eighteenth century to the 1930s (the word itself seems to have entered Russian usage only in the 1860s, however), and the present-day Soviet dissidents are in many ways the intelligentsia's spiritual heirs. What links the historical intelligentsia and its latter-day successors, and serves as their defining characteristic, is precisely a concept of individual sovereignty. Their effort to assert a "sense of self" against a political and social environment hostile to it has been, and remains, the source of their dissent from the *status quo*.

No one ever doubted the existence of the intelligentsia or the crucial role it played in tsarist Russia's intellectual and political history. Yet there was no agreement on exactly what the intelligentsia was, or who its members, the *intelligenty* (plural of *intelligent*), actually were. An extensive literature stalked the elusive intelligentsia through the dense forests of Russian social thought, and the question "what is the intelligentsia?" received a number of conflicting answers. Should it be defined in socioeconomic terms, that is,

12

according to its economic function, the type of work it performed, or its source of income? Was it an intellectual brotherhood united only in its common adherence to certain ideas, or a "moral category" embracing those individuals selflessly dedicated to "the people's" welfare? Each of these definitions had some element of truth to it, but they were all inadequate or misleading even as a working definition of the intelligentsia and its place in Russian society, and they all raised more questions than they answered. Official Soviet usage compounds the problem by applying the term much more broadly than was the case in prerevolutionary times, to embrace all those engaged in mental as distinct from manual labor.

The intelligentsia to date has successfully resisted any attempt to confine it within a rigid sociological or ideological framework. In more elastic but still useful terms, however, we can identify who the *intelligenty* were and what they had in common. The intelligentsia consisted of the educated critics of the Russian political and social order. It can best be visualized as the second in a nest of three concentric circles.[3] The largest of the three circles is the Western-educated stratum of Russian society, that relatively narrow layer of the population familiar with the modern secular knowledge of Western Europe. The intelligentsia was drawn from this stratum but was not coterminous with it. There were government officials and churchmen, for instance, who were soundly educated in the Western sense but were not critics of the existing order, except in the most loyal terms, and expressed no dissident views. Even among writers and other intellectuals there were those who rejected the secular progress and individualism represented by the West – Tolstoi and Dostoevsky immediately come to mind; they, too, though important members of the educated elite, were not part of the intelligentsia. (For this reason the word "intellectual" is not an appropriate translation of *intelligent,* and it is best to retain the Russian term with all its special connotations.) The smallest of the three circles contains the revolutionary activists who appeared in the latter nineteenth century and came mainly from the ranks of the intelligentsia. By no means were all *intelligenty* revolutionaries, however, for even among the most adamant critics of the tsarist regime there were many who rejected violent revolution as an effective or desirable means of changing it. Therefore the intelligentsia, while smaller than the Western-educated stratum, was always larger than the ranks of the revolutionaries. It comprised those individuals whose Western education led them to question the very foundations of the tsarist system. The political conclusions and programs generated by this questioning were numerous and varied, but what all *intelligenty* had in common was their repudiation of the most basic principles and institutions of the existing order. The process by which eighteenth-century Russian conditions began to produce such critics is what concerns us in this chapter.

Writing in 1909, one exasperated critic of the intelligentsia referred to it as "this creation of Peter's . . . the window that Peter cut into Europe."[4] In more ways than it usually cared to admit, the intelligentsia was one of Peter the Great's many legacies to modern Russia. Nowhere does the centrality of state action in Russian history manifest itself more visibly, or more ironically, than in the fact that the educated critics of the state were themselves a byproduct of its policies. The genesis of the intelligentsia lay in Peter's massive attempt to modernize Russia by Westernizing the way of thinking of his subjects, or at least of their uppermost stratum.

The borrowing and imitation of Western techniques was in itself nothing new for Russia. For more than two centuries before Peter's reign (as sole ruler, 1696–1725), Russia had been adapting Western techniques and organizational forms to its military, economic, fiscal, and other institutions. Peter greatly increased the pace and scope of these borrowings, importing them wholesale instead of piecemeal. But at the same time he introduced a crucial qualitative difference into the process of Westernization. He set out not simply to alter the way his subjects performed their tasks but to change their very consciousness. His aim was to replace their religion- and tradition-centered world-view – one which was still medieval by Western standards – with the rational, secular, dynamic outlook on life he so admired in Western Europe. Peter completed the process by which, in the words of the great prerevolutionary historian Kliuchevsky, Russians had begun to regard the West not just as a factory turning out useful goods for sale but as a school that taught Russians how to live and think.[5]

Peter's methods for transforming his subjects were crude, coercive, and highly autocratic. In attempting to recast their self-image, he began with their external appearance. In one of the most famous and colorful episodes in Russian history, he forced his courtiers and officials to shave off the long flowing beards they traditionally sported (a practice which was not merely decorative but had religious significance), giving them an assist with his own pair of scissors. He also required them to exchange their loose, robelike garments for Western-style breeches and coats. They even had to reorganize their social life and attend Western-style balls and receptions. Having shaved his officials and dressed them in new clothes, Peter began to send them to school. His overriding ambition was to make Russia one of the great powers of Europe, and a great power needed shipbuilders, artillery specialists, competent civil servants, and a host of other trained individuals. Peter therefore imposed on the nobility, the class that supplied the state with its officials and military officers, the obligation to master the fundamentals of reading, writing, mathematics, and geometry. Then, at a certain age, each young noble was examined by the state and assigned to a military or civil post or to further training. A network of new educational institutions was created, and when suitable instruction was not available in Russia, young nobles were sent abroad to complete their studies. Thus even the rank-and-file members of the nobility were forcibly immersed in a new world of secular, practical learning, and required to approach life and work in terms of a rationalistic set of values very different from those in which they had been raised.

It would be a serious mistake to think that overnight the nobles of Russia began to dance their nights away at glittering balls and chatter in perfect French, as they so often do in nineteenth-century novels. The average Russian noble was very poor, and at the outset there was little in his consciousness or way of life to distinguish him from the few serfs he might own. Most such nobles were highly bewildered and disoriented by the new demands being made on them, and adjusted to them only with great difficulty. (The other classes of Russian society, particularly the peasants, remained largely untouched by Western culture.) Their assimilation of the new ways was often very superficial, and beneath the surface they remained the same crude country folk they had been before. Those whose financial and cultural position permitted more than a skin-deep adoption of Western manners and attitudes were a small minority concentrated in Moscow and in St. Petersburg, the new Western-oriented capital that Peter built on the Gulf of Finland. Yet, for even the humblest provincial noble the terms of his existence had changed drastically. If not his consciousness, then that of his children underwent a profound transformation as a result of Peter's efforts. The nobility – or at least its most aware members, its educated elite – began to acquire new values, new habits of mind, new ways of looking at themselves and their society. In short, they began to develop a new set of standards shaped by Western education and culture. These new standards encouraged them to undertake a reevaluation of their familiar Russian environment, which they had hitherto taken for granted.

Peter the Great's role in the Westernization process was more than that of instigator and enforcer; he also provided the educated nobility with a model. Throughout his reign, Peter offered a visible and dramatic example of a Russian who had broken with his traditional way of life and expected pattern of behavior. Peter's break with tradition began in his childhood and adolescence. Political circumstances removed him from the Moscow court, with its traditional piety, rigid ceremonials, and strict etiquette, and left him pretty much to his own devices on a suburban estate outside the city. There, instead of the religious and scholastic education a *tsarevich* would normally have received, he embarked on a highly unconventional program of self-education, which included the mastery of modern military skills and exposure to the social life of Moscow's foreign colony, the so-called German Suburb. His attitude toward religious practice became, at worst, one of scorn, and at best, one of willingness to exploit it as an instrument of state. Immediately after coming to the throne he made a prolonged journey to Western Europe, the first trip abroad by a ruler of Muscovy. He even worked as a carpenter at a Dutch shipyard to satisfy his curiosity about shipbuilding, for he always wished to see at first hand just how things worked. Throughout his reign he was an activist monarch who accompanied his armies into battle, traveled all over Russia and abroad, and took a direct hand in the running of the country. He was a radically different sovereign from his predecessors on the Russian throne and even from his own father Alexis, who had presided over his subjects with the exemplary piety, patriarchal dignity, and ceremonial pomp of the traditional Muscovite tsar. It was Peter who adopted the Western term emperor (*Imperator*) as the official title of Russia's rulers, although the Russian term tsar (derived from *Caesar*) continued in popular usage.

In rejecting his own past and creating a new self-image based on Western principles, Peter in a sense became the first Russian *intelligent*. It was he who, not only by his policies but by his personal example, taught his subjects to reject Russian traditions and practices as backward and uncivilized. It was he who encouraged the Westernized nobility to criticize Russian conditions and try to improve them in accordance with a more progressive set of values and objectives. And it was from that Western-educated nobility, which Peter in effect created in his own image, that the intelligentsia was later to emerge.

Obviously, the criticism that Peter and his successors on the throne encouraged was meant to be strictly limited to state tasks: to make Russia stronger, more productive, more influential in the world. Peter's objective was not to weaken autocracy but to make it more efficient and effective. Here was the source of potential conflict between the state and the Western-educated elite. It proved impossible to confine within such narrow channels the critical faculty that Peter planted in the nobility and his successors nurtured. Slowly but inexorably, some Westernized nobles began to delve into areas where the autocracy would tolerate no discussion on the part of its subjects. The Westernization of the Russian nobility, it subsequently turned out, was a kind of Pandora's box; once Peter opened it, all sorts of unanticipated ideas flew out that would eventually come back to plague the state.

In the period between the death of Peter the Great in 1725 and the accession of Catherine the Great in 1762, Western culture penetrated more deeply into the Russian nobility. This was a period of political instability in Russia during which a number of weak and incompetent rulers succeeded one another, frequently as a result of uprisings by the Guards regiments. Few major political or social initiatives could be attempted – thus providing the country with a much-needed respite after the exhausting reign of Peter the Great – but there was considerable achievement in the cultural and educational spheres. A number of new institutions began to expose the Russian educated elite to the literary and philosophical culture of Western Europe rather than merely to its fashions and technological accomplishments. The Empress Anna (1730–40) established the Corps of Cadets, a military training school for young nobles. In addition to technical and military subjects, the curriculum of the school included training in Western social graces as well as some acquaintance with Western languages and philosophy. Many of Russia's first poets and playwrights were former students of the Corps of Cadets. Just after Peter's death the Petersburg Academy of Sciences came into being. The Academy was a body of scholars (most of them Germans at this time) who introduced European scholarly standards into Russia; it had a university and a gymnasium attached to it, and another university was later established in Moscow. In the 1750s, Russia's first literary journals began to appear. Their readership for the time being was very limited, but they were the forerunners of those "thick journals" of the nineteenth century that were to provide the intelligentsia with much of its intellectual sustenance. Probably the most effective cultural instrument in this period was the theater, which presented translations or adaptations of Western plays and made new ideas available even to the semiliterate. In the 1750s, state theaters were founded in Petersburg and Moscow, while some wealthy, stage-struck nobles established elaborate domestic theaters on their estates.

The court was a major source of cultural patronage, providing both encouragement and financial support for many of these institutions. Even more important, the court continued to set a cultural example for the educated elite. The Empress Elizabeth (1741–62), Peter the Great's daughter, appointed Russia's first court poet, and she herself dabbled in poetry. Like most of Europe, Elizabeth's court aped the Versailles of Louis XV, and French speech and manners now became the aspiration, if not always the achievement, of the Russian nobility. Thus the court served as a cultural medium and model, helping to transmit the new Western educational, literary, and philosophical standards into Russia and bestowing the monarchy's seal of approval on them.

If Western culture in the broad sense of the term had been trickling steadily into Russia in the decades after Peter, under Catherine (1762–96) that trickle became a flood. Catherine herself was undeniably the most cultivated monarch Russia ever had. A minor German princess by birth, she came to Russia at the age of fifteen to marry the heir to the Russian throne, the future Peter III. She soon found herself isolated and lonely, and, as she tells us in her memoirs, in these early years at the Russian court she devoted herself to reading (in addition to the love affairs and political intrigues that occupied the rest of her time). She familiarized herself with the writings of the *philosophes* and thus with the most advanced and progressive thought of the Enlightenment. Nor was this merely an adolescent whim, for after she came to the throne she conducted a correspondence with Voltaire and several of his fellow *philosophes,* received visits from them, and patronized their literary activities.

Much has been made of Catherine's "hypocrisy" in her relations with the *philosophes:* here was the Empress of Russia proclaiming herself a disciple of Voltaire while consolidating her autocracy and tightening the screws of serfdom on the Russian peasants. Certainly there was a deliberate "public relations" element in her relationship with the *philosophes,* and she was by no means above exploiting the prestige the *philosophes* gave her in Western Europe for political and diplomatic purposes (a prestige which helped to obscure the fact that she had usurped the throne in a *coup d'état* from her husband Peter III, who was subsequently murdered). The fact remains, however, that no other Russian monarch, before or after Catherine, could have discoursed at any length with the leading European intellectuals of the day. For a country newly wrenched from medieval patterns of life and thought, and still in the process of forming a modern secular culture, this was a highly important example of cultural leadership.

Upon coming to the throne Catherine made a considerable effort, especially in the early years of her reign, to create an educated reading public conscious of national issues and capable of taking an interest in them. In 1767, for instance, she convened her famous Legislative Commission, composed of delegates from all over the country, to discuss the revision of Russia's laws. To serve as the basis for the commission's deliberations she issued a *Nakaz,* or Instruction, a reasoned discussion of political and legal principles gleaned in large part from her readings in the Enlightenment. In 1769 she founded a weekly satirical journal called *This and That,* to which she herself made anonymous contributions. Her own collected writings fill twelve volumes and range from legislative projects to comic operas. Her efforts to arouse the minds of her subjects were successful in that her reign saw the appearance of such important contributors to Russian letters as the journalist Nicholas Novikov, the playwright Denis Fonvizin, and the novelist and historian Nicholas Karamzin. Yet, by the end of her reign she was imprisoning writers whose views she found uncongenial and suppressing precisely the kind of discussion of public affairs she had done so much to foster. It was Catherine's unhappy fate to reap an abundant cultural harvest and then find some of its first fruits bitter to the taste.

The rise of a critical attitude toward the Russian political and social order cannot be explained solely by the fact of increased exposure to Western ideas. There was nothing automatic about the radical impact of such ideas on the Russians, whose social and cultural environment was so different from that of Western Europe. To most Russian nobles Western thought was at best a fashionable amusement, on the same level as French dress or English carriages; they might admire it, but it did not occur to them to apply it to Russian conditions. In Kliuchevsky's incomparable description, it was decorative rather then functional: "The free-thinking cosmopolite of Tula would enthusiastically read and reread pages on the rights of man with a Russian serf girl by his side, and then, while still a humanist at heart, go out to the stable to deal with a servant who had vexed him."[6] The ideas of the Enlightenment became truly meaningful to some members of the educated nobility, not simply by virtue of their intellectual cogency but as a result of changes occurring in the life of the nobility itself. Those changes were helping to give the more conscious and thoughtful members of the educated nobility a new conception of themselves, a new self-image that found confirmation in the Western ideas to which they were now being exposed. It was the interaction of the nobility's social evolution with its cultural development that gave rise to the expressions of criticism Catherine found increasingly disturbing.

The Russian nobility differed from the nobilities of Western Europe in that it was so much a creation of the state. It is often said that Russia had a state before it had a society, in reference to the early rise of a strong centralized monarchy which imposed a sociolegal structure on Russian society from above. As a result of this process, the rights and privileges of each group within the society were defined according to that group's obligations to the state. The nobility's obligation was service, in either a military or civil capacity, in return for which it received its most significant privilege, the exclusive right to own land worked by serfs. This system, under which the nobility served the state while the serfs served the nobility (by providing the latter with its subsistence), had been developing since the fifteenth and sixteenth centuries, and it was completed by Peter the Great. Now all nobles were required by law to serve the state for life, while non-nobles could attain ennoblement upon reaching a certain rank in the state service hierarchy. Although the concept of nobility retained a hereditary element, the definition and confirmation of noble status in Russia was more intimately connected with service to the state than it was elsewhere. The whole political, economic, and social position of the Russian nobility, its self-definition, revolved around its function as a state service class. Unlike its counterparts in the West, it had no independent status resting on tradition, law, or local self-government, and its sense of itself as a corporate entity separate from the state was very weak.

This set of social and political arrangements altered drastically in 1762. The most important act of Peter III (the grandson of Peter the Great), who reigned but six months before his wife Catherine supplanted him, was to free the nobility from compulsory service to the state. Nobles were still encouraged to serve, but they were no longer obliged to do so; except in times of national emergency they could retire from the service at any time or remain outside it entirely. Undoubtedly some nobles, particularly the wealthier ones who could best enjoy their newfound leisure, welcomed the abolition of compulsory service. The reaction of the rank-and-file nobility, however, seems to have been something less than joyful (as suggested, not least of all, by the absence of any strong opposition to Peter's overthrow among the nobles he had emancipated). True, for decades the nobility had pressed for a reduction of the service obligations Peter the Great had imposed, which were personally and financially onerous. To a considerable degree, however, those obligations had already been lightened in the years after Peter's death, and there was actually little pressure to eliminate them entirely. For one thing, the state now paid its servitors a salary and, meager though it might be, it was a financial necessity to the average nobleman with relatively little land and few serfs. Second, service to the state was the very essence of the Russian nobility: it was state service that gave the nobility its definition as a class and the individual noble the meaning and purpose of his life. Understandably, then, Peter III's decree, which broke the hitherto indissoluble link between state service and noble status, proved bewildering and unsettling.

There is considerable weight to the argument some recent historians have advanced that the decree of 1762 did not so much emancipate the nobility from the state as free the state from the nobility. By now, the monarchy had built up a professional bureaucracy, many of whose members were of foreign or non-noble origin. Lacking the traditional social or economic status of the established nobility, they were entirely dependent on the favor of the sovereign, and their loyalty could be counted on. Even when such officials attained nobility by rising through the Table of Ranks, the state service hierarchy, they continued to identify their interests with the state rather than with the class they had now joined. In other words, increasingly the state's officials were not so much nobles serving the state as state servitors who happened to be nobles. By ruling through this professional bureaucracy, the autocracy could ensure that the nobility as a class would never be able to add a dominant position in the government to its social and economic predominance and demand a share of political power from the monarchy. In retrospect, it may seem unlikely that the Russian nobility, deeply fragmented politically and economically and always closely identified with the autocracy, would have presented such a demand. That was not so apparent in the eighteenth century, however, with its succession of monarchs seated and unseated by the Guards regiments, whose officers were drawn from the leading noble families. Thus the emancipation of 1762 was a major step on the road to the Russian nobility's removal from political influence. Individual nobles, of course, continued to occupy high official positions, and most nobles continued to spend at least part of their lives in service to the state. The nobility as a whole, however, after 1762 was gradually transformed from a class of state servitors into a class of land- and serfowners.

The emancipation of the nobility had a number of far-reaching consequences, which ultimately contributed to the rise of the intelligentsia. First of all, it removed the chief justification for serfdom. The nobility no longer owed service to the state, yet it retained all of its traditional social and economic privileges, including, above all, its right to own serfs. More than a century earlier, the state had established and enforced serfdom on the grounds that it was necessary for the support of the service class. Now the nobility's obligations to the state had been terminated, while the peasants' obligations to their masters remained unchanged. This anomaly now became one of the forces working to undermine the foundations of serfdom.

Second, the emancipation from obligatory service began to alter the Russian noble's image of himself and his purpose. Until now he had been a compulsory servant of the state, spending most of his life subject to the military discipline of the army or in the militarylike atmosphere of the civil service. In these strictly hierarchical relationships he owed unquestioning obedience to his superiors, just as the serfs owed unquestioning obedience to their masters. After 1762, however, he could no longer identify himself so closely with the state, and state service could no longer completely determine his self-image. Some nobles now began to make use of their new sense of distance from the state, as well as their newfound opportunities for leisure, to develop a broader conception of themselves as human beings. With the help of Western thought, they began to see themselves not as mere servants to be ordered about at the whim of their superiors but as free individuals, endowed with certain human rights and an autonomous destiny.

Third, Peter's decree created, or, more accurately, made manifest a political situation in which such a noble found it more and more difficult to defend his new sense of individual worth and dignity. Increasingly supplanted in the central offices of the state by more willing instruments of the autocracy, the nobility found itself subject to the arbitrary authority of bureaucrats whom its political impotence prevented it from curbing or resisting. In an earlier age such despotism might have been accepted as part of the natural order of things, and undoubtedly much of the nobility continued to view it in this light and merely grumbled at its fate. To some, however, such treatment now began to seem an intolerable infringement of their basic rights as human beings. The traditional paternalism of the Russian political system was coming into conflict with the new self-image that was developing within the educated elite of the nobility.

This was the fertile soil upon which the ideas of the Enlightenment fell as they penetrated Russia in the second half of the eighteenth century. The Russian nobility, both as a class and as individuals, was undergoing a profound alteration of status and function after 1762, though the full implications of this were by no means understood, and Western ideas current at the time met the new needs and feelings this shift provoked. Thus, instead of remaining mere fads or playthings, those ideas took firm root and began to sow the seeds of political protest.

One of the first examples of this process at work was Nicholas Novikov (1744–1818). Novikov first achieved prominence in the early 1770s as the editor of a series of satirical journals modeled on Catherine's own magazine, *This and That*. The purpose of such publications was self-improvement, to encourage the reader to correct his behavior by lampooning such human follies and vices as greed, foppery, or ignorance. Unlike Catherine, however, Novikov began to move away from the generalized drawingroom setting in which these follies and vices were usually portrayed and to embody them in specifically Russian figures such as landowners and government officials. To describe masters mistreating their serfs and bureaucrats abusing their powers verged on social criticism of Russian conditions rather than the universalized criticism of human frailties that Catherine had meant to encourage. Although Novikov was far from radical, Catherine made her displeasure known and Novikov prudently retired from the publication of satirical journals. He subsequently became one of the leading figures in the Masonic movement and participated in the various publishing and philanthropic activities of the Freemasons in Russia. Catherine, increasingly annoyed at the social initiative displayed by a private organization independent of the government, and increasingly prone to regard Freemasonry itself as an international conspiracy of subversive intent, finally shut down the Masonic lodges and sentenced Novikov to fifteen years' imprisonment. He was released after her death by the Emperor Paul.

The new self-consciousness of members of the educated elite like Novikov finds clear expression in an editorial he wrote in 1777 for the first issue of a Masonic journal that he helped to publish for the next several years. In this essay Novikov exalted the nature of man in the secular, humanistic terms familiar in the West since the Renaissance (which Russia, in her cultural isolation, had never experienced) but still quite new in Russia. Man, he wrote, is "the focal point of this created earth and of all things," created by God to be the master of nature. "Everything proves to us that among the tangible objects with which we have become familiar over many long years, there is nothing finer, nobler, or more majestic than man and his qualities, which flow from the source of all good."[7] From this point of view, man is a creature of considerable dignity and moral worth; he is a morally responsible being who has been endowed with a great potential for good as well as for evil. Moreover, each individual must exercise this moral responsibility for himself, choosing virtue and shunning vice. The key to the proper exercise of moral choice, Novikov and his contemporaries believed, in true Enlightenment fashion, was education. It was to the promotion of moral education by praising virtue and discouraging vice that Novikov and his fellow Masons dedicated their journal. Elsewhere in his writings Novikov stressed the importance of upbringing, the creation of a domestic and pedagogical environment conducive to "teaching [children] to use their reason correctly and helping them to recognize truth and goodness."[8]

Novikov exemplifies the rise of a secular concept of individualism among the more thoughtful members of the educated elite. He expresses their growing awareness of themselves as individual human beings, with their own value and moral purpose, rather than mere extensions of family, religious community, or state. As yet, this new sense of individualism was confined largely to the moral and spiritual plane: for Novikov, as for the Freemasons generally, it was a matter of self-knowledge and of education in virtuous behavior. He attributed the misery of the serfs to "abuse of noble privilege,"[9] criticizing the abuses without calling the privilege itself into question. Moral persuasion and education rather than a change in political and social institutions were the means to correct the injustices he perceived in Russia. Nonetheless, there were important political implications embodied in his outlook. First, if the individual was morally responsible for his actions, if the choice of virtue over vice was his to make, then he must enjoy a certain degree of moral and intellectual autonomy. He must be free to educate himself, to order his moral existence, to develop his conscience. Second, Novikov made the individual an end in himself, his highest purpose being the fulfillment of his moral responsibility. He could no longer be regarded simply as a means to the pursuit of some larger social or political end, and his well-being must be protected and promoted. In both respects Novikov's individualism ultimately was bound to clash with an institutional environment based on the principles of paternalism, hierarchical authority, and servitude. Autocracy and serfdom gave the individual precious little freedom to make his own moral choices, and they treated him not as an active subject but as a passive object.

Denis Fonvizin's comedy *The Minor,* completed in 1782, marks a further step in the development of critical thought. Fonvizin was Russia's foremost playwright of the eighteenth century, and *The Minor* was his outstanding work. Like most eighteenth-century literature, particularly in Russia, the play is didactic – or, less kindly, one might say preachy – for literature was meant not merely to amuse the reader but to uplift and improve him. Educated Russians of this period were so conscious of their mission to enlighten their fellow citizens that the temptation to deliver sermons was often irresistible, even for a writer with the literary talent of Fonvizin.

As so often happens in didactic literature, the representatives of virtue are really less interesting than the representatives of vice, because the latter seem so much more human in their villainy. The monotonously virtuous Starodum and his equally monochrome niece Sophia, whom he saves from the threat of a forced marriage, are less memorable characters than the comic but illiterate and barbaric provincials from whom Sophia is rescued: the coarse and despotic Mrs. Prostakov; her lazy, boorish son Mitrofan; her brother Skotinin, whose one and only passion is for pigs. The message of the play is abundantly clear: Starodum's sense of duty to his country, his honesty and straightforwardness, and his love of justice are contrasted to the greed and savagery prevailing in the Prostakov household. For the most part virtue is praised in the abstract, in Starodum's lengthy admonitions to his niece. What is significant about the play for our purposes is that vice is vividly depicted in terms of real Russian social and political conditions. Mrs. Prostakov tyrannizes not only her family but her serfs as well; she squeezes them dry financially, and she is free with her fists. When told that she does not have the right to mistreat her servants, she asks incredulously: "The noble, when he feels like it, isn't free to beat up his servant? Then what's this directive about the freedom of the nobility given us for?"[10] Starodum, in explaining why he retired early from state service, has some harsh words about the atmosphere at the imperial court. He was repelled by the selfishness and obsequiousness of court life: "I realized that it was better to lead my life in my own house than in someone else's vestibule . . . I left the Court without estates, without decorations, without rank, but I brought myself home unharmed – my soul, my honor, my principles." When it is suggested that people like him should remain at court and try to cure it of its ills, Starodum replies with the most radical statement in the entire play: "It's folly to call a doctor to the incurably ill. The doctor can do no good and will himself get infected."[11]

With this one possible exception, however, *The Minor,* like Novikov's satires, locates the source of the evils it depicts not in institutions themselves but in abuses of those institutions. As mere abuses, they can be remedied within the existing system, thus avoiding fundamental changes. The remedy consists of good upbringing and moral education, the inculcation of virtue in the people who run the system, as Starodum repeatedly urges; or, in the last resort, the removal of the wicked individuals who give rise to abuses and their replacement by better individuals. It is on this note that the play reaches its happy ending. Pravdin, a state official, takes custody of the Prostakovs' estate and serfs in the name of the government, with the observation that Mrs. Prostakov is an "inhumane mistress whose evil conduct in our benevolent state can no longer be tolerated."[12] She is punished and her serfs are liberated from her despotism; Sophia is rescued from the dismal prospect of marriage to Mitrofan and reunited with her true love; evil is vanquished and virtue triumphs – but the principles of neither serfdom nor autocracy are challenged, and the system is depicted as correcting its own defects. *The Minor* was an important milestone in the development of critical opinion, for its satirical references to the actual conditions of Russian life bit more deeply than most contemporary works. But it did not probe the real source of those conditions, the absolute power that Russian institutions permitted some human beings to exercise over others. As long as good individuals were placed in charge of those institutions, the play implied, such power would be exercised benevolently and was therefore justifiable.

It was Alexander Radishchev (1749–1802) who drew the logical social and political conclusions from the new sense of individualism that Novikov had expressed. Radishchev's major writing, a book entitled *A Journey from St. Petersburg to Moscow,* which appeared in 1790, was Russia's first modern work of political protest. Printed on Radishchev's private printing press and then offered for public sale, it was immediately confiscated by Catherine the Great's police and its author condemned to death, a sentence later commuted to Siberian exile. The book is cast in the form of a travelogue, in the then popular style of Laurence Sterne. In the course of a journey from Russia's "new" capital to its "old" capital, the anonymous narrator describes the people, places, and conditions he encounters.

The most striking aspect of the book is its uncompromising attack on serfdom. The narrator speaks to, or hears accounts of, serfs in a variety of situations, and the picture of serfdom that emerges from this series of vignettes is one of unrelieved misery, cruelty, and exploitation. Criticisms of serfdom, even bitter criticisms, were not in themselves something new; as we have seen, authors like Novikov and Fonvizin had already drawn attention to the abuses serfdom was capable of generating. Radishchev was unique, however, in that he did not portray these abuses as defects that could be rectified. Serfdom as he depicted it was inherently evil, for the absolute power it gave the master over the serf violated the fundamental moral rights of the individual. Even if all masters could be persuaded to treat their serfs humanely – and the brutal landowners who fill the pages of the *Journey* make it clear how unlikely Radishchev found such a possibility – serfdom would still stand condemned, for the relationship on which it was based was immoral in principle.

A typical example of Radishchev's attitude is his description of a group of serfs who are being sold into the army as recruits and are chained together to prevent their escape. They had been fictitiously emancipated and sold to a commune of crown peasants, which was now using them to fulfill its own recruitment quota. The narrator exclaims at this sight: "Free men, who have committed no crime, are fettered, and sold like cattle! O laws! Your wisdom frequently resides only in your style! Is this not an open mockery? And, what is worse, a mockery of the sacred name of liberty."[13] It is of particular note that this scene echoes an earlier literary depiction of serfdom, a comic opera of 1779 called *Misfortune from a Coach* by Iakov Kniazhnin. In that work a Frenchified landowner was callously planning to sell one of his serfs in order to buy a new French carriage. Similarly, in Radishchev's account the hapless serfs had belonged to "a landed proprietor who needed money for a new carriage."[14] In Kniazhnin's work, however, all ends happily: the landowner is persuaded to abandon his plan, and the serf hero and serf heroine are reunited. Radishchev's narrator, after an unsuccessful effort to intervene in the serfs' behalf, is forced to abandon them to their sad fate. There is no implication that the abuses of serfdom are remediable, either by moral persuasion or by the removal of evil landowners. Instead, the implication is that serfdom inevitably degrades human beings to the level of livestock.

Radishchev by no means advocated rebellion or revolution. He did warn of a repetition of the Pugachev peasant uprising if nothing were done to improve the condition of the serfs, but there is no indication that he would have welcomed such an event. The unmistakable message of his book, however, was that serfdom must be abolished, preferably by state action. The very principles on which it rested made it an irredeemable institution. It is this fundamental rejection of serfdom and of what it represented that establishes Radishchev as "the father of the Russian intelligentsia."[15]

What remains to be explained, however, is how Radishchev arrived at such an independent and, indeed, risky position in regard to one of the integral features of Russian life. Serfdom, after all, had been a familiar part of the Russian scene for generations. Radishchev himself was the son of a serfowner, and serfdom was approved, or at least accepted, by everyone whose opinions he had been brought up to respect, from his parents to his sovereign. What motivated him to break with the prevailing standards of his society and condemn an institution from which he personally did not suffer and on which, in fact, his own economic and social position rested?

The clue lies in those parts of the *Journey* that do *not* deal with serfdom. The book is justly famous as a protest against serfdom, but it is considerably more than that. There are episodes revealing the arbitrariness of the imperial administrative and judicial systems; examples of the selfishness and corruption of important officials and the persecution of honest, high-minded reformers; and a discourse on the evils of censorship, which takes up the longest chapter in the book. In short, Radishchev was criticizing and condemning the actions of the autocracy and its officials as much as the actions of Russia's serfowners. The immediate victims of autocracy, however, were in most cases not the serfs but the nobles. The average serf, living under the manorial jurisdiction of his master, had few direct encounters with officialdom and little use for civil liberties. The despotism of the bureaucracy and the restraints it imposed on individual self-expression victimized the nobility most of all, especially the educated nobility, and Radishchev's book contains a number of instances in which educated nobles are thwarted, abused, or broken. Paternalistic arbitrariness pervaded the entire Russian institutional structure, and the educated elite was becoming increasingly sensitive to it and resentful of it.

In Radishchev's early years we can trace the process by which educated nobles in this period grew conscious of their individual worth and then indignant when those in authority failed to respect it. Radishchev had the good fortune to receive a far better education than most other provincial noblemen of his time. He was born in the eastern frontier regions of Russia, but at the age of seven he came to Moscow to live with the family of the director of Moscow University, to whom he was related. Several years later he entered the Corps of Pages, a special school for young nobles attached to the imperial court of St. Petersburg. In his formative years, in the cultural capitals and elite educational institutions of the empire, he was introduced to new ideas and experiences quite different from those that shaped the assumptions and habits of mind of the provincial gentry. Then, at the age of seventeen, along with several other young Russians, he was sent to Leipzig for five years by the Russian government to study law. There he was able to familiarize himself with many of the works of the Enlightenment and to experience a social and intellectual climate notably freer than that of Russia. Nothing could better illustrate how the Russian government contributed to the rise of the intelligentsia by its efforts to educate its own officials.[16]

It was in Leipzig that he was most brutally exposed to the arbitrary despotism of authority – or at least that he was first mature enough to take offense at it. Radishchev and his fellow students were severely mistreated and exploited by the Russian supervisor whom the government had appointed to watch over them. According to Radishchev, this petty bureaucrat misappropriated the funds provided for the students' maintenance and kept the young men wretchedly housed and ill fed; when they complained, they were subjected to a form of house arrest and solitary confinement. The impression this experience left on Radishchev is reflected in his *Life of Ushakov,* which he published in 1789, a year before the appearance of the *Journey.* It is really less a biography of Ushakov, one of the Russian students who accompanied Radishchev to Leipzig and died there, than an account of the injustices Radishchev and his friends suffered and their efforts, long unsuccessful, to obtain redress. Significantly, Radishchev traced these injustices ultimately to the autocracy itself: an autocratic sovereign who rules by whim rather than by law "encourages every official to think that in the exercise of his share of unlimited power he is as much a master in particular as the sovereign is in general."[17]

Upon his return to Russia in 1771 and entry into government service, he was a witness to despotism on a much larger scale. Appointed to serve in the First Department of the Senate (the Senate was Russia's highest administrative and judicial institution), he encountered numerous cases of official corruption, lawlessness, and abuses of serfs. By now, he was in a position to evaluate and criticize "Russian reality" rather than merely to accept it as natural and familiar.

The development of a critical perspective did not take place overnight. His recognition of the institutional bases of arbitrary authority took its final, concrete form only in the *Journey,* where the noble's power over his serfs is viewed as a reflection of the bureaucracy's power over the nobles, and both are denounced in terms of natural rights and individual moral autonomy. In his *Life of Ushakov,* Radishchev, like many later memoirists, undoubtedly exaggerated in retrospect the immediate impact of his Leipzig experiences on his consciousness of despotism. The *Journey* was the culmination of a long and complex process in which personal experiences and Western ideas interacted with and reinforced each other to produce a growing awareness of the political roots of oppression. It is a process we shall have occasion to trace again in later *intelligenty.*

The philosopher Nicholas Berdiaev once wrote that the Russian intelligentsia was born when Radishchev penned the sentence that comes at the opening of the *Journey:* "I looked about me – my heart was wounded by the

sufferings of humanity."[18] Berdiaev was justified in placing such importance on this statement, for it captures succinctly the dynamics of the intelligentsia's development. The educated nobleman was now becoming fully
aware of himself as an "I," an individual personality worthy of respect for his
human dignity and freedom for the judgments of his mind and heart.
Thanks to the state, which provided him with education, exposed him to
advanced Western ideas, and sometimes even financed his first experiences
of Western life, he began to look at Russian conditions from a new point of
view; Radishchev's statement suggests how acutely he felt that the scales
had fallen from his eyes as a result of his newfound enlightenment. The
crucial element in crystallizing his new, critical perspective was his personal
experience of the gap between his new ideals and Russian conditions, when
he found that his own individuality was neither secure nor free to express
itself but was subject to the whims of the autocracy and its officials. Only
then did he become fully aware of the sufferings of others – most notably, of
the serfs. Educated nobles like Radishchev, though privileged, began to
turn against the existing order because they had come to realize how insecure their position actually was. Though in different ways and to different
degrees, the Russian system victimized noble and serf alike, reducing them
to playthings of another's arbitrary will and thereby denying them full
recognition as human beings. A deeply personal, emotional involvement in
the situation helps to explain the intensity of feeling and the willingness to
take risks in expressing it that characterized Radishchev and his successors.
Their newly developed consciousness of themselves as individuals, so sorely
threatened by the Russian system of paternalistic authority, gave rise to a
new social conscience, a feeling of empathy with other casualties of this
system and a determination to liberate all victims of oppression.

Despite the radical implications of his criticism, Radishchev displayed
some ambivalence about the autocracy. In the *Journey,* amidst the descriptions of the evil consequences of tyranny, he relates a dream in which Truth
materializes and reveals the real state of affairs to the sovereign – who then
proceeds to correct all the things that are wrong with the system. Here, it
seems, is yet another appeal to the "good autocrat," a reflection of the
traditional Russian reliance on reform from above, and it will recur in the
subsequent history of the intelligentsia. Whether Radishchev merely
wished to flatter Catherine in order to soften the impact of his book, or
whether he truly believed that she could be persuaded to limit the prerogatives she so evidently enjoyed, is difficult to determine. In any case, one
could hardly expect this isolated individual, stepping forward at the very

beginning of the intelligentsia's history, to present a fully consistent and well-wrought program of political reform. Radishchev's ambivalence was resolved by the Decembrists, who completed the intelligentsia's formative process. Like Radishchev, the Decembrists looked to the state for progress and improvement, but instead of merely hoping that the autocrat would perceive the truth and act upon it, they set out in 1825 to seize the state and restructure it in order to make it a more effective instrument of change.

Once again, it must be stressed that the government of Alexander I (1801–25), like that of his grandmother Catherine, was not hopelessly stagnant or reactionary. Alexander, educated by Catherine in the principles of the Enlightenment and coming to the throne after the brief but despotic reign of his father, Paul (1796–1801), seemed bent on liberalization. He promoted higher education and commissioned projects from his officials for far-reaching legal and administrative changes; he granted the Kingdom of Poland a constitution in 1816 and insisted that the restored Bourbons grant one in France; and he hinted at the possibility of a constitutional system for Russia as well. It was the high hopes raised by Alexander, and his failure to fulfill them, that turned the future Decembrists against him, for in the end Alexander proved unwilling to accept any real limitations on his cherished autocratic powers. Disillusionment with a government that encouraged and exemplified commitment to progress and reform, then failed to live up to its own ideals, produced the first open confrontation between the autocracy and members of the intelligentsia. Under the guise of altering the succession to the throne at Alexander's death (they attempted to force the accession of his purportedly "liberal" brother Constantine – who had secretly renounced his rights to the throne – instead of his other brother Nicholas), the Decembrists sought to take control of the state and use it to implement a program of reform.

The origins of the abortive uprising of December 1825 (hence the name "Decembrists") lay in the series of secret societies that began to form in the aftermath of the Napoleonic wars. The men who founded them had several characteristics in common: they were relatively young, well-educated nobles, mostly military officers who had seen service against Napoleon. They had in many cases been exposed to the ideas and ideals of Freemasonry, and, like Radishchev before them, had had an opportunity to observe the West at first hand in the course of the wartime campaigns. Upon their return to Russia, their acute sense of having saved their country from foreign conquest combined with the tradition of state service, which was still strong in their class, to produce a feeling of personal responsibility for Russia's social and political progress. They developed fundamental reservations about the twin pillars on which the existing system in Russia rested: autocracy and serfdom. The terms in which they began to repudiate these institutions are exemplified in the memoirs of Ivan Iakushkin, one of the early conspirators. Iakushkin attests to the impact on him of the year he spent in Germany and the several months he spent in Paris during the war. Now, he wrote, when he and his friends saw the Russian police brutalizing a crowd, or Alexander on horseback angrily chasing a peasant who accidentally got in his way, they became indignant at such barbarism and began to doubt Alexander's willingness to curb it.[19] In other words, they had begun to measure their familiar environment in terms of new standards, and what struck them most forcefully was the everyday violation of basic human dignity in Russia.

Recent Soviet research has shown the Decembrist movement to be a more complex phenomenon than previously thought. There is evidence of a "generational change" as the movement developed: many of the older, higher-ranking officers had left the secret societies before 1825. Those who actively participated in the uprising were younger men (too young to have served in the Napoleonic campaigns) of more junior military rank, and therefore, perhaps, more willing to turn to armed rebellion rather than the educational and propagandistic tasks the Decembrist societies had earlier set for themselves.[20] The entire Decembrist movement, however, was marked by confusion about its ultimate goals and the most effective means of achieving them. The various programs and projects the Decembrists drew up as their secret organizations evolved reflected serious differences of opinion on many issues as well as a considerable lack of reality, and in retrospect the uprising seems to have been doomed from the start.

The best reflection of the mood and feelings of the Decembrists, as is so often the case in the history of the intelligentsia, is a literary work. Alexander Griboedov captured much of their spirit in his *Woe from Wit,* a play in verse completed in 1824. Griboedov was a diplomat who was acquainted with many of the Decembrists and was himself implicated in the conspiracy, though he was later exonerated. The hero of his play, Chatsky, is in many respects the quintessential Decembrist. He is very young, probably no more than twenty – to the extent that their age can be determined, more than half of the active participants in the Decembrist uprising were under twenty-five – and youthful idealism is the hallmark of his character. He too has traveled in the West, and when he returns to Moscow he is repelled by the dullness, the pettiness, and the hypocrisy of the empty life its fashionable citizens lead. The trait that most closely links him to the Decembrists –

and to all the precursors and early representatives of the intelligentsia – is his rejection of the servility the state demanded of the individual. When it is suggested to Chatsky that he enter government service, he replies: "I would be glad to serve, but servility is sickening!" This remark is followed by a lengthy attack on the kowtowing and self-abasement of the would-be favorites at the imperial court.[21]

Griboedov's young hero was not the first to voice this sentiment. We have already seen how Starodum, in Fonvizin's *The Minor,* carefully distinguished between service to one's country and servility before the sovereign. Similar passages appear in Radishchev's *Journey.* And in words very close to those of the fictional Chatsky, in 1819 the future Decembrist Michael Orlov rejected the idea of assuming an important official post in St. Petersburg: "You know me: am I like a courtier, and is my spine sufficiently supple for bowing and scraping?"[22]

The tension between service and servility is one of the principal legacies bequeathed by the eighteenth-century nobility to the nineteenth-century intelligentsia. None of the historical or literary figures we have discussed showed any inclination to resolve the tension by simply withdrawing into a private world and devoting himself exclusively to personal cultivation. The growing individualism of the educated elite was accompanied by a strong sense of social mission, a desire to serve and enlighten one's fellow men. In fact, one of the most striking characteristics of the Russian intelligentsia throughout its history is that it always conceived individual liberation in social terms. The liberation of all men, or at least of all one's countrymen, was the essential condition for self-liberation and the only context in which individual fulfillment was deemed possible. The significant change here was the growing feeling that *state* service was the road not to liberation but to servitude. Particularly after the Decembrist uprising, the notion of service as the activity of the worthy man was transferred from the state to the society or nation, and, ultimately, to "the people," or the peasants, or the workers. It was never abandoned, however, and the Russian intelligentsia persisted in casting its individualism in social terms: the individual could be truly free only when those around him were equally free, and vice versa.[23]

Another eighteenth-century legacy to the intelligentsia is the theme of national consciousness, which now begins to find expression in Russian letters. Satirical criticism of Russians who mindlessly worship all things foreign, and efforts to rediscover native virtues, mark the writings of all the figures we have discussed, from Novikov and Fonvizin to Radishchev and the Decembrists. The Russian dandy who attempts to ape French fashions and winds up making a fool of himself was a particularly frequent target, and none hit the mark better than Kniazhnin in his comic opera *Misfortune from a Coach*. Here a Russian landowner laments the hopeless ignorance of his peasants, who, unlike the more cultured peasants of France, are simply unable to speak French. As we have seen, his Francophilia nearly brings ruin to his peasants when he sets out to sell one of his serfs in order to purchase a new French carriage. With Radishchev's adaptation of this episode for his condemnation of serfdom, the theme of national consciousness became a component of the intelligentsia's social protest; the "derussified" – and corrupt and oppressive – noble would now be contrasted to the traditionally Russian, morally pure peasant.

Why did the imitation of foreigners and of foreign culture become a matter of concern and even scorn to the Russian educated elite at this time, whereas it had not appeared to trouble the Westernized nobles of the generation of Peter the Great? The answer is suggested by the element most frequently emphasized in discussions of the subject: the humiliation entailed in groveling before foreign ways. Those who rejected Russian culture as worthless were denying their own worth as individuals, for their Russianness was an integral part of their character. To be imitation Frenchmen, second-class Westerners, was an intolerable affront to the new self-image the educated elite was beginning to develop. The rise of a feeling of individual dignity led inevitably to a search for national dignity, for the positive merits of Russian culture that would give it equal status with Western culture. The best-known effort in this direction came ultimately from the Slavophiles of the 1840s, who argued that the distinctive features of Russian political, social, and religious life were not signs of backwardness but evidence of the superiority of Russian over Western culture. The search for national virtues had begun earlier, however. The Decembrists, for instance, tried to "Russify" their projects by giving medieval Russian names to constitutional bodies that were clearly modeled on contemporary Western practice. Yet an earlier example is Fonvizin's Starodum: his very name means "Oldsense," and he speaks out in defense of the plain old Russian virtues that supposedly prevailed before the adoption of frivolous foreign ways. The difficulty Starodum and his successors faced in ransacking the Russian past for its native values is that all too often they were likely to find none other than the Prostakovs, that is, ignorance, cruelty, and barbarism. One of the unresolved dilemmas of the Russian *intelligent* – and one that confronts his Soviet counterpart as well – was that Western culture, with its ideals of individual worth and personal autonomy, was the indispensable source of his new self-image but at the same time posed a threat to it: he needed it in order to reject the native conditions that oppressed him, yet in so doing he risked denigrating an essential element of his own personality.

With the Decembrists the Russian intelligentsia finally crystallized, and the movement of political and social dissent associated with it would now become a permanent feature of imperial Russian history. The mere fact of opposition to the existing order was not what distinguished the intelligentsia, however. The rise of autocracy and serfdom had been accompanied over the centuries by various manifestations of protest, the most recent being the Pugachev peasant uprising of 1773–4. In order to understand the intelligentsia's significance we must determine what distinguished its opposition from past movements and currents. What made the intelligentsia's protest new and different was also what enabled it to sustain itself despite the isolation and persecution of so many of its members, and ultimately to bring about the downfall of the tsarist regime.

Even before the latter eighteenth century Russia's rulers had been the object of criticism and protest emanating from elements within the nobility. The earliest expression of such criticism had come from the boyars, the great landowners and military warriors of medieval Russia. Throughout the fifteenth and sixteenth centuries the princes of Muscovy had persistently undercut the position of the boyars, restricting their privileges, increasing their obligations, and gradually supplanting them with a new class of military servitors (the forerunners of the eighteenth-century *dvorianstvo,* or service gentry) more dependent on the monarchy for their economic and social status. In the mid-sixteenth century, Prince Andrei Kurbsky wrote his famous letters to Ivan the Terrible protesting the treatment he and other boyars had received at the tsar's hands.[24] Much later, in the eighteenth century, the gentry had an opportunity to vent its grievances through the Guards regiments. The Guards were the elite units of the Russian army, and in the period between Peter and Catherine (and once again in 1801) they overthrew a number of monarchs in a series of palace *coups d'état* and replaced them with rulers more to their liking.

Kurbsky's cry of indignation, on the one hand, and the Guards' actions on the other, were the products of vastly different historical circumstances. Yet they shared one significant feature: both accepted the principle of autocracy, the principle that the will of the sovereign was the rightful source of all rewards and punishments. Kurbsky in his epistles condemns the tsar's arbitrary behavior and pleads eloquently for justice and fair treatment. Yet, he is unable to articulate any alternative to autocracy. He seems to accept Ivan's image of his subjects as his servants and of himself as their master; he insists that he and the other persecuted boyars have been faithful servants of the tsar, and he goes no further than to lament Ivan's ingratitude toward them. Similarly, the Guards regiments made no effort to change the foundations of the monarchy. Their objective was to secure greater privileges and rewards for themselves and for the particular groups that had won their support. Therefore they sought an autocrat who would favor them over others, but they had no desire to limit the monarch's ability to bestow privileges and rewards by curtailing his autocratic powers.

Popular protest movements displayed the same limitations. In the seventeenth and eighteenth centuries, the consolidation of serfdom provoked a series of peasant uprisings led by Cossack elements and originating in the frontier regions of the east and south where government control was weak. The two most serious outbursts were those led by Stenka Razin in the 1670s and by Emelian Pugachev during Catherine's reign a hundred years later. One of the most striking and most characteristic features of these revolts against the existing order is that they were carried out in the name of the tsar. To the laboring classes the tsar had become a symbolic, almost mythical figure: the all-good, all-merciful Little Father who wanted only to improve the lot of his people. His failure to do so was blamed entirely on the wicked officials and landowners who surrounded him, deceiving him and thwarting his wishes. Or, it was blamed on the fact that the present occupant of the Russian throne was not the rightful, legitimate tsar but an impostor or usurper, hence the frequent appearance of a Pretender to the throne at the head of these movements. Despite the vehemence of their protest and the destruction they left in their wake, the peasant uprisings remained within the ideological framework of the paternalistic political order even while rebelling against its works.[25] Lacking any new principles of social and political organization, they were unable to generate a clear sense of purpose or positive goals, especially in the face of military reverses; they arose spontaneously and sooner or later collapsed and subsided without a trace.

A more complex and enduring movement was that of the Old Believers, the sizable minority of the population that refused to accept the reform of the Orthodox Church rituals in the middle of the seventeenth century. The protest of the Old Believers was purely religious in origin and directed only against the leaders of the established church. Inevitably, however, it took on political overtones because the defender of the established church was the tsar, whose duty it was to punish those whom the church deemed heretics. Hence the religious demands of the Old Believers became intertwined with other grievances against the existing order and figured prominently in both the Razin and Pugachev uprisings. Yet the Old Believers, too, failed to provide any alternative to the existing framework of political and social relations with which they had come into conflict. They continued to regard the tsar as the head of the church and kept hoping to persuade him to support their views. When they failed to do so, they concluded that the reigning monarch was not the real tsar but Antichrist, whose orders could legitimately be disobeyed. Like the peasant rebels who followed the Pretenders, the Old Believers did not repudiate the principle of autocracy. Instead, they rationalized their opposition to the present occupant of the throne by insisting that he was not the rightful tsar – who obviously would have favored their cause – but an infernal impostor. Ultimately, the Old Believers retreated into Russia's wilderness regions and formed their own communities. There they were able to maintain their religious traditions and pursue their own way of life, but they had little impact on the larger society and its values.

Thus despite their different social origins and objectives, the currents of social and political protest that preceded the intelligentsia shared two characteristics. First, each was in its own way faithful to the concept of the autocratic tsar, whether he was viewed as the dispenser of rewards and privileges, the benevolent father of his people, or the head of the Orthodox community of the faithful. His right to exercise autocratic power, that is, to rule according to his will, was not fundamentally challenged, only some specific applications of that power. Second, these were essentially selfish protests, which never rose above the interests of a clique or, at most, of a particular class. With the partial exception, perhaps, of the Old Believers (whose narrowness was of a different kind), they could not conceive of a struggle for the welfare of all Russians, much less of all mankind.

In both respects the intelligentsia introduced something significantly new into the history of protest in Russia. The intelligentsia urged political and social change not just for its own benefit but for the benefit of others. In fact, some of the changes it urged were plainly detrimental to the position of the class from which it originated, the nobility. Furthermore, the intelligentsia called into question the very principles on which the Russian social and political order was based, and it offered an alternative to them. It was not yet in a position to elaborate specific programs of reform (although the proposals drawn up by the Decembrists, schematic and unrealistic as they were, marked a beginning in this respect), but it was developing fundamental principles and values very different from those of the paternalistic Russian system, most notably a new concept of the individual.

Western ideas played a crucial role for the intelligentsia because, as the history of earlier challenges to autocracy and serfdom demonstrates, there was no "usable past" in Russian thought or experience to support the intelligentsia's values. Newly conscious of themselves as individual personalities, members of the Western-educated elite were highly receptive to the thought of the Enlightenment, with its defense of the individual's reason, moral worth, and capacity for judgment. (Christianity, of course, sanctioned the concept of individual moral dignity, and traces of the Christian tradition can be found in Novikov and Radishchev. The strong element of worldly passivity embedded in Russian Orthodoxy, coupled with the autocracy's firm institutional control over the church, limited the contribution Russian religious tradition could make to the modern, secular needs of the intelligentsia. As will be seen, however, elements of that tradition would later be "rediscovered" and would play a role in the intelligentsia's history.) In place of the hierarchical, paternalistic, inherently arbitrary system of authority that ruled Russian life, the intelligentsia upheld the ultimate value of the individual and defended his right, and capacity, to shape his own destiny. Firmly in possession of these ideological principles, the intelligentsia was able to create a movement of dissent that could be kept alive from generation to generation, one that could neither be bought off by the grant of special privileges nor crushed by physical defeats.

3

The formation of a Russian *intelligent*

It is only a personal injury that proves mortal; one can get over injuries to other people.

Michael Bakunin, 1870.[1]

In the hundred years from the formation of the Decembrist societies to the Russian Revolution of 1917, social theories and political organizations rose and fell within the intelligentsia in rapid succession. The post-Decembrist generation, the "men of the forties," exemplified by Alexander Herzen, were dominated by German idealist philosophy and the controversy between the Westernizers and the Slavophiles over Russia's relationship to Western culture. It was also this generation that began to study French socialism. The next generation, the "men of the sixties," with Nicholas Chernyshevsky as their chief mentor, adopted materialism and scientism as their philosophical creed and socialism, based on the Russian peasant commune, as their political program. Also in the 1860s, following the emancipation of the serfs in 1861, the revolutionary movement got under way in earnest. The Populist movement, with its commitment to peasant socialism and its willingness to engage in antigovernment terrorism to achieve it, dominated the 1870s, while Russian Marxism, committed to proletarian socialism, arose in the eighties and nineties. These two socialist currents competed for the intelligentsia's loyalties and were joined at the turn of the century by a revitalized liberal movement, which also sought fundamental changes in the existing order, particularly a parliamentary political system, but preferred legal methods of activity.

The intellectual and political history of the intelligentsia has received considerable attention from historians. What concerns us here is the personal side of the intelligentsia's development: the biographical process that led individuals to sever their traditional loyalties to family, class, and state, renounce the expectations of their parents, and join the ranks of those opposed to the existing order of things in Russia. As time went on, such individuals came from more and more varied backgrounds. Not only the philosophical and political commitments of the intelligentsia but also its social composition underwent considerable change as the nineteenth century progressed. At first it remained confined almost entirely to the gentry, the only class exposed to the primary generating force of the intelligentsia: Western education. Until the last decades of the nineteenth century, nongentry elements remained a negligible portion of the intelligentsia. As educational opportunities began to widen late in the century, however, the ranks of the intelligentsia began to include non-nobles as well as representatives of the national minorities. At the same time, Russian society was undergoing fundamental changes: the emancipation of the serfs finally removed the most glaring social injustice from the Russian scene, while the gentry lost its previously unchallenged social and economic predominance.

And yet, the opposition movement that had its roots in the latter eighteenth century continued without interruption, despite the great changes taking place both in the protestors themselves and in the conditions they were protesting against. The causes of the intelligentsia's dissent went deeper than the troubled status of the nobility or the revulsion against serfdom, the initial context within which the intelligentsia originated. The *intelligenty* were people who had developed an acute consciousness of themselves as individuals and who found their personal development threatened, or thwarted, by the paternalistic arbitrariness that continued to pervade Russian society even after the emancipation of the serfs. At first, it was only the educated nobility whose social and educational position permitted the crucial development of a heightened sense of individual worth, but as time went on the same individualistic consciousness began to filter down to other strata of Russian society. Paternalistic authority molded the entire Russian system; it had colored the relationship between master and serf, and it continued to pervade relations within the family as well as the political relationship between tsar and subject. Therefore dissent could be voiced by non-nobles as well as nobles and could continue even after the abolition of serfdom. The true basis of the intelligentsia's protest was rebellion in the name of individual autonomy, against arbitrary authority. Thus it could begin at any point in the system – family, society, or state – wherever the individual, through personal experience, encountered the system's underlying principles and was made inescapably aware of their threat to his individuality. In this chapter we shall trace some examples of how individuals experienced that confrontation, and how their experiences, in turn, shaped their views of human liberation in general.

One of the most significant results of the Decembrist uprising was the definitive break it effected between the state and the educated elite. Until now, critics of the existing order had trusted in the monarchy's commitment to progress and had appealed to it to introduce timely change. The Decembrists themselves had at first intended to use their positions in the military and civil service to influence the government's policies. It was only in the last years of Alexander's reign that the conflict within the monarchy itself between commitment to progress and commitment to autocratic prerogatives became fully clear, and the Decembrists began to think in terms of capturing and reforming the state rather than merely persuading it to change its ways.

With Nicholas I (1825–55) there was no problem of disappointment and disillusionment, for he had raised no hopes of liberalization in the first place. He was considerably younger than Alexander, his education had not been supervised by their grandmother Catherine, and he had not been so fully exposed to the thought of the Enlightenment. There was no streak of liberalism in his make-up to compete with his autocratic instincts and produce the ambivalence that Alexander had displayed. His thirty-year reign, however, was not a time of unrelieved darkness and persecution, as the intelligentsia's accounts of it often suggest. It was under Nicholas, for example, that Russia's laws were finally rationalized and systematized – a project started but never completed by the enlightened monarchs Catherine and Alexander. Oppressive as the intellectual atmosphere of the 1830s and 1840s was, it was not so oppressive as to prevent the remarkable flowering of Russian thought and literature that took place in these years. Nevertheless, the educated elite was subjected to the constant interference of a heavy-handed censorship, surveillance by the Third Section (a political police Nicholas had established to counter subversion and prevent any repetition of the Decembrist uprising), and the imprisonment and exile of some of its leading representatives. It is not surprising, therefore, that this stratum of Russian society tended to experience Nicholas's reign as a period of unmitigated reaction, repression, and intellectual suffocation.

With the failure of the Decembrist uprising a new attitude toward the state began to pervade the disaffected segment of the educated elite. The hope of working with and through the state for progressive change was now

largely discarded. The last vestiges of the link between the disaffected segment of the educated elite and service to the state were severed, and the
intelligentsia, while still almost entirely of noble origin, emerged from the
nobility as a fully distinct group. This break between state and intelligentsia had two serious consequences. In the first place, it opened the way for
the revolutionary movement that was to preoccupy so much of Russia's
political life until 1917. Active revolutionary conspiracies did not begin to
make their appearance until the 1860s, but their seeds were planted in the
1830s and 1840s. The state, which had been the source and instrument of
progress since the time of Peter the Great, was now perceived as the enemy
of progress. It was no longer considered amenable to reform, as the Decembrists had intended; it was a roadblock that had to be destroyed before
meaningful social and political change could occur. The revolutionaries
turned away from the state and began to look to popular forces as the agent
of change.

Second, the intelligentsia now found itself without a meaningful role to
play in Russian society. Given Russia's economic backwardness and its
stratified society, virtually the only occupations open to a noble in the
Russia of Nicholas I were military or civil service, or the life of a serfowner.
The disaffected members of the educated elite could no longer regard such
positions as acceptable, however, for they implied identification with autocracy and serfdom, the two institutions the intelligentsia abhorred. They
might enter state service for a time, as their families expected them to do,
and they often continued to draw their economic subsistence from the family estates, but neither as servicemen nor as serfowners could they be con-
tented or fully engaged. As a result, the intelligentsia hovered in a kind of
social limbo. Ideologically and emotionally it identified more and more
with the laboring classes, in whose life it could not participate; culturally
and intellectually it still had much more in common with the state and the
privileged segment of society, in whose life it would not participate. In this
period, the best of its members devoted themselves to philosophical and
literary pursuits, and this commitment now became the hallmark of the
intelligentsia.

The foremost representative of the post-Decembrist generation was Alexander Herzen (1812–70), whose brilliant autobiography, *My Past and
Thoughts,* one of the monuments of Russian literature, epitomizes the development of the intelligentsia in the reign of Nicholas. Herzen was such a
vivid and forceful individual, and his autobiography such a personal state-

ment, that considerable caution must be exercised in treating him as a "typical" *intelligent*. But in his autobiography he traces a series of formative experiences, and reactions to them, that recur in a closely similar pattern in the memoirs and fiction of other *intelligenty* throughout the nineteenth century. At least in its broad outlines, therefore, *My Past and Thoughts* depicts not just a unique personality and intellect but a prototype of the Russian intelligentsia.

The central figure in the first part of the memoirs is not so much Herzen himself as his father, an excellent specimen of the "superfluous man" who haunts Russian literature throughout the nineteenth century. The superfluous man was an educated, sensitive individual whose life was made empty and useless by his inability to apply his talents under Russian conditions. Herzen's father, a member of a wealthy old noble family, seems to have fallen victim to this conflict. Having received an education, served in the military, and traveled abroad, he retired after the Napoleonic wars at the age of thirty-one and lived out the rest of his days in Moscow as an increasingly eccentric recluse. Herzen attributes his father's shattered life to the negative effects of Western education. The contradiction between the values acquired by exposure to Western culture and the values contained in one's Russian environment were a fruitful source of energy and aroused consciousness in some, but a source of intellectual and emotional paralysis in others. As Herzen puts it, his father was "spoilt for Russia by Western prejudices and for the West by Russian habits."[2] The superfluous men were direct descendants of Kliuchevsky's eighteenth-century landowners, who wept over a sentimental French novel, then mercilessly flogged their serfs. Like Herzen's father, as well as a number of the other figures who appear in *My Past and Thoughts*, they frittered their lives away in meaningless pursuits or quietly moldered in their townhouses and country estates.

Retired from the service, Herzen's father became a hypochondriac and a petty despot who spent half his day tyrannizing his household servants. (Though Herzen describes his tyranny as only half serious, its consequences for the servants were often very serious indeed.) The household revolved entirely around his whims and eccentricities. Herzen himself was the product of one of those whims. His mother was a German woman, the daughter of a petty official, whom Herzen's father had brought back to Russia from one of his foreign trips but never formally married. Their son was therefore illegitimate, and instead of his father's family name, Iakovlev, he received the surname Herzen (from the German *Herz,* heart). This note of sentimentality was not generally characteristic of the relationship between Herzen's parents, however. Herzen's mother remained part of the Moscow household but was kept totally dependent and subordinate as a result of her ambiguous position. Here was a glaring case of patriarchal despotism, which might well have given Herzen food for thought from his earliest years. Herzen gives no indication that this was the case, however, and the mother plays only a fleeting, shadowy role in her son's memoirs.

Unlike serf-bastards, who were usually brought up as peasants in the villages, Herzen was raised as his father's son and heir – perhaps in recognition of his mother's higher station, perhaps merely as another of his father's whims. Despite the father's refusal to regularize Herzen's status, he enjoyed the conventional childhood and adolescence of the wealthy Moscow gentry: he was pampered by the servants, indulged by his father, and well educated by private tutors, an education supplemented by his father's large library of Russian and Western literature. Added to what was obviously a high degree of innate intelligence and awareness, this was an upbringing amply conducive to the formation of a strong personality, one with a heightened consciousness of his needs and feelings as an individual and the expectation that the rest of the world recognized and respected them.

One of the earliest indications that this expectation might not be fulfilled came when, as Herzen tells it, he was thirteen, although in fact he was only eight. He relates in his memoirs how he overheard a conversation in which his father was discussing Herzen's future with a friend who referred to the difficulties the boy's "false position" might raise. Thus Herzen learned of his illegitimate birth and of the possible stigma that might attach to it. His reaction, as he describes it, is very revealing. Its principal effect, he claims, was to give him a new sense of independence from his environment and its values. "I felt myself more independent of society, of which I knew absolutely nothing, felt that in reality I was thrown on my own resources, and with somewhat childish conceit thought I would show the old generals what I was made of."[3] He does not dwell on this incident, however, and dismisses it rather quickly. But almost immediately thereafter – whether by design or unconsciously – he embarks on a lengthy description of the sufferings and humiliations of his father's serfs, for whom he had great affection and sympathy.

Thus, in selecting the formative experiences that he believed had shaped his life (and every memoirist makes such choices), Herzen juxtaposed the discovery of his own vulnerability to a heartrending account of the vulnerability of the serfs. It is difficult to believe, as Herzen intended us to, that at the age of thirteen (or, even less likely, at the age of eight) this rather spoiled and self-willed boy had perceived the evils of serfdom and become a champion of freedom. That could result only from a broader and more complex set of experiences and reflections. But there is no reason to dismiss Herzen's implication that a sense of injured pride at the realization of the somewhat blemished image he presented to the world played a role in his development of a social conscience. Russian gentry society was tolerant of bastards and was prepared to accept Herzen as his father's son and heir. On the other hand, Herzen had at least one half-brother and a variety of cousins – including his future first wife – who were the children of serf women; they were either brought up as peasants in the country or, as with his wife and his brother, were subjected to an endless series of persecutions and humiliations.[4] He had every reason to sense that his own much more favored position in life had been a very close call, an accident or a mere whim. Not overnight, perhaps, but with gradually deepening perception, a realization of his own insecurity revealed to him the insecurity of others; the vulnerability of his own pride and dignity sensitized him to the vulnerability of others and made their suffering and humiliation real to him.

That Herzen first began to perceive the evils of serfdom by identifying with its victims is suggested not only by the sequence of episodes in his memoirs but by his description of serfdom itself. What he stresses again and again is not the physical abuse of the serfs, their material deprivations, or interference in their traditional way of life – things that the serfs themselves might have placed at the head of their list of grievances – but their humiliation and helplessness in the face of their masters' arbitrary authority. For example, he dwells on a theme that had appeared in Radishchev's *Journey* and was to reappear later in Peter Kropotkin's memoirs: the tragedy of the educated serf who finds himself still treated like a slave and is morally crushed. Such cases have been documented,[5] but were they as frequent as their recurrence in the intelligentsia's writings would lead us to believe? How many of the serfs themselves, if asked to record their grievances against serfdom, would have cited cases of this sort? What most repelled Herzen and other *intelligenty* about serfdom was its denial of the serf's human dignity and freedom (a repulsion not necessarily belied by the fact that Herzen as a young man was not above seducing his servant girls). The most tragic victim of serfdom the *intelligent* could imagine was the serf who, through education, had become conscious of himself as an individual, who had acquired a degree of pride and self-respect, and then found himself still subject to the whims of his master, a mere instrument of another's will. Such consciousness, however, was far less likely to arise among the serfs, preoccupied with their daily struggle for existence, than among the pampered, leisured, educated gentry. Thus the suffering serfs who inhabit the pages of the intelligentsia's writings are in many cases thinly veiled reflections, or self-projections, of the suffering *intelligenty* – *intelligenty* such as Alexander Herzen, growing up as the illegitimate son of a cranky and unpredictable father.[6]

The politicization of Herzen's sense of estrangement from and grievance against the existing order was neither inevitable nor swift; it was the product of a series of episodes that progressively opened his eyes to what was going on in the society around him. He was only about thirteen when the Decembrists' uprising occurred, but several years later, inspired by their example, he and his friend Nicholas Ogarev (also the illegitimate son of a rich and overbearing landowner), stood on the Sparrow Hills of Moscow and vowed to sacrifice themselves for the good of mankind. The specific objectives of the Decembrists appear to have eluded these restless teenagers (as they eluded many actual observers of the tragedy of 1825). What they saw in the Decembrists was a revolt against oppressive, arbitrary authority in the name of freedom and justice, and these were sentiments they were perfectly capable of sharing. It is highly revealing of the intelligentsia's development that they resorted to Western literature in order to express feelings generated by their personal experience: their oath on Sparrow Hills was derived from Schiller's play *Don Carlos*, which had a great impact on both Herzen and Ogarev.

In 1829, when he was seventeen, Herzen entered Moscow University. This was a new departure for the gentry, and it reflected the changing relationship between the state and the educated elite. Until now, the sons of the wealthier, more aristocratic gentry had been educated at home by tutors or in elite schools such as the Corps of Cadets. They had then entered the service, particularly the Guards regiments. Now, disaffected members of the educated elite were shunning the service and preferred to devote themselves to philosophical studies at the universities. For Herzen, the university also provided scope for his growing rebelliousness. He became one of the ringleaders in an episode in which the students drove an unpopular professor from the lecture hall with hisses and catcalls. For their efforts, Herzen and his collaborators were confined – though not uncomfortably – in a detention house that the university used to punish errant students.

Until now, Herzen's rebellion had been directed against the paternalistic authority he encountered in his daily life: his father, the university officials. In 1834, an event occurred that contributed to the politicization of this unfocused rebelliousness. A group of young men were arrested for singing "subversive" songs at a party. In the course of the investigation Ogarev was implicated and, through him, Herzen. Though Ogarev and Herzen had already come to the attention of the police, neither had participated in the affair, which, according to Herzen, involved nothing more than a few satirical lyrics. But Nicholas I, fearing the rise of new secret societies on the order of the Decembrists, insisted on dealing very harshly with all concerned. After ten months in prison Herzen was exiled for an indefinite term to the remote provincial town of Viatka. For the first time in his comfortable existence he had been exposed, directly and personally, to the supreme arbitrariness and disrespect for the rights of the individual that the Russian autocracy was capable of displaying.

Herzen spent five years in exile, first in Viatka and then in another provincial town, Vladimir, somewhat closer to Moscow. Here he served as a clerk in the provincial bureaucracy. (It was only one of the many eccentricities of the tsarist system, and a reflection of its unslaked thirst for competent officials, that a man accused of activities against the government should be given a position of some responsibility in that same government.) He was able to take a close look at just how the administrative and legal system worked, and what he saw was an appalling picture of corruption, despotism, and lawlessness. Now painfully sensitive to injustice, like Radishchev in his post-Leipzig work in the Senate, Herzen could understand the full import of what he observed: arbitrariness pervaded every level of Russian life, and no individual, whatever his class, could be assured of his legal rights or personal inviolability.

Herzen was finally allowed to settle in St. Petersburg but was soon rearrested and exiled again. The incident that precipitated his second arrest was even more absurd and trivial than the first. In a letter to his father he had made a derogatory remark about the St. Petersburg police. The letter was intercepted by the authorities, and Herzen was charged with spreading false and harmful rumors concerning the forces of law and order. When confronted with the charge, and the new sentence of exile that accompanied it, Herzen writes in his memoirs, he could scarcely believe his eyes: "such complete absence of justice, such insolent, shameless disregard of the law was amazing, even in Russia."[7]

It is equally amazing to recall that Herzen's father was very wealthy and belonged to a distinguished noble family. Yet his mail was read by the police, his son was arrested and exiled on a trumped-up charge – and he was powerless to prevent it. This incident reveals the striking helplessness of even the highest-ranking nobles vis-à-vis the autocracy and its officials, a helplessness echoed in the warning with which Herzen's father had sent him off to Nicholas's capital: "For God's sake, be careful . . . Do not trust anyone. Petersburg nowadays is not what it was in our time. There is sure to be a spy or two in every company."[8] The social, economic, and cultural privileges of the gentry enabled people like Herzen to cultivate the sense of individual autonomy and self-respect that nurtured revolt against despotism. That revolt, however, could not be carried out in the name of the gentry itself. On the one hand, serfdom tied this class inextricably to the existing social order, while, on the other, its subordination to the bureaucracy rendered it politically helpless. "Gentry radicals" such as Herzen had to repudiate the class that had given them birth but could not defend their cause, and had to create a new group loyalty and identity in the intelligentsia.

In his second exile, in the ancient but dreary town of Novgorod, Herzen again served in the bureaucracy, this time in a higher position than before, because he had received a service promotion! His new post dealt particularly with serfdom, an experience that sharpened his perceptions of injustice and provided concrete evidence for his previous conclusions about the Russian system. Eventually, after eight years of almost continuous imprisonment and exile and an additional five years under police surveillance in Moscow, he was allowed to travel abroad. He never returned to Russia, devoting his talents instead to the creation of the first significant Russian émigré press in Western Europe, which enabled him to publicize and encourage the voices of dissent at home.

We should not, of course, accept Herzen's descriptions of his experiences uncritically. Like most memoirists, he was reviewing his life through the prism of his mature attitudes and image of himself, and he undoubtedly exaggerated the impact of some events and understated the significance of others. As a great writer, he was not immune to the temptation of embellishing his narrative for the sake of literary effect. And as an avowed enemy of autocracy and serfdom he had no interest in presenting a balanced picture of those institutions. It is not necessary to verify each episode in his account, however, in order to discern the overall pattern of his development. Here was an individual whose social position, upbringing, and education had bred within him an acute sense of his own importance as an individual and an insistence on the freedom to develop his personality and form his own judgments. At the same time, he experienced an increasingly painful series of confrontations with a system – familial, social, political – that denied the individual's importance and freedom. Only because he was a victim him-self, though a privileged one, to be sure, was Herzen able to attain full awareness of the victimization of others, particularly the serfs. Seeking to liberate himself from the trammels of paternalistic authority, he was in-exorably drawn into a struggle for the liberation of others. By this process the son of a serfowning nobleman became the enemy of a system that had endowed him with enviable economic privilege and social status.

The lives of other noble *intelligenty* repeat the broad outlines of Herzen's development. Herzen's friend and contemporary, Michael Bakunin (1814–76), was raised on a country estate where his father, a man of consid-erable culture, gave him a liberal, fully Western education based on En-lightenment principles. Bathed in the values of the latest European thought, Bakunin wrote later, he and his brothers and sisters "lived, so to speak, outside of Russian reality, in a world full of sentiment and fantasy, but stripped of all reality."[9] Russian reality intruded harshly when, at the age of fourteen, he left this idyllic environment and was sent to the Artillery School in St. Petersburg to prepare for a career in military service. Soon he was writing to his parents that "the petty peculiarities of military service and discipline are unpleasant, for instance, the fact that in military service you never have rights before your superiors."[10] Eventually irritation ripened into repugnance, and in search of personal freedom Bakunin left the service to live in Moscow and devote himself to philosophical studies. His father's anguished and bewildered response to his eldest son's new life is revealing: "True philosophy consists not in dreamy theories and idle talk," his father wrote in an effort to persuade him to resume his service career, "but in fulfilling the family, social, and civic obligations of our milieu." Having given his son a liberal, enlightened education, the elder Bakunin now urged him to come to his senses and be "a good and obedient son."[11]

A few years later, Prince Peter Kropotkin (1842–1921) followed a pat-tern of development similar to that of Herzen and Bakunin. Like Herzen, Kropotkin's early life was privileged but lonely. The son of a wealthy but rather cold and rigidly conventional Moscow noble, Kropotkin lost his mother at an early age and had a tense and hostile relationship with his stepmother. He, too, turned to the house serfs for attention and affection, to some extent even identifying with their helplessness against the author-ity of his parents. His recollections of his childhood contain sympathetic descriptions of the mistreatment of serfs closely similar to those of Radishchev, Herzen, and other *intelligent* writers. After receiving his early education at home from Russian and foreign tutors, Kropotkin, like Bakunin, was sent to a boarding school in his early teens, in this case the socially prestigious Corps of Pages in St. Petersburg. There he received a good formal education as well as extracurricular exposure to the principal intellectual trends of the period. At the same time, he was outraged by the harsh forms of discipline practiced at the school, the bullying inflicted by the older pupils, and the incompetence of some of the staff. He was not slow to act on his indignation, and the school gave Kropotkin an opportunity for his first acts of rebellion against the accepted order of hierarchy and subordination.

Kropotkin was also repelled by the obsequiousness that prevailed at the imperial court, where he and his fellow students served as pages, and which he criticizes in his memoirs in terms very much like those of a Starodum or a Chatsky. In a particularly notable comment, he provides a clue to the psychological process by which a strictly personal reaction against arbitrary domestic authority could widen into political or social rebellion. Alexander II ended a speech to Kropotkin's graduating class at the Corps of Pages with an angry threat of punishment for those who proved disloyal. Remembering that scene, Kropotkin associates the tsar with his father, and the young pages with the serfs: "His voice failed; his face was distorted by anger, full of that expression of blind rage which I saw in my childhood when my father screamed at the peasants and servants: 'I'll skin you under the birch rods.' Several similarities between my father and the tsar flashed through my mind."[12]

Finally, again like Herzen, a brief tour of duty in provincial government confirmed his growing sense of antagonism toward the autocracy. As a young military officer after his graduation from the Corps of Pages he served in the administration in Eastern Siberia, where he tried to help implement the various reforms that accompanied the emancipation of the serfs. He experienced first-hand the abuses and incompetence of the autocracy's officials as well as the growing conservatism of the Petersburg government. "I soon realized," he writes in his memoirs, "the absolute impossibility of doing anything really useful for the mass of the people by means of the administrative machinery . . . I lost in Siberia whatever faith in state discipline I had cherished before."[13] Reflecting the increasing intransigence of the autocracy's critics as the century wore on, Kropotkin's disillusionment with the tsarist government would ultimately ripen into the theory of anarchism that he propounded in his maturity. Back in St. Petersburg, he was soon drawn into the budding revolutionary movement, was arrested, made a daring escape from a prison hospital, and in his long years of West

European emigration succeeded Bakunin as the patriarch of Russian anarchism.

The impact of their educational experiences is particularly striking in the evolution of these three "gentry radicals." A privileged upbringing and exposure to Western thought bred a sense of individual worth in men like Herzen, Bakunin, and Kropotkin. Their self-esteem received further confirmation when they entered institutions of higher learning, especially the more prestigious ones, for they could not help but see themselves as a tiny but highly significant elite in a backward and ignorant country. Yet, despite the good education they usually received, they found their pride and dignity violated by the atmosphere of the schools themselves. The constant surveillance and rigid, sometimes brutal discipline that pervaded these institutions reflected both the mores of a paternalistic society and the suspicions of the autocratic government, which financed and controlled most of Russia's secondary schools and all its universities. Throughout the nineteenth century, the tsarist government faced an intractable dilemma in regard to higher education. It could not dispense with it, on pain of economic and technological death, as Russia's humiliating defeat in the Crimean War demonstrated; and in fact, in the latter part of the century the government undertook a remarkable expansion and improvement of the country's system of higher education. But at the same time the government had reason to fear the independence of mind aroused by its own educational efforts, particularly when the revolutionary movement arose and a number of students and former students turned up in its ranks. The government sought to tighten its controls over the institutions of higher learning in order to produce useful but nonsubversive graduates – and succeeded in turning more and more of them against the tsarist system.[14]

Russia's defeat in the Crimean War of 1854–5 raised anew the challenge of modernization that had had such far-reaching consequences under Peter the Great. Russia was bested on its own soil by the relatively small seaborne forces of England and France and was forced to acknowledge the backwardness of its military system, transportation facilities, and economic organization. As serfdom was the cornerstone of all Russia's social and economic arrangements, and those arrangements had proved inadequate for the modern age, emancipation was clearly the first step toward a new and more viable order. In 1861, Alexander II (1855–81) abolished serfdom, and the pressure that Russia's most glaring social and moral problem had been exerting on the tsarist system was at last alleviated.

Alleviated, but by no means eliminated. In the countryside, mass distress actually grew rather than diminished, for the peasants were now freer but poorer. Under the terms of the emancipation, the gentry landowners retained nearly half the land, the rest going to their former serfs. The rapidly growing peasant population found itself with insufficient land to support itself, while its poverty and backwardness prevented it from exploiting more productively the land it did have. The peasants saw only one solution to their plight: to get hold of the gentry estates and divide them up among themselves. As the government would not expropriate the gentry by legal means, the peasants' objectives could be achieved only extralegally, and this kept the peasantry a potentially revolutionary force right up to 1917.

The emancipation of the serfs was accompanied by a number of other reforms in the social, economic, and legal spheres during the 1860s and early 1870s. In the cities and towns, the abolition of serfdom opened the way to Russia's belated industrialization, which attained massive proportions by the last decade of the nineteenth century. In the long term, industrialization offered the benefits of mass production and a higher standard of living. In the short term, however, it created a proletariat afflicted with all the social ills the early phase of industrialization generates: low wages, wretched living and working conditions, insecure employment. Concentrated in the towns and organized by the factory system itself, the industrial workers, though far less numerous than the peasants, were potentially an even more explosive source of social unrest.

The period of the "great reforms" no more satisfied the educated segment of the population than it did the laboring classes. The judicial system was reformed and considerably strengthened; the *zemstvo* – an elective organ of local administration – was established in the rural areas, along with the municipal *duma,* or council, in the towns; a more regular and humane system of military recruitment was introduced; the universities received greater autonomy, censorship was relaxed, and even the restrictions on the Jews were eased. Some of these changes went too far for conservative tastes and were curtailed by Alexander himself in the latter years of his reign and, even more, by his successors. But they did not go nearly far enough to satisfy the disaffected elements of the educated elite, for they entailed no reform of the autocratic political system. Alexander made it clear that he was just as devoted to the principle of autocracy as his predecessors had been, and that he would permit no public participation in government and no restrictions on his ability to act at will through his chosen officials. In

1862, when a group of liberal gentry merely suggested the desirability of a constitutional form of government, Alexander's testy response was to clap them in jail.

Thus the reform period failed to dry up the sources of dissent that had given rise to the intelligentsia. The educated elite was still denied any degree of self-government or meaningful participation in public affairs; its freedom of expression continued to be restricted by censorship and other police measures; and it remained subject to arbitrary treatment at the hands of officialdom. This is not to deny that the reign of Alexander II was a marked improvement over the reign of Nicholas I. But the reforms had the effect of whetting the appetite for personal security, self-expression, and political responsibility rather than satisfying it. As a result, the disaffection the educated elite had displayed before the reform period continued and even intensified. With the increase in social mobility and educational opportunity after 1861, the intelligentsia was ceasing to be the exclusive preserve of the gentry and began to include educated commoners. Although many *intelligenty* still came from a noble background, they were joined by *raznochintsy,* or "men of all ranks" – sons of parish priests,[15] petty officials, or merchants. In fact, the distinction between noble and non-noble was no longer very meaningful, now that the nobility had lost its most important privilege, the right to own serfs. Nevertheless, the intelligentsia's protest displays a striking psychological continuity. The grievances of the educated elite against the tsarist system remained essentially the same from the late eighteenth century to 1917, regardless of the changes that took place in Russian society and in the composition of the educated elite itself. Despite differences of style or tone, educated nongentry individuals reacted against Russia's paternalistic society and government in much the same way, and for much the same reasons, as their gentry predecessors.

One important example of this continuity is Nicholas Chernyshevsky's novel *What Is to Be Done?*. Chernyshevsky, the son of an Orthodox priest, became one of the leading mentors of the generation of the late fifties and early sixties. His journalistic writings helped to develop the doctrines of Populism, or peasant socialism, which dominated the intelligentsia's thinking and the emerging revolutionary movement throughout the sixties and seventies. His most influential work, however, was his novel, written while he was in prison (he had been arrested for spreading radical ideas) and published in 1863. To the modern reader it leaves much to be desired from a literary point of view: it lurches fitfully from episode to episode, it is filled with sermons and moral lessons, and its characters seem cut from cardboard rather than fashioned of flesh and blood. Yet, it had an enormous impact on the emotional and moral consciousness of the educated young Russians coming of age in the reform period, and it left an indelible mark on the Russian intelligentsia. Its heroes became models for contemporary *intelligenty* and even for succeeding generations.

The central theme of the novel is the effort of a group of educated young people to free themselves from oppressive social conventions and prejudices and to structure their lives according to their own principles and personalities. In this fundamental respect the heroes of the novel are the direct successors of Griboedov's Chatsky, Herzen, Bakunin, and Kropotkin, all of whom were seeking freedom to develop their personalities in the face of a paternalistic, hierarchical social order. The social setting has significantly altered, however: Vera Pavlovna, the heroine, though educated and sensitive, comes from a family that can be described, at best, as lower-middle class, while her male friends are poor St. Petersburg medical students. At the beginning of the novel, Vera Pavlovna is faced with the prospect of marriage to a rich young man whom she dislikes intensely. She is being pushed into the match by her mother, a coarse, grasping woman reminiscent of Mrs. Prostakov in *The Minor* – and, like her, the most human figure in a work whose characters are for the most part abstract message bearers.

A new group of victims makes its appearance in this novel to typify the injustice and brutality of a social order resting on paternalistic authority. The serfs had been freed from the arbitrary authority of their masters; here, their place as exemplary victims of another's whim is taken by women. The plight of Vera Pavlovna is treated in much the same terms as the intelligentsia had traditionally treated the plight of the serfs. The theme of abduction, or forced marriage, of serf girls, had a long history in Russian critical literature. Numerous examples appear in the comic operas of the late eighteenth century, many of which, like Kniazhnin's *Misfortune from a Coach,* had village settings. Other examples appear in Radishchev's *Journey* and Kropotkin's *Memoirs.* In Fonvizin's play and Chernyshevsky's novel the same theme appears on a higher social plane, while Michael Bakunin's first challenges to his father's patriarchal authority involved the younger Bakunin's efforts to "liberate" one or another of his sisters from what he considered a degrading match. In all of these instances, the plight of women is treated in universal, rather abstract terms: they are examples of worthy but helpless individuals whose fundamental human rights are being violated. In Vera Pavlovna's case, she is very much the counterpart of the educated serf, a personality awakened by education to a consciousness of its own individuality but stifled by a society where someone is allowed to be master of another's fate. Instead of serfdom, the institution responsible for this violation is the family, with its traditional parental authority. The status of women obviously was a real social problem in imperial Russia. But, like serfdom, the treatment this problem received in the intelligentsia's writings was more often than not a projection of the intelligentsia's own general preoccupations, which the abolition of serfdom did not resolve. Thus Chernyshevsky states the book's central issue in the following words: "O human degradation! Depravity! to *possess!* Who dares possess a human being? One may possess a pair of slippers, a dressing-gown. But what am I talking about? Almost every one of us, men, *possesses* some one of you, our sisters! But what kind of sisters can you be then? You are our servants."[16]

Vera Pavlovna's ambition is to attain her rightful share of human freedom: freedom from despotism, and freedom to shape her life in accordance with her own impulses. "I wish neither to dominate nor be dominated," she declares. "I wish to be independent and live in my own fashion."[17] Most of the novel relates her successful escape from the clutches of her family, with its hypocrisy, greed, and social aspirations – what a later age would call "bourgeois values" – and her construction of a new life based on reason rather than subservience. (In the next chapter we shall look more closely at the role of reason in the lives of Chernyshevsky's heroes.) To ensure that she will not simply be trading her mother's despotism for her husband's, she and her fiancé, Lopukhov, agree that after they marry each will have his/her own room, which the other may enter only with permission, and between them a "neutral" living room where the couple can meet for tea. (Lest this image of marital bliss seem overly schematic, it should be noted that Chernyshevsky and his wife maintained a similar arrangement in their own marriage.)

In addition, Vera Pavlovna insists on establishing economic independence from her husband. "Whoever has money has power and freedom," she reminds Lopukhov; "then, as long as woman lives at man's expense, she will be dependent on him, will she not? . . . I know that you intend to be a good and benevolent despot, but I do not intend that you should be a despot at all."[18] She proceeds to establish a seamstresses' cooperative, which proves highly successful (a slightly veiled socialist theme in a work whose propaganda content had to be muted to pass the censorship). In this way she puts her own liberation to work for the benefit of others. "The words 'I feel joy and happiness' mean 'I would like all men to be joyous and happy,'" Chernyshevsky observes; "it is human; these two thoughts are but one."[19] The

Vera Pavlovnas of the world, by liberating themselves from family conventions and social prejudices, achieve personal autonomy and fulfillment and at the same time contribute to the betterment of society as a whole.

In Maxim Gorky's memoirs of his childhood we find the formation of an *intelligent* taking place even farther down the social scale than in Chernyshevsky's novel. When Gorky (the pen name of Aleksei Peshkov, 1868–1936) was a young child his father died, and he was taken to live with his maternal grandparents, the Kashirins, in the Volga River town of Nizhny-Novgorod. His grandfather, formerly a barge hauler on the Volga, was now the proprietor of a small dyeworks, and the first part of Gorky's memoirs, "Childhood," is set in his grandfather's household in the 1870s and 1880s. Though he was eventually to become one of the most prominent supporters of the Bolsheviks, Gorky places little emphasis on the economic aspect of the household. Its atmosphere, as he describes it, was determined not by what a Marxist would term its petty-bourgeois economic activity but by more elemental forces of good and evil. On the one hand were Gorky's uncles, almost bestial in their uncontrollable cruelty, greed, and violence. On the other was his grandmother, one of the most vivid characters in all of Russian literature, overflowing with a spontaneous goodness, piety, and strength, an earth-mother figure who seemed to have sprung from one of the fairy tales she told so well. In the center of the picture was his grandfather, a sternly patriarchal character before whom the rest of the household cowered.

What Gorky traces in "Childhood" is the emergence of an individual consciousness. We see the quarrelsome, greed-ridden Kashirin household through the eyes of a small boy, bewildered, often frightened and lonely, but detached and increasingly critical. He likens himself to a beehive, to which various people brought "the honey of their knowledge and views of life, each of them making a rich contribution to the development of my character."[20] It is a character that emerges from this dark and squalid background much as a piece of sculpture emerges from the unformed clay. What enabled him to assert himself against such a suffocating environment, to remain detached from it and eventually liberate himself from it, instead of unthinkingly accepting its values? Like Radishchev, Herzen, and his other *intelligent* predecessors, unusual personal experiences jostled Gorky out of the course his life would normally have taken, giving him a heightened sense of self-consciousness as an individual and equipping him to view his surroundings from a critical perspective. The essential element was his knowledge that he was a Peshkov, not a Kashirin. This is stressed several times in the narrative. He retains memories of his early life with his father and mother, a life far happier and more loving than what he experiences in his grandfather's house.

I knew no other life, but I had a vague recollection that my mother and father had not lived like that; they had spoken other words, known other amusements, and had always sat and walked alongside of each other, close together . . . I felt like a stranger in [grandfather's] house, and the life about me pricked me with a thousand needles, rousing my suspicions and forcing me to watch everything with strained attention.[21]

We have seen how changes in the life of the gentry in the late eighteenth century bred a new sense of individual dignity and self-respect, confirmed by the exposure to Western culture and the experience of European travel. In Gorky's vague remembrance of a household in which people treated each other with respect and consideration, we find an analogue to the educated noble's experiences in an earlier era: a vision of a more humane, more civilized way of life that provides a critical yardstick against which to measure Russian reality. And even in the case of the largely self-educated Gorky, his childhood perceptions and feelings were confirmed and consolidated by the wide reading in Western literature that he undertook in his adolescence.[22]

His acute awareness of self, and of his vulnerability, sensitized Gorky to the feelings of others. Shortly after coming to live with his grandparents he got into mischief and, for the first time in his life, was beaten unmercifully and fell ill. "The days of my illness were important days of my life," Gorky tells us. "During that time I seemed to suddenly grow older and develop a new quality – that of being deeply concerned about all people. It was as though the skin had been torn off my heart, making it unbearably sensitive to every injury, my own or another's."[23] Only a very self-conscious individual, with a highly developed ego, would have been so deeply offended at treatment which, by Gorky's own account, was a commonplace in this environment. We may remain skeptical about the immediacy and clarity of the youthful Gorky's reaction to this particular episode, and regard it as perhaps an interpretive reconstruction by a memoirist. But there is no reason to doubt that the mental process he describes was a significant motif in his overall development, even if a slower and more complex one than his account might suggest.

The final step in Gorky's emergence as an *intelligent* came when his critical attitude toward his surroundings led him to reject the entire conception of good and evil that prevailed in his environment and to begin making his own moral judgments. Here is the final link, crucial to the history of the intelligentsia, between consciousness and conscience. In a pivotal chapter of his autobiography, Gorky describes the two very different concepts of God held by his grandmother and his grandfather respectively. His grandmother prayed to an all-good, all-merciful God, submitting herself joyfully to a deity who was "equally kind and equally dear to everything on earth."[24] His grandfather, on the other hand, prayed to an authoritarian God, a cruel and punishing God, "a raised sword, a lash held over the heads of the wicked."[25] Yet, different though they seemed on the surface, these two images of the deity had much in common. Both held that God played an active role in the daily affairs of men, that he was the sole author of all the rewards and punishments in their lives. In the grandmother's case, this belief induced a childlike passivity, an unquestioning endurance of suffering as an act of God; in the grandfather it bred a less attractive but equally childlike acceptance of cruelty – his own as well as others' – as a legitimate element of human existence, as part of the natural order of things. To both, good and evil were external, cosmic forces visited upon man from without. He might hope, and pray, to enjoy the one and avoid the other, but in the end he could only submit to whatever God's will imposed upon him.

Gorky rejects both attitudes in the name of individual moral responsibility. Interestingly, it is an *intelligent,* evidently a Populist revolutionary, who first voices this principle to the young Gorky. A rather mysterious and taciturn young man, whom Gorky dubs "That's Fine," lodges for a time in his grandfather's house and is subsequently arrested. One evening this *intelligent* hears Gorky's grandmother reciting one of her folktales and, deeply moved by the moral it teaches, repeats over and over: "It's wrong to let someone else act as your conscience!"[26] The next day he makes a point of impressing this message on Gorky. Through this figure, Gorky draws the connection between the Russian intelligentsia and the idea of responsibility for one's own moral behavior. In rejecting both his grandmother's passive acceptance of arbitrary authority and his grandfather's active identification with it, he is, like the rest of the intelligentsia, rejecting serfdom and autocracy – not just as external institutions but as internalized principles of human behavior.

In a provocative essay on the young Gorky, Erik Erikson has characterized the new outlook Gorky develops as a Russian version of a "protestant morality."[27] This is a useful notion (protestant being used here in the broad sense), for the protest of the intelligentsia was, like the Protestant Reformation, at its deepest level a protest against paternalistic authority in the name of individual conscience and moral responsibility. Just as the Reformation in the West had far-reaching repercussions beyond the strictly religious sphere, the Russian intelligentsia's protest occurred on a number of different planes: because paternalistic authority permeated every aspect of Russian life, the battle for individual autonomy had to be fought simultaneously on the political, social, familial, and religious fronts. Erikson links the origins of this protestant outlook in Russia to industrialization, which was just getting under way at the time, unleashing new energies and disrupting age-old traditions and superstitions. As we have seen, however, the origins of Gorky's outlook go back to the eighteenth century and the impact of Enlightenment thought on Russia. Because of its isolation from the West, Russia had not experienced at their source the Renaissance, the Reformation, or the scientific revolution. The humanistic precepts those currents generated did not strike Russia with full force until the eighteenth century. Then, embedded in – and considerably radicalized by – the Enlightenment, they were adopted by the newly Westernized educated elite, with explosive results. Thus Gorky was heir to an intellectual tradition that was already more than a century old. Like an individual whose stages of growth repeat the evolutionary history of his species, Gorky, in his journey from his grandparents' house to his association with the revolutionary movement, recapitulated the path that the intelligentsia as a whole had been traveling since the time of Peter the Great.

Finally, we come to Leon Trotsky (born Lev Bronstein, 1879–1940), whose memoirs appeared in 1930 under the title *My Life.* In his brief account of his formative years, there are elements that seem to make him a typical *intelligent.* Trotsky's social origins were even humbler than Gorky's. He was born in the Ukraine, in an area on the northwest coast of the Black Sea called New Russia. The territory had been acquired from Turkey only at the end of the eighteenth century. To populate it rapidly, Catherine the Great had opened it to colonists on liberal terms and had allowed even Jews, who were generally barred from landholding in the Russian Empire, to acquire land there. As a result, Trotsky's father was that rare phenomenon in Russia, a Jewish peasant. He was what was called a *kulak,* a well-to-do peasant able to hire laborers to work for him. It was a hardworking and thrifty environment, and also, like Gorky's, one that was often harsh, grasping, and exploitative. Trotsky was by no means mistreated, but such an intelligent and thoughtful boy was bound to feel cramped in this culturally barren and intellectually narrow atmosphere.

Like Radishchev, Trotsky was able to break out of his provincial rut at an early age, thanks to relatives who lived in a big city. At the age of nine he went off to Odessa to attend school. Odessa, one of Russia's major ports, was a colorful and cosmopolitan city, rich in cultural and educational opportunities. Trotsky was exposed to a variety of new ideas and attitudes, including the more mannerly and refined home life of his cultured relatives. As he puts it in his memoirs:

Mine was the grayish childhood of a lower-middle-class family, spent in a village in an obscure corner where nature is wide, and manners, views and interests are pinched and narrow. The spiritual atmosphere which surrounded my early years and that in which I passed my later, conscious life are two different worlds, divided not only in time and space by decades and by far countries, but by the mountain chains of great events and by those inner landslides which are less obvious but are fully as important to one's individuality.[28]

The "inner landslides" began in Odessa, where "every day there was revealed to me some aspect of a cultural environment greater than that in which I had passed the first nine years of my life."[29]

In Trotsky's early years, also, there is the element of personal injury and experience of injustice that appears to have been crucial in the making of the *intelligent*. In his autobiography, Trotsky pays little attention to the fact of his Jewishness, and later in his career he displayed no sense of Jewish identification. Whatever his degree of Jewish consciousness, however, he could not escape the numerous forms of discrimination to which Jews were subjected in the Russian Empire of the 1880s. Alexander III (1881–94), coming to the throne at the assassination of his father, Alexander II, adopted a policy of Russification in regard to the empire's numerous national minorities. His government set out to impose cultural and religious conformity, and thereby, it hoped, political loyalty on the empire's diverse population. Alexander II's liberal policy toward the Jews was reversed, and they now found themselves among the foremost victims of this discriminatory program. Thus, upon arriving in Odessa, Trotsky was forced to postpone his enrollment in a school for a year because the recently imposed Jewish quota had been filled. Here was a personal taste of arbitrary injustice and victimization of the sort that we have found so closely connected with the development of a social conscience. By the age of seventeen, he asserts, "life had stored within my consciousness a considerable load of social protest. What did it consist of? Sympathy for the downtrodden and indignation over injustice – the latter was perhaps the stronger feeling."[30] More concretely, Trotsky describes how he grew increasingly aware of the injustices to which students were subjected at his school and, on visits home, began to perceive how harshly his father treated the long-suffering peasant laborers on the farm.

In looking at the case histories of individual *intelligenty* and their evolution into opponents of the existing order, the importance of temperament must, of course, be recognized. Each of these rebels was a unique individual with a unique personality structure. An intensive psychoanalytic examination of each one might, perhaps, help to explain why he made the choices he did. Such an examination, however, is inherently limited by the fragmentary nature of the evidence available for it, and it is unlikely that its findings would be either persuasive or very substantial. We have confined ourselves to delineating some of the experiences common to the educated elite in the nineteenth century, and to showing the recurrent patterns in the way a series of individuals reacted to those experiences. As to why they reacted as they did, while others ostensibly like them reacted differently, or did not react at all, we can only agree with Chernyshevsky's assessment of one of his heroes: "His past life may have counted for something, it is true, in the formation of his character; but he could not have become such an uncommon man if he had not been specially endowed by nature."[31]

To summarize, the central feature of life in prerevolutionary Russia was paternalistic authority. It was often benevolent but inherently arbitrary in its treatment of the individual, and it pervaded every institution, from the family to the political structure. Members of the educated elite, privileged in some ways but themselves victims of paternalistic authority, were in a unique intellectual and moral position to criticize this principle of authority and pose an alternative to it. The hallmark of the intelligentsia's protest was its vision of a different order of human relationships, one in which the individual would be free to pursue his own destiny and to develop his full potential as a human being. To be sure, not all of the tsar's revolutionary opponents shared this libertarian vision or held it to the same degree. But it is what gave the intelligentsia's struggle not only its idealism and nobility but its drive and persistence from generation to generation.

And yet, with Trotsky, a subtle but important difference makes itself felt. On the whole, Trotsky minimizes the significance of his early years and formative experiences. Unlike the other memoirists we have considered, he devotes only a small portion of his autobiography to these experiences, and he does not dwell on them in loving detail. In particular, he takes great pains to deny the influence of anti-Semitism on his development. After recalling one or two instances of petty discrimination, and the fact that the *numerus clauses* had forced him to lose a year of school, he states that this issue "probably was one of the underlying causes of my dissatisfaction with the existing order, but it was lost among all the other phases of social injustice. It never played a leading part – not even a recognized one – in the lists of my grievances."[32]

In short, Trotsky himself denies the personal roots of his rebellion against the existing order. Instead, he treats it as an "objective" process, an abstract, intellectual rather than emotional repudiation of injustice.

Beginning with my earliest childhood, in all the impressions of my daily life human inequality stood out in exceptionally coarse and stark forms. Injustice often assumed the character of impudent license; human dignity was under heel at every step. It is enough for me to recall the flogging of peasants. Even before I had any theories, all these things imprinted themselves deeply on me and piled up a store of impressions of great explosive force.[33]

But why did these impressions make such an impact on a child growing up in the narrow rural environment Trotsky describes? Where did he find a standard of justice and human dignity different from that of his parents and the other authority figures around him, if not in his own feelings? Could his intense commitment to fairness and humane treatment have been generated by purely intellectual experiences, the reading of books and exposure to ideas? Trotsky's formative experiences closely parallel those of other *intelligenty,* yet he refuses to acknowledge the possibility that his social conscience had a personal component: an intense belief in the value of one's personality and a deeply felt sense of vulnerability, leading to an identification with all the downtrodden and oppressed.

Part of the explanation lies in the circumstances surrounding the composition of his memoirs. He wrote them in the first year after his expulsion from the Soviet Union, and his unsuccessful power struggle with Stalin colored his whole account of his life. He was less concerned with self-examination and self-understanding than with refuting the calumnies that were being leveled at him and with proving himself a more faithful Leninist than Stalin. Therefore he skims lightly over his early years and concentrates instead on his political development and revolutionary career. Also, as a Marxist, he tended to underplay the personal, individual sources of historical movements and to concentrate on impersonal, objective, social and economic factors. But his rejection of *feeling* as irrelevant to political activity, and possibly even a distraction from the revolutionary cause, goes deeper than his rivalry with Stalin or his Marxist ideology. At work here is an attitude that lodged itself within the intelligentsia in the course of its development and found its strongest expression in Bolshevism. This attitude proved fateful for the intelligentsia. It helps to explain why the long-sought overthrow of the tsarist system failed to achieve the humanistic, individualistic ideals that lay at the heart of the intelligentsia's dissent, and, instead, destroyed the intelligentsia itself.

4

Reason and revolution

Often I found that a human and sympathetic Communist was a bad Communist to the extent that he was human and sympathetic, and that he was well aware of this himself.

Stephen Spender, *The God That Failed*. [1]

If the ultimate objective of the Russian intelligentsia's dissent was to liberate the individual from arbitrary authority, something clearly went wrong. The tsarist order toppled, but this long-sought political change, instead of removing the obstacles to the individual's development, opened the way to the new and far more repressive system of Stalinism. Obviously, the new Soviet order was the product of complex historical, cultural, and material circumstances. But contradictions within the intelligentsia's own thinking contributed to the rise of Stalinism, or at least rendered the intelligentsia itself unable to resist it – as many *intelligenty* themselves realized only too late. From the very beginning of its history, one of the major concerns of the intelligentsia, a group whose very identity rested on its educated consciousness, was the role of reason in human affairs. The evolution of the intelligentsia's attitude toward reason and the relationship of reason to individual freedom provides one of the keys to its decline and fall at the hands of Stalin.

From the outset of its struggle for personal liberation, the Russian intelligentsia regarded reason as its chief weapon. Again, it was the state, intent on creating a modern educated class, that first implanted this notion. Peter the Great, finding that the nobility was resisting the new educational requirements he had imposed on it, decreed that without a minimum of education a noble was to be considered a perpetual minor: unless he could read and write he could not inherit property, become an officer, or even get married. Hence the intelligentsia, emerging from the nobility, was well disposed to adopt the emphasis on education embedded in Enlightenment thought.[2] To people like Novikov, education meant not only intellectual training but moral growth. Good behavior was a matter of eradicating ignorance and prejudice, and there was an indissoluble connection between reason and virtue, education and moral responsibility. The plays of both Fonvizin and Griboedov blame ignorance and backwardness for the problems of their heroes and heroines, who are notable for their cultural and intellectual development as well as for their integrity. Subsequently, faith in reason found expression in the rationalistic philosophies and ideologies that dominated the intelligentsia's history – from Hegelianism in the forties to scientism in the sixties to Marxism in the nineties.

As in the West, this rationalistic orientation did not go unchallenged. Some eighteenth-century Russian writers, including Radishchev, reflect the Rousseauist cult of simplicity. In some of his passages on the serfs, Radishchev contrasts the moral superiority of rural life to the corrupting overrefinement of the towns – a theme even echoed in a comic opera attributed to Catherine the Great – and finds virtue in naturalness rather than conscious deliberation, in unlettered simplicity and spontaneity rather than education. The emphasis on the peasants, whose culture remained virtually untouched by the Westernizing reforms of Peter the Great, found even stronger expression in the nationalism of the Slavophiles. In opposition to "Westernizers" such as Herzen, the Slavophiles of the 1840s rejected Western Europe as a model for Russia and harshly criticized what they regarded as the one-sided rationalism, legalism, and formalism of Western life. They were conservative romantics, their outlook closely tied to the landowning nobility from which they came. Their vision of society was deeply patriarchal, emphasizing the organic communal bonds that had supposedly prevailed in the pre-Petrine past and were supposedly preserved in the life of the unspoiled peasants. They idealized the family, the peasant commune, and the church, while sharply criticizing the Westernizing and modernizing course the Russian state had been following since Peter the Great. They were not reactionaries: their resentment of bureaucratic despotism and their opposition to such institutions as censorship and serfdom made them suspect to the government of Nicholas I and even earned them some active persecution. But the paternalistic communal forms of the past could hardly provide support for the individualistic aspirations of the intelligentsia, and Slavophilism as an ideology soon disintegrated. Some of the philosophical and religious components of Slavophilism, however, would be employed by later generations in an attempt to rescue those aspirations when the embrace of rationalism proved too suffocating.

For most *intelligenty,* however, the cultivation of reason remained the road to personal emancipation and self-development. Then, in the 1860s, just as the revolutionary movement was getting under way, two famous novels appeared that posed the question of the proper role of reason in the sharpest terms. The first, Ivan Turgenev's *Fathers and Sons,* published in 1862, expressed doubt that reason was the universal solution for mankind's problems. The second, Chernyshevsky's *What Is to Be Done?,* which appeared a year later, reaffirmed the intelligentsia's confidence in reason. It did much more than that, however. Chernyshevsky's novel stated the case for reason in such a way as to raise the danger that reason might become the master of man rather than man the master of reason.

Both novels portray the "men of the sixties," as the generation of the intelligentsia that came of age at the time of the Great Reforms is called. These young men – and, in appreciable numbers for the first time, young women – cherished reason in the specific form it takes in the natural sciences. Bazarov, the young hero of *Fathers and Sons,* delights in shocking his elders by rejecting all accepted moral and philosophical assumptions, aesthetic tastes, even polite manners. Turgenev terms him a nihilist, defined as "a person who does not look up to any authorities, who does not accept a single principle on faith, no matter how highly that principle may be esteemed."[3] (Later, this term misleadingly came to be applied to revolutionary terrorists.) Bazarov, however, like his real-life counterparts, did accept some principles, namely, the methods and standards of the sciences. His watchword is "two and two make four; the rest is all nonsense."[4] He is a medical doctor, absorbed in biological research, and he declares that a chemist is worth a score of poets. He is prepared to discard any principle or sentiment that cannot measure up to his utilitarian and materialist criteria, and he spends his spare time dissecting frogs in search of useful knowledge.

It would not be wholly unfair to summarize *Fathers and Sons* as a novel about a young man who believes that cutting up frogs is the means to universal happiness until he discovers girls. His scientific principles fail him and the methodical framework of his life begins to collapse when he falls hopelessly in love with an attractive young widow who does not return his feelings. Early in the story, Bazarov scornfully dismisses his antagonist in the novel, Paul Petrovich, a "man of the forties" whose life has been shattered by an unhappy love affair: "I must say, though, that a man who has staked his whole life on the card of a woman's love and who, when that card is trumped, falls to pieces and lets himself go to the dogs – a fellow like that is not a man, not a male."[5] But it is precisely the "male" aspect of his own nature that Bazarov is now forced to confront: the unpredictable and uncontrollable element of passion. Unlucky in love, he too begins to "fall to pieces." He soon dies an untimely death, having neglected to take proper precautions against infection while performing an autopsy on a peasant. Was his death really an accident or a form of suicide? Perhaps Bazarov himself is uncertain of the answer. In any case, his rigorously rationalistic principles have proved inapplicable to his emotional life. The human personality, Bazarov's fate suggests, is too complex and too varied in its needs to be compassed by science and logic. It is too unique, too spontaneous and unpredictable – too human, in other words – to conform entirely to the rules of reason.

Chernyshevsky's *What Is to Be Done?*, following immediately on the heels of *Fathers and Sons* (which had aroused a storm of protest within the intelligentsia), presents the men of the sixties and their convictions in a very different light. In part it appears to be a reply to Herzen's *Who Is to Blame?*, published in the 1840s. Both novels describe a love triangle in which two men are in love with the same woman. Herzen's novel, however, is peopled with "superfluous men" and tearful idealists who, despite their high-minded principles and noble sentiments, succeed only in destroying each other. Chernyshevsky's "new men" and "new women" are, as we have already seen, clear-eyed, clear-headed, and decisive. (The dialogue that these two novels conduct between the men of the forties and the men of the sixties is echoed in *Fathers and Sons* in the conflict between Bazarov and Paul Petrovich.) More importantly, Chernyshevsky's novel is a direct response to Turgenev's. Bazarov's tragic fate suggested that the bold principles of the "nihilists" were sterile and abstract, incapable of providing for the happiness of flesh-and-blood individuals. Chernyshevsky's heroes were designed to prove exactly the opposite.

In the last chapter we left Vera Pavlovna and her husband Lopukhov in their rationally planned three-room apartment. Lopukhov, like his best friend Kirsanov, is a medical student. Lest an inattentive reader fail to perceive their role as rejoinders to Bazarov, Chernyshevsky carefully informs us that in the course of their research they "had exterminated an enormous quantity of frogs."[6] The guiding principle of all these "new people" is rational egoism, a Benthamlike belief that if each individual pursues his own self-interest with proper care and calculation, such behavior will lead to the happiness of society as a whole. The principle of mutual self-interest underlies the successful seamstresses' cooperative that Vera Pavlovna establishes. The same principle resolves the love triangle that develops in the course of the novel. Rational as they are, Chernyshevsky's characters are not devoid of human emotions, and Vera Pavlovna soon realizes that, much as she admires and respects Lopukhov, she is really in love with Kirsanov. Lopukhov, coolly analyzing the situation, decides to bow out of the picture: he ingeniously fakes a suicide (the incident with which the novel opens) and clears the way for Vera Pavlovna and Kirsanov to marry. Several years later a mysterious figure named Beaumont appears on the scene – it is obviously Lopukhov, who has spent several years in America since his disappearance. He marries another "new woman" who is better suited to him than Vera Pavlovna, the two couples move into adjoining apartments, and all live happily ever after.

Throughout the novel, Lopukhov and the others maintain, insistently and at great length, that they are acting purely on the basis of rationally calculated self-interest. The modern reader may or may not find these assertions convincing, but the happy ending, at which everyone is more fulfilled than he was at the beginning, was clearly intended by the author as proof of their validity. Reason is capable of resolving even the tangled problems of love. The reconstruction of society as a whole, foreshadowed in Vera Pavlovna's cooperative, is simply a matter of extending the same rational principles that govern personal life. Far from being irrelevant to individual happiness, reason is a liberating force, enabling each and every man to throw off the fetters of ignorance, prejudice, and convention, and to reconstruct both his personal relations and his social life in a fully satisfying manner. This was Chernyshevsky's message to the men of the sixties, and the intelligentsia found it far more persuasive than Turgenev's cautionary tale, despite the latter's incontestably superior literary merits.

So far, however, *What Is to Be Done?* has presented little that is really new. Vera Pavlovna, Lopukhov, and Kirsanov are merely an extreme expression of the intelligentsia's traditional faith in reason as the road to personal liberation. It is another character in the novel, Rakhmetov, who signifies a new and fateful departure. Rakhmetov appears but briefly; his abrupt entrances and departures are only tenuously related to what there is of a plot. The leitmotif of Rakhmetov's existence is self-discipline. The son of a rich landowner, he has renounced all personal pleasures in order to devote himself to "duty" – the nature of which is never explained, in order to evade the tsarist censorship. The reader, as usual more perceptive than the censor, can easily infer that it involves revolution. This "rigorist," or "uncommon man," as Rakhmetov's friends call him, follows "special rules for the government of his physical, moral, and intellectual life . . . a complete system, to which he always held unchangeably."[7] He reads only what is useful, eats quantities of red meat to build up his muscles, sleeps on a bed of nails to test his endurance, and – in marked contrast to Bazarov – resists entanglement with a rich young widow to whom he is strongly attracted. "I am no longer free," he tells her, "and must not love."[8] Chernyshevsky makes it clear that Rakhmetov represents a higher, more advanced human specimen than even the liberated Vera Pavlovna and her friends. The Rakhmetovs of the world constitute a small but dynamic elite. They "are few in number, but through them the life of all mankind expands; without them it would have been stifled."[9]

Rakhmetov is a new and different model for the intelligentsia. Previous *intelligenty,* as we have discussed, arrived at a position of political radicalism through their struggle for self-liberation. They had first freed themselves from blind obedience to external forces and traditional authority by developing their individual reason, by asserting their educated consciousness. Their political objective, a world in which every man would be able to live his life in the light of his own reason, was a culmination of their personal quest; they sought social justice as an extension and guarantee of their individual freedom and fulfillment. Rakhmetov, however, stands for a denial rather than a fulfillment of self. He regards his feelings, his urges, the promptings of his ego, not as the legitimate demands of a unique personality but as distractions, or temptations, which must be resisted. And he is the real hero of the novel – even Vera Pavlovna agrees that concern with personal fulfillment is a sign of limitation of character:

The Rakhmetovs are another sort of people: they are so much concerned about the common welfare that to work for public ends is a necessity to them, so much so that to them altruistic life takes the place of private life. But we do not scale these high summits, we are not Rakhmetovs, and our private life is the only thing, properly speaking, that is indispensable to us.[10]

Reason now demands the suppression, or at least the indefinite postponement, of individual happiness, for the sake of achieving the happiness of mankind as a whole. Chernyshevsky terms Rakhmetov's path a matter of "scaling the difficult points in order to enter into the immense prairies fertile in all sorts of joys."[11] Until those sunny plateaus are reached, however, the individual must renounce all personal fulfillment – social, economic, even erotic – in order to concentrate on climbing the mountain peaks standing in the way.

Rakhmetov's historical significance lies in the fact that he did become a model for the intelligentsia, particularly for the revolutionary activists who were beginning to make their appearance in the late nineteenth century. The impact Chernyshevsky's novel made on Lenin is an outstanding example of this. According to Nicholas Valentinov, a Social–Democrat who was for a time closely associated with him, Lenin professed an unbounded admiration for *What Is to Be Done?*.

Only Chernyshevskii had a real, overpowering influence on me before I got to know the works of Marx, Engels, and Plekhanov, and it started with *What is to be Done?* Chernyshevskii not only showed that every right-thinking and really honest man must be a revolutionary, but he also showed – and this is his greatest merit – what a revolutionary must be like, what his principles must be, how he must approach his aim, and what methods he should use to achieve it. [12]

Lenin bristled at any suggestion that the work had literary shortcomings and insisted that it provided "inspiration for a lifetime." The most obvious sign of his admiration was his adoption of Chernyshevsky's title for one of his own major works. Lenin's *What Is to Be Done?* dates from 1902, and it spelled out his views on the organization of the Social–Democratic Party and the character of its members. If, as is generally agreed, Lenin's most original contribution to Marxism was his concept of the Party, then this pamphlet expresses the essence of Leninism. It laid down the fundamental principles that were to govern the theory and practice of Bolshevism.

The prevailing theme of Lenin's work is discipline – ideological, political, and personal. Only unquestioning, undeviating adherence to the "scientific" theories of Marx can guarantee the revolutionary triumph of the working class. Therefore the Party must not seek mass membership, which might dilute its doctrinal purity, but should restrict itself to an elite of dedicated, conscious Marxists. (This was the issue that ultimately produced the split between the Bolsheviks and Mensheviks.) This elite must be tightly organized in order to deploy its forces to the best advantage. And its members must be not amateur enthusiasts but full-time revolutionary activists, or, in Lenin's words, "professional revolutionists." Party membership is to be limited to "persons who are engaged in revolution as a profession and who have been professionally trained in the art of combating the political police."[13] "Give us an organization of revolutionists," Lenin summed up in a famous paraphrase, "and we shall overturn the whole of Russia!"[14]

Lenin did not require that Party members consume red meat or sleep on beds of nails. The impression made on him by Rakhmetov, however, as well as by the real-life Populist revolutionaries of the seventies, who were equally selfless and determined and to whose "militant centralized organization" Lenin paid tribute in *What Is to Be Done?*, is unmistakable. Certainly his own life was one of single-minded dedication to the revolutionary cause. He had an enormous amount of self-discipline, his personal life was austere and carefully regulated, and his literary and artistic tastes were utilitarian. He gave up chess, which he loved passionately, because it distracted his mind from political concerns, and he complained that listening to classical music made him feel too sentimental. Equally significant is an element of his outlook that has frequently been noted, his ambivalence toward the intelligentsia. He considered the intelligentsia indispensable for the success of the revolution, for it alone had the educated consciousness, the broad outlook and understanding of ultimate goals, which the unlettered workers, with their undisciplined, spontaneous energies, lacked. At the same time, however, he disdained much of what the intelligentsia stood for: its idealism, its sentimentality, its humanism. These were qualities he considered "soft" and liable to undermine the will to revolution if not carefully resisted and suppressed.

If, as he himself avowed, Lenin drew a "lifetime of inspiration" from Chernyshevsky's novel, the object of his admiration was not Vera Pavlovna and her friends, whose central preoccupation was self-liberation and self-development, but Rakhmetov, who rigorously channeled all his personal impulses and energies into work for the "cause." With Bolshevism, the evolution of the Russian intelligentsia's attitude toward reason took yet another step. Embodied in the "scientific" ideology of Marxism, reason now became an external force, existing outside of and above the individual. Instead of an internal instrument of self-awareness and self-emancipation, reason became a new deity to which the needs and aspirations of the individual must, if necessary, be sacrificed. In order to liberate all men, each man must accept the dictates of a higher reason, that is, the objective laws of historical development as formulated by Marx and interpreted by the Party.

Against this background, the self-image Trotsky attempts to project in his autobiography becomes more comprehensible. As part of his demonstration that he was a good Bolshevik – and as he joined the Party only in 1917 his credentials were always open to some suspicion – he discounted the impact of personal feelings and experiences on his development as a revolutionary. In his school years in Odessa, he tells us, he had already conceived a hatred of oppression.

During my school years I held no political views, nor for that matter had I any desire to acquire them. At the same time my subconscious strivings were tinged by a spirit of opposition. I had an intense hatred of the existing order, of injustice, of tyranny. Whence did it come? It came from the conditions existing during the reign of Alexander III; the high-handedness of the police; the exploitation practised by landlords; the grafting by officials; the nationalistic restrictions; the cases of injustice at school and in the street; the close contact with children, servants and laborers in the country; the conversations in the workshop; the humane spirit in the Schpentzer family; the reading of Nekrassov's poems and of all kinds of other books, and, in general, the entire social atmosphere of the time.[15]

Trotsky attributes the growing social conscience of his adolescent years not to any particular personal events or experiences that forcefully brought home to him the arbitrariness of the existing order – even though, as his very next paragraph relates, he was himself on occasion the object of anti-Semitic prejudice – but to an impersonal perception of the political, social, and economic defects of the tsarist system. More specifically, he states that "the feeling of general over particular, of law over fact, *of theory over personal experience,* took root in my mind at an early age and gained increasing strength as the years advanced."[16] He presents himself in his memoirs not as a sensitive individual whose own feeling of humiliation or subjugation led him to identify with all the victims of arbitrary authority, but as a vessel of an "objective," Marxist consciousness of the forces of social development.

Trotsky's image of Lenin is cast in the same mold. In the biographical study he began in the early 1930s, Trotsky drew a sharp contrast between Lenin and Lenin's older brother Alexander, who was executed in 1887 for involvement in an abortive attempt on the life of Alexander III.

As a type, Alexander was more like a knight than a politician. This created a psychic barrier between him and his younger brother, who was far more elastic, more opportunistic in questions of personal morals, better-armed for the struggle, but in no way less implacable toward social injustice . . . Alexander had not the will to power, the ability to harness for a cause not only the virtues but the weaknesses of others and, should need arise, to proceed despite considerations of individual personality. *He was too subjective, too much a prisoner of his own experiences .`. .*[17]

Putting aside the question of how accurate these characterizations are, is this Trotsky arguing – with himself, perhaps – the necessity of being "hard"? Is it the voice of the *intelligent* who has felt those "considerations of individual personality" but suppressed them for the sake of revolutionary victory? Whatever the answer, Trotsky's words succinctly describe the demands made on the *intelligent* who wished to be considered a "good Bolshevik."

Though firmly established in Bolshevism and other radical currents, the rationalism, materialism, and utilitarianism of the men of the sixties never achieved a total monopoly on the intelligentsia's thinking. One of their severest critics was Dostoevsky, whose *Notes from the Underground* appeared in 1864, the year after Chernyshevsky's *What Is to Be Done?*. Dostoevsky's "underground man," an embodiment of the dark, irrational sides of human nature, suggests that the object of human life lies in the endless but creative process of striving, rather than in a specific goal. For any such goal "must always be expressed as a formula, as positive as twice two makes four, and such positiveness is not life, gentlemen, but is the beginning of death . . . I admit that twice two makes four is an excellent thing, but if we are to give everything its due, twice two makes five is sometimes a very charming thing too."[18]

The most searching and comprehensive critique of this outlook appeared shortly before its elevation to an official ideology in 1917. In 1909, a collection of seven articles by some of Russia's leading intellectuals appeared under the title of *Signposts* (sometimes translated *Landmarks*). This was a rich and provocative volume in which the varied philosophical, cultural, and political tendencies of Russia's "Silver Age" found expression. The book aroused widespread interest and provoked a storm of controversy, thanks in part to the participation in it of such prominent political and philosophical figures as Peter Struve, Nicholas Berdiaev, and Sergei Bulgakov. Most of the contributors had at one time been Marxists (Struve, in fact, had drafted the program for the first congress of the Russian Social–Democratic Party in 1898) but now, particularly after witnessing the violence of the 1905 revolution, had rejected Marxism and turned to constitutional liberalism (a political evolution that was becoming increasingly common in the early years of the twentieth century). The book's main purpose, however, was not political analysis but a moral and philosophical examination of the commitment to revolution, which the authors felt had fatally affected much of the intelligentsia.

One general theme that ran throughout *Signposts* was a criticism of the extreme rationalism of the intelligentsia's successive ideologies, especially the various forms of socialism, of which Marxism was only the latest. This inflexible rationalism, the authors felt, was philosophically narrow and sterile, and it was incapable of resolving the vital ethical questions of human existence. Some, notably Bulgakov, condemned the Enlightenment itself for what he saw as its one-sided and destructive emphasis on reason, echoing a theme in Russian intellectual history that went at least as far back as Peter Chaadaev and the Slavophiles, and reflected the general revolt against "positivism" that was occurring in Western thought at the end of the nineteenth century. To supplement this meager diet of rationalism, *Signposts* urged the intelligentsia to open its mind to the idealist and religious currents in Russian thought – as represented by such thinkers as the Slavophiles, Dostoevsky, and the late nineteenth-century philosopher Vladimir Solovyov – which it had long dismissed or ignored.

A second major theme was criticism of what the authors termed the "nihilism" of Russian radical thought, its Bazarovlike utilitarian and materialist approach to cultural matters. *Signposts* deplored the tendency to reduce all cultural activities and institutions to a mere reflection of material forces and class antagonisms, or to view them simply as instruments for social and economic change. Berdiaev's article, for instance, lamented the intelligentsia's attitude toward philosophical inquiry: "The intelligentsia's basic moral premise is summed up in the formula: let truth perish, if by its death the people will live better and men will be happier; down with truth, if it stands in the way of the sacred cry 'down with autocracy'."[19] Philosophy, art, religion, the family, the nation, the state – all have an independent, objective validity, *Signposts* contended. Through them man expresses his human identity and develops his consciousness of himself and of the world around him. They are absolute, not relative values, and to sacrifice them to the search for social and economic justice is to sacrifice an essential dimension of human existence.

The most significant aspect of the book in relation to our theme was *Signposts'* contention that the intelligentsia's single-minded striving for social revolution contradicted the absolute value of the individual. The intelligentsia elevated into objects of worship one abstraction or another – "the peasantry," "the proletariat," "the people" – whose salvation became the sole object of concern even at the risk of sacrificing real individuals to the cause. The philosopher Semyon Frank, in perhaps the most penetrating of the seven articles, warned that "the abstract ideal of absolute happiness in the remote future destroys the concrete moral relationship of man to man and the vital sensation of love for one's neighbor, for one's contemporaries and their current needs." The revolutionary socialist "is striving for human

happiness, but he does not love living ⟨...⟩ f
universal human happiness. Since he sa⟨...⟩ ⟨...⟩
not hesitate to sacrifice others as well."² ⟨...⟩
philosophical contradiction between a ⟨...⟩
ideology, on the one hand, and the inte...ɡ....ɪ.. a....u.., on tne other,
observed: "The best members of the intelligentsia were fanatically prepared
for self-sacrifice and just as fanatically professed materialism, which denies
all self-sacrifice."²¹

To most of the *Signposts* authors, these contradictions could be resolved
only by some form of religious faith. They saw the radical intelligentsia's
unquestioned atheism as one of its most glaring and dangerous failings, and
they sought the meaning of human existence in a divinely created universe.
If man was created in the image of God, they felt, and human history was
the result of a divinely ordained plan, then each individual had objective,
absolute, moral significance, both in himself and in relation to others, and
could not be reduced to a mere means to some other end, whether social,
economic, or political. *Signposts* here reflected the religious renascence of
early twentieth-century Russia, one of the distinctive elements of the Silver
Age, and two of its contributors, Berdiaev and Bulgakov, went on to become noted religious philosophers.

Unlike other attacks on the intelligentsia and its world-view, *Signposts*
was itself a product of *intelligenty*, who, while criticizing the intelligentsia,
were also criticizing themselves and their own past. The book reaffirmed
what had been the central objective of the intelligentsia since its inception:
the liberation of the individual within a context of social justice. Although
some of the authors were influenced by such thinkers as the Slavophiles,
these were not conservatives nostalgic for an idealized past. In the idealist
and religious tradition of Russian thought they were seeking firmer support
for the absolute moral value of the individual – his right to security, personal development, and moral responsibility – than they felt a rigidly
rationalistic and materialist ideology could provide. At the same time, they
by no means were suggesting that the intelligentsia abandon its campaign
for social justice. Instead, they sought to restore the delicate balance that
had to be maintained between individual liberation and social improvement. *Signposts* warned the intelligentsia that its drive for social justice was
submerging its commitment to the individual, a commitment that formed
the real ethical basis of its protest against the existing order. Despite assertions to the contrary from its critics, *Signposts* as a whole did not urge the
intelligent to withdraw from external concerns in order to cultivate an inner,

purely spiritual freedom; it recognized that inner freedom must manifest itself in concrete terms if it is to be truly meaningful.[22] Therefore the struggle to improve the conditions of everyday life – to introduce the rule of law, raise living standards, spread education, foster social equality, etc. – must continue, but to be truly productive it must be based on more solid moral and philosophical foundations. *Signposts* attempted to find a religious resolution of the contradictions inherent in the intelligentsia's commitment to revolution; subsequent generations, whether they accepted or rejected this particular approach, would be forced to confront those contradictions in increasingly acute form in the decades after 1917.

The Revolution of 1917 – or, rather, the two revolutions, that of February, which overthrew the tsarist regime, and that of October, which overthrew the Provisional Government and brought the Bolsheviks to power – and the ensuing civil war that lasted until the end of 1920, plunged Russia into the worst turmoil it had experienced since the early seventeenth century. It was a time of political, cultural, even moral collapse, in which the whole fabric of social relations in Russia seemed to have come unraveled. Spontaneous violence, sectarian strife, and social atomization marked the daily life of this era. For all its heroic, even epic quality, the period of the Revolution and civil war brought with it an ominous depreciation of the value of individual life, a legacy that contributed substantially to the making of Stalinism in the 1930s.

The Soviet twenties, however, sandwiched between the upheaval of the Revolution and the terror of the Stalin period, were years of relative tranquility. The position of the intelligentsia was a highly ambiguous one in this decade. On the one hand, its place in the new society was no more secure than it had been in the old. Physically, it had been decimated by death and emigration during the civil war. Nor did political repression cease when the civil war came to an end. By 1922, all the non-Bolshevik parties had been suppressed, and even within the Bolshevik Party itself the decisions taken by the Tenth Party Congress of 1921 were stifling dissent on the part of the rank and file. Also in 1922, a number of prominent nonpolitical intellectuals, including such figures as Nicholas Berdiaev, Sergei Bulgakov, and Semyon Frank, who had contributed to the *Signposts* symposium, were deported to Western Europe. For those who remained, the suspiciousness of the state was supplemented by a degree of endemic popular hostility, for the Revolution had not overcome that dual alienation which permanently afflicted the intelligentsia. The automatic association in the popular mind between the educated elite and the privileged classes placed the intelligentsia in a particularly insecure position at a time when the privileged were under concerted, at times violent, attack. A startling passage from the memoirs of the Soviet writer Konstantin Paustovsky provides an illustration:

It took Mama and Galya two weeks to walk to Kiev [in 1919]. They deliberately dressed to look like beggars; in actual fact, this is what they were. Galya went without glasses, and walked holding on to Mama's shoulder, like a blind woman. No one would have believed them to be poor if Galya had worn her glasses. Everyone treated people in glasses suspiciously in those violent times. They thought them cunning enemies, and hated them bitterly. It is amazing that this distrust of people wearing glasses has persisted up to the present time.[23]

Nevertheless, despite these conditions, the Soviet twenties also produced some efforts to put into practice the ideals of the intelligentsia. The relaxation of economic tensions under the New Economic Policy (NEP), with its concessions to peasant agriculture and petty trade and manufacture, had its parallels in other areas of Soviet life. Certain developments in the social and cultural life of these years, in some cases sponsored and in other cases tolerated by the Bolshevik Party (now renamed the Communist Party), reflect the intelligentsia's quest for individual liberation. For all its limitations and shadows, the twenties – roughly from the end of the civil war to the introduction of the first Five Year Plan in 1928–9 – can be considered the one time in Russian history when an attempt was made to put into effect some of the intelligentsia's libertarian aspirations.

The most striking, and certainly the most publicized, effort in this direction was the attempt to resolve the "woman question," which Chernyshevsky had discussed decades earlier. The foremost exponent of the emancipation of women was Alexandra Kollontai, who became associated with the idea of "free love." Like so many of Russia's revolutionaries, Kollontai came from an upper-class background: her father was a general who came from an old Ukrainian family. Drawn into the radical movement, she separated from her husband, became a Bolshevik, and after the Revolution had a distinguished diplomatic career. In publicizing the notion of free love, Kollontai did not mean to encourage promiscuity. She was attempting to implement the ideal that had been preached by Chernyshevsky and actually put into practice within their own circles by many of the Russian radicals who came after him: that no individual should be imprisoned in an outworn relationship, forced by legal or economic bonds to remain wedded to another. The family, in its traditional form that rendered a woman subservient to the male breadwinner, would, like the state, "wither away" under communism. The following was Kollontai's vision of the future status of women and the relationship between the sexes:

The family is ceasing to be a necessity of the state, as it was in the past; on the contrary, it is worse than useless, since it needlessly holds back the female workers from more productive and far more serious work. Nor is it any longer necessary to the members of the family themselves, since the task of bringing up the children, which was formerly that of the family, is passing more and more into the hands of the collectivity. But on the ruins of the former family we shall soon see rising a new form which will involve altogether different relations between men and women, and which will be *a union of affection and comradeship, a union of two equal members of the communist society, both of them free, both of them independent, both of them workers. No more domestic "servitude" for women! No more inequality within the family!*[24]

The leadership of the new Soviet state was not quite as enthusiastic about the demise of the family as Kollontai and her adherents. Lenin particularly, whose own family life was as impeccably bourgeois as Marx's had been, and who did not on the whole share the intelligentsia's libertarian personal ideals, was skeptical of such efforts. In regard to Kollontai's notion that making love should be as casual an act as drinking a glass of water, he reportedly questioned whether a normal man would wish to drink out of a glass "with a rim greasy from many lips."[25] Nonetheless, in the twenties Soviet social and legal policies did diminish the strength of family ties and attempted to liberate women from their previous constraints. Both marriage and divorce were simplified and became matters of mere registration. Common-law unions were put on a par with officially registered marriages, the legal distinction between legitimate and illegitimate birth was erased, and abortions were made readily available. At the same time, because Marxist ideology attributed the subjugation of women primarily to their economic dependence, particular efforts were made to liberate women as workers: new careers were opened to them, and the principle of equal pay for equal work was proclaimed. To be sure, the new regime's attitude toward the family was in part a reflection of its antireligious stance, as traditional family relationships in Russia had owed a good deal to religious considerations. But this attitude also reflected a deliberate effort to liberalize the strongly patriarchal Russian family structure and to free its individual members.

Similar efforts were made in the field of education, where the ideas of John Dewey, and of progressive education in general, had a considerable vogue in the twenties. Here, too, as in social policy, there was a desire to abolish "bourgeois" tradition and to substitute for the competitiveness and authoritarianism of the past a new atmosphere of egalitarianism and free individual expression. Parallel developments occurred in the arts, where many of those avant-garde artists who remained in Russia tried to put their talents at the disposal of the revolutionary new society they believed was arising. The result was the continuation into the twenties of the avant-garde currents and experiments that had marked the Silver Age in the years before the Revolution. Abstract and futuristic art forms found striking application in theatrical productions, book design, graphic art, and even in such mass consumption items as crockery and furniture. Whether it was a matter of recasting the family, the school, or the aesthetic environment, the twenties saw an attempt to release the pent-up creative energies of the individual.

It would be a mistake to glorify this era, which to some Soviet citizens, in the light of what the thirties and forties were to bring, came to represent a kind of Golden Age. Creative energies were not entirely free to pursue their own course, and the incorrigible nonconformist was treated none too gently. Osip Mandelstam, to cite just one example, a nonpolitical but intensely independent poet, remained largely unpublished, virtually ostracized by the literary establishment, and subjected to an increasing number of harassments and persecutions. Within the political and ideological limits imposed by the new regime, however, there was a widespread belief that the individual had at last been released from the constraints of social hierarchy, patriarchal authority, and outworn tradition, that the Revolution and its Marxist ideology had definitively established the social and economic conditions that would enable him to cultivate his talents and apply them freely for the benefit of society.

The most forceful description of the new human freedom that many of the defenders of the Revolution believed imminent came from the pen of Trotsky. In *Literature and Revolution,* published in 1924, Trotsky sketched a vision of the future in which man's creative talents, released at last by the communist reorganization of society, would remold both man himself and his environment. It is a vision of man artistically reshaping the earth in his own image, through science and technology: "Through the machine, socialist man will command nature in its entirety, with its grouse and its sturgeons. He will point out places for mountains and for passes. He will change the course of the rivers, and he will lay down rules for the oceans."[26] Social life as well as nature would become the object of reason and planning: "Communist life will not be formed blindly, like coral islands, but will be built consciously, will be tested by thought, will be directed and corrected.

Life will cease to be elemental, and for this reason stagnant."[27] Finally, man would be in a position to master his own nature, to gain control over his physiological and psychological impulses and put them to conscious use. "He will try to master first the semiconscious and then the subconscious processes in his own organism, such as breathing, the circulation of the blood, digestion, reproduction, and, within necessary limits, he will try to subordinate them to the control of reason and will."[28] Trotsky ends with a description of man raised to new heights of achievement under communism: "The average human type will rise to the heights of an Aristotle, a Goethe, or a Marx. And above this ridge new peaks will rise."[29]

Trotsky's vision of liberation had a long genealogy in Russian thought. What man needs to be liberated from, according to Trotsky, is obedience to blind, spontaneous forces that act upon him as a mere plaything. Those "coral islands," as he terms them, unquestioned accretions of tradition, were all too numerous in Russian life: the despotism of autocracy and serfdom, the backwardness and poverty of Russian society, the impulsive crudeness of the Prostakovs or of Vera Pavlovna's mother, the passive submission to supernatural powers by Gorky's grandparents. The weapons the intelligentsia had taken up to do battle with these dragons were reason, consciousness, self-assertion; the objective was to master those elemental, uncontrolled forces swirling in and around man, for only by opposing and conquering them could the individual assert his full humanness. The "new man" whose emergence Trotsky foresaw under communism was in fact an image older than Russian Marxism and older even than the intelligentsia itself. It reached all the way back to Peter the Great, who, by conscious opposition to tradition, had sought to Europeanize and modernize his backward subjects. The new man had been reincarnated in Russian radical thought, most notably in the figure of Rakhmetov, and had been inherited by Bolshevism. Trotsky adds a specifically Marxist element with his celebration of modern industrial technology. But the concept of the new man, emancipated from the play of spontaneous natural forces and blind instinct by the assertion of reason, long antedated the reception of Marxism in Russia. It had accompanied the birth of the intelligentsia and of modern Russia itself.

The assumption that reason was the royal road to individual liberation had been subjected to criticism from various quarters in the past, and even now it did not go unchallenged. Several literary works of the twenties raised serious doubts about the kind of technological utopia Trotsky had sketched and the prospects it offered for individual freedom. The authors of these works saw not harmony but inherent antagonism between the ideological principles to which the new regime was committed and its professed goal of human liberation. Like many prerevolutionary writers, they feared that the first would inevitably overwhelm the second. Now, however, the rationalism, materialism, and scientism they were calling into question were not just one current of thought competing freely with others for the intelligentsia's loyalty, but were enshrined in the official Marxism that formed the basis of the new government's legitimacy. Criticism of this outlook consequently took on political overtones it had not had in the past and could incur serious penalties.

One of these works was perhaps the most outstanding Russian literary production of the twenties, the novel *We* by Evgeny Zamiatin. It was written in 1920–1 but was not accepted for publication – one indication that even in cultural affairs the twenties were not as liberal as later generations liked to think. The novel has never, in fact, been published in the Soviet Union; its author emigrated in 1931 and died in the West. *We* is an antiutopian novel, in many respects a forerunner of two better known works, *Brave New World* and *1984*. It is set in the more or less distant future, in a political entity called the One State. A remote and omnipotent dictator called the Benefactor presides over the One State, which is governed by ruthlessly rationalistic principles. Individuals bear not names but numbers, and every moment of their daily lives is regulated by a timetable, the Table of Hours. The novel is in the form of a diary kept by the hero, D-503, a mathematician, who describes life in the One State as follows:

Every morning . . . at the same hour and the same moment, we – millions of us – get up as one. At the same hour, in million-headed unison, we start work; and in million-headed unison, we end it. And, fused into a single million-headed body, at the same second, designated by the Table, we lift our spoons to our mouths.[30]

Science and technology contribute to this uniformity: the One State is a world constructed of glass, and all the inhabitants live in identical transparent cubicles, in an artificial, man-made environment totally devoid of privacy.

As in *Brave New World* and *1984*, the theme of dehumanization and rebellion in Zamiatin's antiutopia centers around sex. Certain hours of the day are set aside for sexual relations, which are carefully regulated by books of pink coupons issued by the state. Hence a spontaneous, illicit love affair of the sort D-503 finds himself drawn into is necessarily a form of political rebellion. Significantly, the mysterious woman who seduces the narrator and makes him rebel against the way of life he has hitherto glorified is named I-330. Their affair is a revolt of "I" against "we," the assertion of individuality, expressed in passion, against the faceless mass.

The world Zamiatin envisioned was one in which science, technology, and reason, far from serving as instruments of liberation, have become forces of repression and dehumanization. In a world ruled by the logic of a timetable, the uniqueness of the individual has no place and must be crushed. The liberating, humanizing marks of individuality in *We* are precisely those forces that do not conform to reason and predictability: nature, emotion, sensuality, creative imagination. The One State has tried its best to obliterate all these forms of spontaneity but has not fully succeeded. The rebellious hero, for instance, has hairy hands, while his best friend – a poet, significantly – has negroid lips; both features are regarded as throwbacks to a more spontaneous, "animal" nature. Even mathematics, usually a sign and instrument of uniformity, yields a symbol of individuality. The hero of *We* is preoccupied with the radical number $\sqrt{-1}$, the irreducible, irrational element that refuses to behave according to the rules; here, it becomes a symbol of the human soul as well as of the "radical number" D-503, who emerges from the mass as an "I." It is interesting to compare this mathematical symbol with the slogan of Bazarov, the "nihilist" of the sixties, to whom the logical purity of "two plus two are four" seemed a liberating, vivifying force.[31] In *We*, as in *Fathers and Sons*, the spontaneous impulse of love – irrational, illogical, uncontrollable – affirms the true humanity of the hero, overwhelming his unnatural efforts to regulate his life according to reason. Finally, nature itself provides an overarching symbol of nonconformity and source of revolt. The One State is surrounded by a wall which protects its technological world of glass and steel from the encroachments of nature. In this green, tangled, but natural environment live those few who have rejected the values of the One State, and it is from this base that a revolution against it is organized. D-503, however, who has now been subjected to an operation to remove the element of imagination from his brain, expresses confidence that "we" shall conquer, for, in the novel's ironical last words, "reason must prevail."[32]

Zamiatin's novel, of course, was written before Trotsky's *Literature and Revolution,* yet it seemed to anticipate Trotsky's vision of the future and respond to it even before it was expressed. It was a criticism not just of the dangers of political dictatorship but of the particular form of rationalism that the official ideology embodied and Trotsky's words reflected. Celebration of the economic productivity of the modern industrial system is an important element of Marxism, which, unlike some other varieties of nineteenth-century socialism, accepted the rise of industry and sought to harness its potential. In Russian Marxism this element grew into a veritable worship of technology, for to backward Russia the forces of modern industry seemed to promise not only economic benefits but a truly civilized existence, an infallible method of catching up with the more advanced West.[33] If this was what the Revolution meant, Zamiatin was warning, it risked enslavement and dessication of the individual instead of recognition of his uniqueness and the opportunity to develop it freely.

Another satirical criticism of what seemed to be the official values of the new Soviet state came at the end of the twenties with the appearance of Maiakovsky's play *The Bedbug* in 1929. Vladimir Maiakovsky's powerful lyric verse had made him one of Russia's leading poets before the Revolution. In the twenties he placed himself at the service of the Soviet government and produced a stream of political slogans, propaganda posters, and hymns of praise to Lenin. Maiakovsky, then, was not a writer who held himself aloof from the new regime from the very beginning, not a "fellow traveler," to use the term Trotsky coined; he had served it faithfully, virtually as its official poet. His disillusionment, therefore, had considerable impact, reinforced by his suicide in 1930.

The first part of *The Bedbug* is set in the 1920s, and it is a satire on the era of the NEP. The central figure of the play, Prisypkin, is a member of the new "ruling class," an unwashed, vulgar, vodka-sodden loudmouth who is enjoying the material privileges and social standing that his proletarian status brings him. Most of the other characters in this first act, among them profiteers and petty traders of the sort that flourished in the NEP, are similarly crude and grasping.

In the course of Prisypkin's drunken wedding celebration the house burns down, and when the firemen douse the flames, Prisypkin is frozen in a block of ice. Fifty years later he is discovered, defrosted, and resurrected in a triumph of futuristic technology. The collectivized world into which he emerges is totally different from the one he has left: it is an antiseptic, artificial world – like the world of *We,* constructed of glass – in which even the fruit on the trees grows in tidy little baskets. Dirt and disease have been abolished, but, Prisypkin discovers, so have vodka, roses, daydreams – and, of course, love. In this setting, the coarse, undisciplined, unhygienic Prisypkin, a figure of unmitigated vulgarity in the first act, becomes a symbol of human vitality, his incurable romanticism and spontaneity threatening to infect the entire society. The play ends with Prisypkin isolated and on exhibit in a glass cage at the zoo, his only companion a bedbug that has been unfrozen along with him. *The Bedbug* raised much the same questions as *We*, though with considerably more humor, about the possibility of dehumanization in a world ruled entirely by reason, science, and technology. Primitive and undisciplined though he is, Prisypkin is fully human, and his very animality becomes an assertion of irrepressible human individuality in a society from which spontaneity and naturalness have been banished.

The anxieties expressed in these literary works of the twenties concerning the fate of the individual seemed to be borne out by the events of the thirties. Under Stalin, the Communist Party, which based its claim to leadership on a "scientific" understanding of the forces of history, shrank the individual into an instrument for the achievement of material progress and the construction of socialism. The liberalization of many areas of Soviet life in the twenties gave way to strict social discipline and cultural conformity. With the advent of the Five Year Plans, the emphasis was now on productivity, work, and self-sacrifice for the collective good as defined by the Party, on harnessing individual energies for the benefit of the state rather than releasing them for the fulfillment of the individual. The efforts to loosen family bonds were reversed and the regulations governing such matters as divorce and abortion were considerably tightened. The educational experimentation of the twenties was abandoned, and traditional classroom discipline as well as a traditional curriculum were reinstated. The arts and literature were brought firmly under state control and were made to serve as handmaidens of official propaganda. In the chilling phrase attributed to Stalin, writers were to be "engineers of human souls."

In part, the new social and cultural conservatism stemmed from Stalin's drive for political mastery over Soviet society. Stalin and his associates wanted to ensure that their policies would not be the object of any sort of criticism or opposition. Therefore they extended the instruments of Party and state control into every facet of Soviet life, seeking to eliminate all pockets of autonomy and sources of initiative from below. In large part, however, the new social policy flowed logically from the decision embodied in the first Five Year Plan to accelerate the pace of Russia's economic growth and transform the country with breathtaking swiftness into a modern industrial society. Such a program required that the country's human, material, and economic resources be mobilized to the utmost and placed at the full disposal of the state. Thus it was essential to stifle the libertarian principles that had been given some leeway in the twenties, with their challenge to traditional social values and forms of authority. The energies of all Soviet citizens now had to be disciplined and directed into productive channels by a state that was once again, as in the time of Peter the Great, dedicated to the goal of modernization above all.

The social and economic policies of the thirties, then, brought with them a deliberate repudiation of the intelligentsia's traditional ideal of individual liberation. At the same time, a social change was taking place that undermined the intelligentsia in another way. Under Stalin's auspices a new generation of political leaders was arising. Many of them were of worker or even of peasant origin (since much of the industrial labor force had itself barely emerged from the peasantry). Like Stalin himself, they were narrowly educated at best, and therefore tended to be culturally conservative; and they had a hard-boiled, realistic view of politics and of life in general. They had neither the life experiences (a taste of social privilege, foreign travel) nor the education that had instilled a conviction of the sanctity of the individual and his fundamental human rights in the old middle- and upper-class educated elite and had enabled it to envision a radically different set of relationships between people from that prevailing under the old regime. Both their political style and their political objectives distinguished them from the generation that had made the Revolution, much of which had its roots in the Westernized intelligentsia.

Several memoirists of the purges have noted a coarsening of manners and a deterioration of cultural levels within the ranks of Soviet officialdom as the thirties proceeded and the new generation began to supplant the old.[34] The most prominent example of this change is Nikita Khrushchev, whose memoirs vividly describe his rise within the Party in the thirties and forties. Of worker-peasant origin (his father was a coal miner, and Khrushchev himself started out in the mines), Khrushchev was quick-witted and ambitious. At the same time, he accepted – and exploited – the extraordinary system of sycophancy, arbitrariness, and self-abasement that was the price of power under Stalin.[35] It was a rough-and-tumble political world in which one could rise rapidly or vanish abruptly. If the top leaders of the country were able to tolerate such despotism and were willing to expose themselves to such risks, it is hardly surprising that they viewed the average citizen as expendable. These were the kinds of people whom Stalin was promoting to prominent positions in various walks of Soviet life in the twenties and thirties, and their support sheds light on Stalin's own staying power as well as the behavior of his regime.

These two factors, the need for social discipline and the changing social composition of the political leadership, help to explain why the purge of the thirties fell so heavily on the remnants of the old educated elite, which had produced the critical and questioning Russian intelligentsia. The so-called Great Purge, the wave of mass terror that broke over Russia in the thirties, began with the assassination of Sergei Kirov in 1934 – a still murky affair in which, it is strongly suspected, Stalin himself had a hand – and came to an end late in 1938, with the replacement of Ezhov, the head of the secret police at the height of the terror, by Beria. The motivations behind the Great Purge were numerous and complex, and they went far beyond Stalin's effort to rid himself of actual or potential rivals for power. That may have been a primary purpose, but with the number of arrests ranging upward to seven or eight million the purge obviously extended far beyond the country's political elite. Ivanov-Razumnik, a writer and critic of Populist persuasion who had achieved literary prominence before the Revolution, left this description of his fellow cell-mates in the Butyrka prison in Moscow in 1937:

There was the former People's Commissar, Krylenko, and a great many Vice-Commissars; an important Soviet general, the "four-rhomboid" General Ingaunis, who had commanded the whole Air Force of the Far Eastern Army under Blucher; the famous designer of the ANT aircraft, A. N. Tupolev; and a whole multitude of others – party bigwigs, lorry-drivers, academicians, chauffeurs and professors. There was General Ozhunkovsky, a former Assistant Minister; there were members of the Comintern. There were youths of sixteen and old men of eighty (including the well-known lawyer, Chibisov, and the Chief Rabbi of Moscow). There were Socialists of various persuasions and KRs ("Counter-Revolutionaries"). There were all sorts of lesser Soviet officials accused of embezzling State funds. There were airmen and students and . . . but why go on? The list was unending! Here one found the "levelling" process in full swing.[36]

The prison cells held an astonishingly thorough catalogue of Soviet social types. The great "show trials," in which the most prominent victims figured, were but the visible tip of the iceberg; beneath the surface, the purge struck not only at anti-Stalinists and alleged anti-Stalinists, but even at pro-Stalinists and at a great many who were simply non-Stalinists.

Not all of the details of the purge were planned in advance, nor did Stalin personally select all of the victims. In the first place, many private scores were settled in the course of the Great Purge. Some people took the opportunity to rid themselves of professional rivals or to shed inconvenient lovers by denouncing them to the secret police. There were even cases of individuals denouncing their neighbors in order to acquire their apartments at a time when housing was in extremely short supply. Second, a large-scale terror campaign inevitably develops a momentum of its own: one suspect implicates others, and each accusation of "conspiracy" breeds a chain reaction of further accusations. Finally, the secret police had a vested interest in maintaining and even accelerating the purge's momentum. By detecting more and more new traitors, they could demonstrate that they were doing their job properly and merited promotions, increased budgets, and greater authority. It seems likely that these factors helped to swell the Great Purge beyond Stalin's original intentions.

There is no evidence that Stalin ever lost overall control of the operation, however, and he was able to bring it to a halt when it had served its purpose. Whatever Stalin may have had in mind at the beginning, as it grew the Great Purge acquired very far-reaching social and political objectives. On the one hand, it turned into a campaign to atomize Russian society, to break up all existing, or potential, group loyalties and solidarities through arrest, fear, and mutual suspicion, so as to leave the individual citizen totally isolated in his confrontation with the state. On the other hand, it aimed at the elimination of all possible criticism of the new order Stalin was forging or even any questioning of the policies he was pursuing. Given these objectives, it was the educated elite that was bound to suffer most heavily, for this was a social stratum interlaced by a complex web of professional and occupational connections and endowed with the greatest potential for critical thought and expression. The mature generation of the educated elite in the thirties had received its education in pre-Soviet times; many of its members had traveled abroad or at least been heavily exposed to Western ideas; and they were fully aware of the ideals and promises in the name of which the Revolution had been carried out. These qualities gave them some independence of mind in viewing the new Stalinist order, and it was that potential for independent judgment that the Great Purge sought to eradicate. What determined the choice of victims in most cases was not any specific act they had performed, or were planning to perform, or were even capable of performing, but their objective characteristics, which gave them the possibility of bringing a critical perspective to bear on their surroundings.

Many of the victims were Old Bolsheviks, that is, people who had joined the Party before 1917 and did not owe either their status or their view of the world to Stalin alone. Many, however, were not Party members at all. One characteristic shared by large numbers of those arrested was that they had experience of foreign travel or foreign contacts. Stalin was obviously well aware of the role that knowledge and experience of the outside world had played in generating the intelligentsia's opposition to the tsarist regime. Therefore anyone who had traveled abroad, had studied or served there, or even corresponded with foreigners for professional purposes was automatically suspect and had a high probability of being arrested. The fact that such objective factors, rather than any specific deeds, frequently determined the choice of victims clarifies some of the otherwise puzzling features of the Great Purge. It helps to explain why certain groups were singled out for particular attention, although they were not inherently more disloyal than others: the diplomatic corps, for instance, or the Russian railroad workers who had served on the Chinese Eastern Railway in Manchuria and were repatriated when the Soviet Union sold the line to the Japanese in 1935. (Russian railway workers in general were heavily victimized in this period. Before the Revolution they had created one of the strongest and best organized unions in the country, and Stalin evidently wished to destroy the remnants of this solidarity.) It also helps to explain why the charges leveled against individuals – industrial sabotage, spying for foreign powers, and so on – were so outlandish, in many cases involving actions that it was physically impossible for the accused to have taken even if they had wished to; and why certain individuals were persecuted while similar individuals, for no obvious reason, escaped attention. The real objective was to decimate certain groups of the citizenry, not to punish specific cases of wrongdoing. Therefore the choice of individual victims was often random, or a matter of the investigative officials' whim, and the charges, while they had to be serious, did not have to correspond to the actual behavior of the accused.[37]

The educated elite found itself in the unenviable position of displaying to the greatest degree the characteristics that most aroused Stalin's suspicions. What the arrests began, the conditions in the labor camps, to which millions were sentenced for long terms, completed. Mistreatment, starvation, and overwork ensured a high death toll. Even in the camps, the authorities were not above utilizing the popular resentment of the educated as a privileged class. Common criminals were generally given the "trusty" positions in the camps and allowed to exploit those sentenced on political charges. The latter, who were most often intellectuals and professionals, were given the heaviest tasks, for which they were physically unprepared, and the shortest rations.

It cannot be said that the Great Purge deliberately set out to annihilate the educated elite inherited by the Stalin regime from the tsarist era, but as it snowballed it came close to doing precisely that. Such was implicitly acknowledged by the authorities themselves when they gave the signal that the purge was drawing to a close. On November 15, 1938, the Central Committee of the Communist Party issued a lengthy statement which included the remark that intellectual-baiting was no longer to be tolerated.

[The Central Committee of the Communist Party] states that despite the extremely important role of the intelligentsia in the Soviet state a disparaging attitude toward our intelligentsia has not yet been overcome. This is a highly pernicious transferral onto our Soviet intelligentsia of those views and attitudes toward the intelligentsia which were widespread in the prerevolutionary period, when the intelligentsia served the landowners and capitalists.[38]

The statement suggests that the regime was now satisfied that the old educated elite, with its potential for criticism, had been replaced by a new, Soviet-trained generation, which could be trusted to remain politically docile while performing its crucial role in the country's economic development.

The efforts of some historians to rationalize the Great Purge of the thirties, to depict it as a somewhat extreme but essentially "normal" feature of Russian history or of the Soviet political system, are unpersuasive. The terror, the violence, and the scale of the arrests and executions were unprecedented in peacetime Russia. This is not to deny, however, that some significant features of the Great Purge had their roots in the Russian past. The social change just described conformed to the autocratic pattern of modernization from above that Russia had been following since the reign of Peter the Great. Modernization required an educated elite, but autocracy required that the elite's education remain within narrow, technical boundaries. The tsarist government's inability to preserve those limits had created out of the educated elite an intelligentsia, increasingly critical of the system that had created it and eager for more freedom and autonomy than an autocracy is usually willing to concede. Now Stalin, as part of his drive for unchallenged supremacy in Russia, was attempting to reduce the Soviet educated elite once more to an obedient instrument of the state's modernization plans. Peter III and his successors, after the emancipation of the nobility from compulsory service in 1762, had relied increasingly on their professional bureaucracy, more dependent and hence more reliable than the gentry class. Stalin, too, sought a more docile group of state servants than those he had inherited from the previous order. Instead of putting the old elite out to pasture on country estates, however, he terrorized it, decimated it, and promoted a new generation to fill the leading positions it had previously occupied.

For those victims of the Great Purge who had never fully reconciled themselves to Communist Party rule – individuals like Ivanov-Razumnik – their experiences merely confirmed, though in particularly brutal fashion, everything they had always believed about the Bolsheviks. Party members, however, who formed a significant proportion of the purge victims, found themselves psychologically and ideologically unprepared to explain the nightmare world of accusation and terror into which they were suddenly thrust. For many years they had obediently followed the dictates of the "objective forces of history" as embodied in the Party's policies. They had fought the Party's opponents in the Revolution and the civil war, they had participated, or at least acquiesced, in the elimination of dissidents both inside and outside the Party in the twenties, and had then helped to impose the immensely destructive collectivization program on the peasantry. They believed that these ruthless measures, unfortunate though they might be in themselves, were necessary steps along the road of historical progress, of which the Party was the chosen instrument and which created a "higher morality" justifying the sacrifice of those classes and individuals whom the Party deemed stumbling blocks along the way. Now, when they themselves, loyal Party members, fell victim to the same standards of judgment, they could find no firm ground, no principled stand, from which to claim exemption. Having reduced the individual to a relative value, whose worth depended on his usefulness to the construction of socialism and the advancement of history, they could evince no compelling reason for protecting any individual against those who claimed to be acting in the name of that higher end. They had been morally disarmed, and although they knew that they were innocent of any wrongdoing, they had no way of challenging the Party's right to treat them as it saw fit. In fact, many of them never denied that the Party should be allowed to destroy those whom, in its infallible wisdom, it chose to destroy. They claimed only that the Party had made a mistake when its choice fell on them[39] – Stalin had been deceived by the wicked officials who surrounded him, and they were merely the victims of a rectifiable error. Like Prince Kurbsky centuries earlier, who implicitly accepted the principle that the sovereign was the legitimate source of all rewards and punishments, they asked only to be rewarded or punished according to their true deserts.

Some, however, reacted differently: their sudden reversal of fortune opened their eyes to the true character of the system they had hitherto supported and forced them to reexamine its fundamental premises. One of the best examples of this process is Eugenia Ginzburg, the author of a poignant memoir of the Great Purge. Ginzburg was a loyal Party member, a university graduate, journalist, and teacher; she was arrested in 1937, at the height of the purge, sent to labor camps after a term of imprisonment, and released only after Stalin's death. Ginzburg's reaction to her arrest and to her prison experience was a rediscovery of the human quality of her fellowman, a process of moral awakening that forms the leitmotif of her memoir.

At the start of her tribulations, as she herself tells us, she was an unquestioningly obedient Party member. "I must say in all honesty that, had I been ordered to die for the Party – not once but three times – that very night, in that snowy winter dawn, I would have obeyed without the slightest hesitation. I had not the shadow of a doubt of the rightness of the Party line."[40] She was prepared to sacrifice herself for what the Party represented, as hitherto she had accepted the sacrifice of others to that same higher purpose. The importance of the political dogmas she has subscribed to and taught to others begins to diminish, however, when she finds herself cast into communal jail cells, surrounded by fellow victims of a faceless terror. "For the first time in my life I was faced by the problem of having to think things out for myself – of analyzing circumstances independently and deciding my own line of conduct."[41] Soon, "the most unorthodox thoughts" begin to pass through her mind, suggesting to her "how thin the line is between high principles and blinkered intolerance, and also how relative are all human systems and ideologies and how absolute the tortures which human beings inflict on one another."[42] Finally, when a fellow Party member asks whether she should report a cell-mate's infringement of the rules to the prison authorities, Ginzburg gives the following advice: "Since we're all naked in every sense of the word, I think you should be guided by the instinct which is generally known as conscience."[43] Through her own suffering and humiliation – "the worst physical sufferings, it seemed to me, would have been easier to bear than the sense of outrage and degradation"[44] – Ginzburg had grown sensitive to the sufferings of others, and loyalty to ideological abstractions began to yield to a reawakening of human values. As a loyal Party member she had accepted the state's suppression of its enemies and alleged enemies in the name of Marxism, progress, the forces of history. Now at last she realized what it meant to be an innocent victim, and the result was a discovery, or rediscovery, of the absolute worth and irreducible equality of all men.

The 1930s completed a long cycle in the history of the Russian intelligentsia. Just as the Russian state in the eighteenth century had demanded uncritical obedience from its subjects in the name of traditional monarchical authority, the Stalinist state demanded the same obedience in the name of Marxist-Leninist ideology. Despite the obvious differences in the legitimization of power, the state in both cases claimed to be the sole arbiter of progress and regarded the individual citizen simply as a tool to be used to that end. The Great Purge forced upon the remnants of the old intelligentsia the bitter acknowledgment that many of them had in fact acceded to the state's demand; in Gorky's phrase, they had "hidden behind another's conscience." They had suspended their individual judgment of right and wrong and abdicated their moral responsibility in favor of the Party's will. Their victimization in the purge reawakened the sense of individual conscience that men like Novikov and Radishchev had first voiced, but for the intelligentsia as a whole it was too late.

Although individuals survived, the Great Purge marked the physical extermination of the old intelligentsia as a recognizable social group, with its gentry and middle-class roots, its close contact with Western culture, and its sense of shared traditions and ideals.[45] But even as it expired, the intelligentsia left an important legacy to the new dissidents who were to arise after Stalin's death. The moral lesson of the purge, the rediscovery of human values and the reaffirmation of the absolute worth of individual life, would prove to be the starting point of the currents of Soviet dissent that began to swell in the 1950s.

5

Khrushchev and the de-Stalinization campaign: the development of literary dissent

We were scared – really scared. We were afraid the thaw might unleash a flood, which we wouldn't be able to control and which could drown us. How could it drown us? It could have overflowed the banks of the Soviet riverbed and formed a tidal wave which would have washed away all the barriers and retaining walls of our society. From the viewpoint of the leadership, this would have been an unfavorable development. We wanted to guide the process of the thaw so that it would stimulate only those creative forces which would contribute to the strengthening of socialism.

Nikita Khrushchev, in *Khrushchev Remembers: The Last Testament.* [1]

By the time Stalin died, on March 5, 1953, he appeared to have succeeded in stifling all criticism and dissent on the part of the Soviet citizenry. The war years, in which some loosening of ideological controls over Soviet life had been permitted, were followed by the massive cultural purge of the late forties. This reimposition of ideological orthodoxy came to be termed the "Zhdanovshchina," after the official primarily responsible for carrying it out, Andrei Zhdanov. It was characterized by a crude campaign against Western influences, and such leading literary figures as the poet Anna Akhmatova and the satirical writer Michael Zoshchenko were savagely attacked for their alleged adulation of "bourgeois" Western culture. The campaign quickly acquired, as one of its corollaries, a broad streak of anti-Semitism masked under the code term "rootless cosmopolitanism." Just before Stalin's death came the announcement of the discovery of a "doctors' plot," in which nine Kremlin doctors were accused of having conspired to assassinate top Soviet leaders by medical means. Most of the accused doctors were Jewish, and the announcement may have been intended as the signal for a further intensification of anti-Semitism, or, more broadly, a resumption of terror on the scale of the Great Purge of the thirties. Whatever this ominous incident portended, it was forestalled by Stalin's sudden death, ostensibly from a stroke.

We have referred a number of times to the central importance of initiative by the state in Russian historical development. Ironically, this factor is again clearly evident in the renewal of criticism and protest in the Soviet Union since Stalin's death. Open criticism of the past and the demand for improvement in the present did not well up spontaneously from below as soon as the heavy hand of the dictator was removed; Soviet society in the preceding decades had been too thoroughly atomized and effectively cowed for that. Instead, criticism filtered down from the very summit of the political structure, initiated by none other than the First Secretary of the Communist Party, Nikita Khrushchev, in his "secret speech" of 1956.

Khrushchev's speech, which proved to be a major turning point in Russian historical development, in more immediate terms marked the culmination of a jockeying for power that had been taking place at the top of the political hierarchy during the three years after Stalin's death. These years saw a general easing of tensions in Soviet life: those accused in the doctors' plot were freed; there was an end to mass arrests; and, in the most dramatic incident of this period, Lavrenty Beria, the chief of the secret police since 1938, was relieved of his post and later shot. Beria's removal had the effect of reducing the influence of the secret police and at the same time seemed to signal a repudiation of mass terror as an instrument of government. Stalin had been succeeded by a so-called collective leadership, a government by committee consisting of the most powerful of Stalin's former associates. Shortly after Beria's downfall, Khrushchev acquired a leading position within the ruling group by being named First Secretary of the Central Committee, or head of the Party. From this political base Khrushchev built his power, as Stalin had done before him and as Brezhnev was to do after him. Given the history of the Bolshevik Party, with its long tradition of one-man rule, collective leadership was likely to endure only until one of its members succeeded in establishing his predominance over the others. The political situation was similar to the one that had prevailed after Lenin's death in 1924, and within three or four years it had produced one-man leadership once again. It was of fateful significance, however, that on this occasion the new leader who emerged was not a Stalin but a Khrushchev.

At a two-day session of the Twentieth Congress of the Communist Party of the Soviet Union, February 24–25, 1956, Khrushchev, to the surprise of most of his colleagues and the undoubted dismay of many, delivered an unscheduled speech roundly denouncing Stalin. It was a secret speech in the sense that it was not intended for public circulation. It was given at a special closed meeting of the Congress, to which only Soviet delegates were admitted, foreign guests having been excluded. Copies were subsequently circulated to Party secretaries throughout the country, and the text of the speech was read at Party meetings and then at special non-Party gatherings as well. Its contents became widely known, but the text itself has never been published in the Soviet Union.[2] The U.S. State Department managed to acquire a copy, however, and translations of it were published in the West. The profound historical importance of this document is yet to be fully measured, for it touched off a movement of intellectual and political ferment whose end is not yet in sight.

Why did Khrushchev take the momentous – and irrevocable – step of exposing Stalin's atrocities and denouncing the methods by which he had exercised power? His motivations, to the extent that they can be ascertained, were diverse and reflected a number of different concerns. It is certainly not inconceivable that he genuinely wished to provide the Soviet people with a greater degree of security in their daily lives by renouncing the use of mass terror. The pervasive fear and insecurity that Stalin had encouraged, and which appeared to be building to a new climax on the eve of his death, were repulsive in their barbarity. Khrushchev was a product of Stalin's system, and a successful one, but he was not entirely insensitive to that barbarity, whose effects he himself had witnessed firsthand in the upper ranks of the political elite. Since his removal from office in 1964 and the partial rehabilitation of Stalin that followed, Khrushchev's commitment to a more humane political system has come to look increasingly consistent and sincere.

At the same time, on a more pragmatic plane, Khrushchev had a strong interest in normalizing and stabilizing the Soviet system. Stalin's methods of rule were not just inhumane; they threatened to paralyze the system itself by so terrorizing those responsible for running it that they could no longer work effectively. The promptings of humanism may well have played a role, but they coincided with the political desirability of reassuring the Party apparatus and, implicitly, the public at large, that there would be no recurrence of Stalin's mass purges and that they would henceforth enjoy some minimum of personal security.

Finally, on the level of intra-Party politics, "de-Stalinization," as the process of shrinking Stalin's reputation and cleansing Soviet life of his methods of rule came to be called, was the instrument Khrushchev selected for winning the power struggle within the Soviet leadership. By donning the mantle of the reformer, he could brand his rivals (who, like himself, had all been Stalin's close associates) as hard-line Stalinists, undermining them and ultimately removing them. This consideration helps to explain why his campaign against Stalinism took the dramatic, semipublic form of a speech to the Congress delegates: he had to seize the role of reformer visibly and forcefully if it was to serve as an effective political weapon. In this he was successful, for by 1957 he had removed from power his main rivals, Malenkov, Molotov, Kaganovich, and others, having labeled them the "anti-Party group" and accused them of upholding Stalinist principles.

Effective as this weapon was in winning the struggle for power, it was not without its dangers for the one who sought to use it. For the rest of his tenure in office, Khrushchev was confronted with what has been called "the dilemma of the reforming despot." He had now identified himself as the leader of the de-Stalinization campaign, and he had made that identification the foundation of his claim to leadership. He could not wholly repudiate de-Stalinization, even if he had wished to, without undermining his own legitimacy. At the same time, however, he had to keep it carefully circumscribed and under control. Like his predecessors, both Soviet and tsarist, he refused to countenance any serious criticism, much less limitation, of his right to exercise as he saw fit the supreme power he had now attained. In the years after 1956 he showed his determination to suppress any aspect or degree of de-Stalinization that might conceivably infringe upon his freedom to wield power. From this dilemma stemmed the erratic series of ups and downs, thaws and freezes, that marked the efforts to liberalize Soviet life under Khrushchev. It was the same dilemma that had previously been faced by Catherine the Great, Alexander I, and Alexander II, all of whose reigns had displayed one or more cycles of reform and reaction, relaxation and retrenchment. In Khrushchev's case, the narrow line the reforming despot had to tread found its clearest embodiment at the very outset, in his secret speech of 1956. Unexpected and shocking though it may have seemed to much of its audience, it very carefully limited the scope of reform and laid down the terms in which criticism of the past would be allowed. Thus it was the state which not only initiated dissent but established the framework within which, at least at the beginning, that dissent was to find expression.

What were the specific counts of Khrushchev's indictment of Stalin? Stalin's rule, after all, had spanned more than half the existence of the Soviet state, and Stalin had been responsible for policies that had shaped the very nature of the Soviet system: collectivization and forced industrialization, the purges, and the conduct of the Second World War, among many others. To subject all of Stalin's actions and decisions to criticism risked calling into question the very system that had brought Khrushchev to power and over which he now presided. He confined himself, therefore, to the denunciation only of carefully selected aspects of Stalin's legacy. His primary accusation was that Stalin had victimized innocent people in his purges of the thirties and late forties. A sizable section of the speech concentrated on "rehabilitating," that is, clearing of charges, some of those falsely condemned individuals – primarily Party members and military men. Second, Khrushchev charged Stalin with misconduct of the Second World War: stubborn misjudgment of Hitler's intentions even in the face of reliable warnings of the impending invasion; panic when the invasion occurred; and incompetent meddling in military operations. Third, Khrushchev condemned the wholesale deportation of several small national minorities (omitting specific mention of some of them, however) whom Stalin accused of treason during the war and forcibly resettled in remote eastern regions, with great suffering and loss of life.

Some of Khrushchev's specific revelations – such as his implication that Stalin had been behind Kirov's assassination in 1934, and his description of Stalin's terror-stricken paralysis in the face of the Nazi invasion – were sensational. While most of these disclosures were already known – or at least suspected – in the West, they had never before been admitted by an official Soviet spokesman. More significant than the revelations, however, were those policies Khrushchev excluded from criticism. For instance, he fully condoned Stalin's defeat of the "right" and "left" oppositions within the Party in the late twenties, moves that consolidated Stalin's power by discrediting such top Party leaders as Trotsky, Zinoviev, and Bukharin. Khrushchev agreed that these "enemies of Leninism" had to be removed from power and that "here Stalin played a positive role";[3] he condemned only their subsequent liquidation. These former oppositionists would not be among those "rehabilitated" in subsequent years, and they have remained in the category of "nonpersons." Collectivization of agriculture and forced industrialization, policies made possible by Stalin's defeat of his rivals, also remained exempt from criticism. In essence, Khrushchev's indictment began only with Kirov's assassination and the start of the Great Purge. Before that date Khrushchev credited Stalin with major accomplishments and important services to socialism and the development of the Soviet Union. By 1934, the essential elements of the Soviet social and economic structure that Khrushchev inherited, as well as the centralized, hierarchical structure of the political system he now headed, were more or less complete. By claiming that only from this point had Stalin gone astray and his leadership degenerated, Khrushchev could denounce "Stalinism" without opening to question the foundations of the Soviet system and the methods by which it had been constructed.

Khrushchev's attack on Stalinism can be summed up in the titles of two nineteenth-century Russian novels, by Herzen and Chernyshevsky respectively: *Who Is to Blame?* and *What Is to Be Done?*. The answer to the first question was simple: Stalin himself, and a few depraved individuals close to him, were responsible for Stalinism. The disease that had infected the healthy system bequeathed by Lenin was the "cult of personality" (sometimes translated "cult of the individual"), that is, the glorification and virtual deification of Stalin's person. The rites of this new religion had, in Khrushchev's words, transformed Stalin "into a superman possessing supernatural characteristics, akin to those of a god," omniscient and infallible.[4] Cult of personality henceforth became the official code word for the entire Stalin era, with the distinct advantage of obviating the use of Stalin's name, which could be consigned to oblivion. According to Khrushchev, "Stalin was a very distrustful man, sickly suspicious," whose "persecution mania reached unbelievable dimensions."[5] His suspicions were fed and played upon by "the abject *provocateur* and vile enemy, Beria," and his orders were carried out by "Beria's gang, which ran the organs of state security."[6] Elsewhere, Khrushchev referred to "the *provocateurs* who had infiltrated the state-security organs together with conscienceless careerists"[7] as the perpetrators of the mass terror. The sources of Stalinism were Stalin's own personality disorder, which, by the thirties, had degenerated into a kind of paranoia, and Beria and his henchmen in the secret police, who were vicious, corrupt, or treacherous. The cure followed logically from the diagnosis: remove the individuals who were responsible for this state of affairs. Stalin and Beria had already disappeared from the scene. Now Khrushchev promised the elimination from Soviet life of all traces of the cult of personality and the explusion of "*provocateurs* and careerists" from the security organs and other positions of responsibility.

Again, what Khrushchev omitted was more significant than what he actually said. Conspicuously absent from his speech was any reference to the legal, political, or institutional sources of Stalinism, and to the necessity of change in these areas. He dealt exclusively with the symptom of Stalinism – the arbitrary misuse of power – while carefully avoiding any mention of its underlying causes, the features of the Soviet system that gave Stalin his power and permitted him to misuse it. In fact, although he promised to restore pure Marxism–Leninism, cleansed of its Stalinist adulterations, as the guiding ideology of the Soviet Union, Khrushchev offered a most "un-Marxist" interpretation of a quarter-century of Soviet history. Avoiding all consideration of underlying social and economic forces and their political manifestations in the thirties and forties, as one might have expected from a Marxist, Khrushchev attributed some of the most significant occurrences of the Stalin years to the arbitrary actions of one man, or, at most, a small group of men. While condemning the cult of personality, he in fact embodied it in his historical explanation of the origins of Stalinism.

More specifically, the central feature of the Soviet political system, the Communist Party's monopoly on power, never came into question in Khrushchev's speech. Instead, Khrushchev sought to dissociate the Party from Stalin's atrocities while crediting it with all the positive accomplishments of the Stalin period. He referred to "the efforts of the party in the socialist transformation of the country," "the party which undeviatingly traveled the path outlined by Lenin."[8] The achievements of the past, the Revolution and the construction of socialism, were products of the Party's leadership, and not, as Stalin had maintained, of his personal leadership. Khrushchev concluded his speech with the ringing assertion that the Party, armed with the decisions of the Twentieth Congress, would lead the Soviet people on to new successes and victories.

The few rotten apples having been removed from the Party barrel, Khrushchev offered the reassertion of leadership by the Party – which had never erred but had merely been eclipsed by the malevolent shadow of Stalin – as the guarantee against a recurrence of Stalinism. The Party would remain the sole judge of how that leadership was to be exercised, however, and of how it was to be applied in the treatment of particular individuals. Khrushchev praised Lenin's use of "the most extreme methods" against "enemies of the Revolution and of the working class" and against "actual class enemies,"[9] and he repeatedly referred to Stalin's misdeeds as violations of "revolutionary legality" or "socialist legality." Thus, ideological and political criteria were to remain the standards for judging people's behavior, and the application of those standards was to be determined by the Party alone. As an autocratic reformer, Khrushchev could hardly proclaim the principle of public accountability for the Party's policies, nor could he accept the notion of inalienable personal rights, guaranteed by strict legal norms, as a bulwark against repetition of the injustices and persecutions of the Stalin era. The Party, guided by the supreme wisdom embodied in its ideology, would continue to exercise final judgment over all Soviet citizens. Khrushchev merely held out the reassurance that the Party would hence-forth exercise its judgment properly instead of allowing it to be usurped by an unbalanced despot.

In effect, Khrushchev's denunciation of Stalinism remained strictly on the level of moral criticism: the Soviet political, economic, and social sys-tem was fundamentally sound, only the defective character of some of the people who had been running it was at fault. Once these bad people were rooted out and replaced by good people, the system would be restored to health. Any attempts to go beyond this level of historical explanation were immediately suppressed. In the wake of the Twentieth Congress, for in-stance, Palmiro Togliatti, then First Secretary of the Italian Communist Party, suggested the need for a more probing analysis, an examination of the origins of Stalinism in social and institutional terms. This effort to adopt a more "Marxist" approach to the subject was promptly squelched, and the "personality cult" continued to shoulder the blame for Stalinism in all official pronouncements.

By and large, unofficial criticisms of Stalinism accepted the limits Khrushchev had imposed on the subject. For the next ten years, until the Siniavsky–Daniel trial of 1966, the voices of dissent evoked by Khrushchev's speech confined themselves largely to the moral plane, call-ing for a change in the character and attitudes of the people running the Soviet system while exempting the system itself from direct criticism or serious analysis. In this first phase of post-Stalin dissent, literature, always an important vehicle of protest in Russia, played a particularly crucial role. Literature is especially well suited for the expression of moral criticism, because moral issues can best be posed in dramatic situations, and moral virtues and failings best displayed by personifying them in literary charac-ters. Not only did dissidents resort to literature to express their views but Khrushchev and his supporters were attempting to bend literature to their own purposes, utilizing it as an instrument of de-Stalinization while at the same time trying to ensure that it did not cut more deeply than they wished. Hence, in the post-1956 period the authorities supervised the practitioners of literature more closely, instructed them more carefully, and scolded them more shrilly than usual. Literature became the most sensitive barometer of de-Stalinization, registering the successive changes in the political weather of the Khrushchev era.

One of the earliest reflections of the thaw after Stalin's death had been a plea, bold for the time, on behalf of greater literary freedom. At the end of 1953, a writer named Vladimir Pomerantsev published an article entitled "On Sincerity in Literature" in *Novy mir* (New World), the literary journal that became the leading exponent of liberalization in the Khrushchev years. (It will henceforth be referred to by its Russian name, by which it is best known in the West.) Pomerantsev attacked the afflictions that had sapped the vitality of Soviet literature under Stalin: the "varnishing of reality," that is, the glossing-over of real problems and the embellishment of actual conditions in the country; the simplification of life's complexities and contradictions; the predominance of the pot-boiler "production novel," in which people are preoccupied with plan fulfillment and speak in slogans rather than in natural human terms. "To say of a writer that his books are characterized by patriotic feeling, love for the people, and faith in the future is to say nothing."[10] Writers must sincerely and passionately feel what they are writing, he maintained, and not merely write to order; and they must be encouraged to depict real people, not the manufactured objects that currently populated their stories and plays.

Pomerantsev's article, along with several by other writers in the same vein, called for more freedom for the writer to register honest feelings, more opportunity to deliver a personal message of his own instead of the one imposed on him by the narrow strictures of "socialist realism."[11] Such an appeal accorded ill with the official view of literature's function that had been inherited from the Stalin era. In September 1954, *Novy mir* was required to publish an official resolution taking the journal to task for some of its recent publications and singling out Pomerantsev's article, among others, for special criticism. Pomerantsev, the resolution charged, "brought literature down from its lofty position of teacher of the feelings and character of the builders of communism." He would have literature express the subjective impressions of the individual writer "isolated from the struggle and creative activity of society."[12] Much of the literary dissent expressed in the Khrushchev period was to revolve around the issues expressed by Pomerantsev. The writers persisted in their campaign for a more honest, more "humanistic" literature with a greater degree of freedom from the crushing burdens of the Party's political objectives and political restrictions. For the moment, however, their campaign foundered and the authorities brought this first thaw to a halt. Among the casualties was Alexander Tvardovsky, the editor of *Novy mir,* who was removed from his post, only to be reinstated in 1958.

Khrushchev's secret speech at the Twentieth Congress touched off a second and more significant thaw, in which the temperature rose much higher than it had in 1953. Again, the first audible responses to the dramatic events of the Twentieth Congress were literary, most notably the second part of a two-volume almanac entitled *Literary Moscow.* One of the stories in this collection, "Levers," by Alexander Iashin, illustrates particularly well the kind of criticism that now began to find expression. A group of peasants on a collective farm are gathered in the village clubhouse; they are the local Communist Party members and are about to hold a meeting. While they are waiting for the meeting to begin, they discuss the village's problems: irrational planning from above, bureaucratic high-handedness and mistrust of the peasants, lack of consultation on local conditions and needs. The moment the Party meeting opens, the warmth, spontaneous harmony, and unspoken consensus that have characterized the discussion end abruptly. Now the participants treat each other with bureaucratic formality, mechanically repeat Party dogmas and clichés, and unfailingly arrive at "unanimous" decisions. "And the meeting was marked by just what these members of the Party organization . . . had just been talking about and criticizing with such frankness and perspicacity – official routine, bureaucracy, and pedantry of word and deed."[13] They cease talking like human beings and begin to perform like "levers in the village," as the Party terms its local members. As soon as the meeting is over, the icy atmosphere immediately dissolves and the cell members once again become "clean, warmhearted, straightforward people – people, and not levers."[14]

The criticism contained in this story was mild indeed. Its targets were bureaucratic formalism, hypocrisy, pedantry, and its plea was for greater feeling, sincerity, and honesty in human relations. In itself, none of this could be objectionable to the authorities. Yet, in its own way, the story was more barbed than might appear at first glance. The peasant Communists depicted here are not individuals of bad character, nor "conscienceless careerists," to use Khrushchev's term. They are decent, honest, goodhearted people, and their soulless Party meeting is clearly a typical occurrence, not an aberration. The failings they display at the meeting, the story implies, are not inherent in their character but are in some way generated by a system that requires people to behave like levers rather than human beings. The objective is still moral reform, but the search for the source of moral decay has subtly shifted direction from a few "rotten apples" to the

barrel that contains them. Even the hopeful reference to the upcoming
Twentieth Congress at the end of the story, with its implication of impending reform, is ambiguous, for the resolutions of a congress can hardly remedy the kind of dehumanization the story has described. The authorities
apparently sensed an attempt to widen the limits they sought to impose on
criticism, and upon its appearance the story was severely attacked.

Another literary example from 1956 of the doubts and uncertainties generated by Khrushchev's attack on the hitherto unquestioned past was a
satirical poem by Vladimir Mass and Michael Chervensky with the sugges-
tive title "2 × 2 = ?". The poem relates the effort of the "best of all verse
writers" to prove "that two times two is four – no more, no less," and his
criticism of other poets for failing to express this truth clearly enough.

> Everywhere his influence seems to lurk,
> And that is what we most of all deplore.
> In drama you can find him and – beware! –
> In music, painting – in fact, anywhere. [15]

Like much of the other critical literature of this period, the poem, with its
echo of the motto of Turgenev's Bazarov, attacked the deadening influence
on cultural creativity of primitive and simplistic ideological dogmas. In
addition, as the title suggests, the poem hinted that perhaps in real life two
and two do not in fact always add up to four with unfailing regularity and
certainty.

The major literary reflection of the second thaw was Vladimir
Dudintsev's novel, *Not by Bread Alone*, first serialized in *Novy mir* late in
1956 and then published in book form. The central theme of the novel is the
struggle of individual creativity against bureaucratic inertia and careerism.
To appreciate the full impact of Dudintsev's work, however, it is instructive
to compare it with a novel that had appeared just two years earlier, Ilia
Ehrenburg's *The Thaw*. Ehrenburg, a Jew, had long been one of the Soviet
Union's leading writers – one of the few to bear both of those attributes and
survive under Stalin. He was one of the first to express a veiled hope that a
new era had begun with Stalin's death, and he was to become one of the
most prominent defenders of literary liberalization under Khrushchev. His
slight novel, published in 1954, gave its name to the transitional period
from 1953 to 1956, when the pressures and tensions beneath the surface of
Soviet life were quietly easing but Khrushchev had not yet broken the ice
with his explicit renunciation of Stalinist practices. Ostensibly, *The Thaw*
charted the decline and fall of a factory manager who is heartless and over-

bearing and neglects the welfare of his workers in a single-minded concentration on increased production. It was a mildly unorthodox plea for greater compassion and human understanding by those in authority rather than an exclusive concern with material values – a theme paralleled by the numerous love relationships that develop among the novel's characters. Within the book, however, there was a much bolder appeal for honesty and integrity in a sphere quite removed from the factory setting, the realm of art. Tucked away among the subplots is the story of two painters: Pukhov, a successful careerist who adheres strictly to the sterile propaganda demands of "socialist realism," and Saburov, who paints unorthodox landscapes and portraits which he cannot exhibit, is poverty stricken, and lives in squalor. What was unusual in Ehrenburg's treatment of this theme was that he made Pukhov, who obediently follows official standards, an artistic hack, an unhappy and unfulfilled individual, while the nonconformist Saburov is portrayed sympathetically and is even admired by Pukhov for remaining true to himself. Here was a defense of artistic integrity against ideological demands, of a sort that would scarcely have been permitted under Stalin. Though the ice may have begun to melt, the waters in 1954 were as yet untested, and the cautious Ehrenburg introduced this sensitive issue only as a subsidiary theme. It was a measure of the impact of Khrushchev's speech that *Not by Bread Alone,* embodying a similar theme, boldly brought it to the forefront and treated it in a considerably more provocative manner.

Lopatkin, the young hero of *Not by Bread Alone,* is a creative artist of sorts: he is the inventor of a new and more efficient pipe-casting machine. Penniless and without influence in high places, he persists in the face of numerous obstacles in the effort to have his design adopted by the appropriate government ministry – not just for his own sake, of course, but out of patriotic devotion to his country and its need to develop its economy. He is opposed, harassed, and ultimately sent to a labor camp by a formidable array of bureaucratic vested interests, all of which feel threatened by his new design. These self-interested careerists, particularly in the person of the bureaucratic factory manager Drozdov (whose disillusioned young wife joins Lopatkin's campaign and ultimately marries him), hide behind the clichés of official ideology in order to protect their social privileges, maintain their power, and, in some cases, mask their gross incompetence.

Dudintsev's novel was a peculiar mixture of conventional socialist realism and relatively penetrating criticism. In form, it closely resembled the standard Soviet "production novel," with its worship of machine and factory and its didactic technical descriptions. Most Western readers would feel, to paraphrase a famous review of a book on penguins, that this work tells them more about pipe casting than they actually wanted to know. Most of the characters, also, were conventional Soviet heroes and villains: the "bad" bureaucrat, such as Drozdov, was a stock figure of officially sponsored "self-criticism," as was the equally conventional "good" Party official who mysteriously appears in the course of the novel, rescues the hero, and selflessly helps him to triumph over his enemies. Typically, such an ending demonstrated the system's ability to correct its defects and proved that they were exceptions to the rule.

Why, then, was the novel a milestone in the development of Soviet dissent? First, though the criticism of the system had definite limits, it was pursued with a depth and a bitterness not found previously in officially sanctioned literature. Lopatkin is not confronting just a few self-serving individuals: he is surrounded on all sides by selfish and ruthless opportunists in the bureaucracy, in industry, even in the august Academy of Sciences. And, although he is vindicated, the villains go unpunished. In the last line of the novel Lopatkin sees a long road unwinding before him, suggesting that he has won a battle but not the war. Although formally the novel observed the conventions of official self-criticism, the evils it exposed were so all-pervasive as to raise questions about the wholesomeness of the system itself. The strong implication of the book was that the Drozdovs were more than just a few aberrant individuals but were to some degree typical figures. Dudintsev was not in any way repudiating the Soviet system, but the message of his novel was that the task of eliminating its afflictions was considerably more complex and arduous than Khrushchev had suggested in his speech to the Twentieth Congress.

This message was made forcefully explicit by the venerable writer Konstantin Paustovsky. In a speech to a meeting of the Writers' Union called to discuss Dudintsev's book, Paustovsky lashed out at "the Drozdovs," whom he identified not as an individual problem but as a sociological phenomenon. The problem Dudintsev had laid bare was not a matter of a few careerists but of "an entirely new social stratum, a new caste of *petty bourgeois*."[16] Paustovsky indicted the Drozdovs for their material privileges, their cultural philistinism – he blamed them for the destruction of leading artists in the purges – and even for environmental damage to the Soviet landscape in the interests of plan fulfillment. He concluded his unusually outspoken statement with an appeal to sweep away the Drozdovs and their works.

Thus, Dudintsev's novel not only created a literary sensation but, at least for a time, lent Soviet dissent a generic name for the privileged and hypocritical bureaucrats who had become the main targets of critical literature. At this point the authorities began to feel that the writers had gone too far, too fast – especially in view of the disturbances in Poland and the Hungarian uprising of late 1956 – and forced a curtailment of such trenchant criticism. The literary thaw after Stalin's death had been followed by a new freeze in mid-1954; now the much more extensive warming trend in the wake of Khrushchev's speech gave way to a severe frost. In the spring and summer of 1957 there was a general crackdown on literature, with *Literary Moscow II* singled out for particularly strong criticism and Dudintsev's novel the object of a vitriolic attack by Khrushchev himself.

The controversy aroused by these works seemed minor compared to the furor over Boris Pasternak's *Doctor Zhivago* in 1958, the greatest literary sensation during the Khrushchev years. The publication of *Doctor Zhivago* in the West won Pasternak a Nobel Prize as well as a torrent of abuse from the Soviet authorities, which finally forced him to renounce the award. Though never published in the Soviet Union, the novel is well known to many Soviet citizens, for the hand-to-hand circulation of unpublished, and unpublishable, manuscripts was commonplace in Soviet literary circles long before the West became familiar with the term *samizdat*. The book is set in the period of the Revolution and the early years of the Soviet state. While not strictly autobiographical, it deals with events that Pasternak himself, who was born in 1890, experienced. Its style, its range of concerns, its characterizations, and its spiritual commitments made it startlingly different from standard Soviet writing; in many ways it was a literary anachronism, a discovery from a lost world. But it was precisely as a voice from the past that this rich and complex novel made its contribution to the developing themes of Soviet dissent. It helped to transmit to the post-Stalin generation the moral individualism that writers of the prerevolutionary period and the twenties had counterposed to the values embodied in the official ideology, but which had subsequently been effaced from Soviet literature, or at least driven underground. *Doctor Zhivago* thus provided support and a fresh source of inspiration for the growing literary response to the criticism of the Stalinist past.

Iury Zhivago is in many ways a typical prerevolutionary *intelligent*: he is well educated, has been brought up in a cultivated home, and thus has the essential *intelligent* element of consciousness, the ability to reflect on his surroundings and the events taking place around him. In addition, Pasternak carefully places Zhivago in a twentieth-century context by making him a professional man, a medical doctor. He is not one of those "superfluous men" who filled the ranks of the intelligentsia in the mid-nineteenth century, searching in vain for a satisfying outlet for their energies. By the turn of the century the intelligentsia more and more consisted of professionally trained individuals who occupied – or could have occupied, if they had chosen to do so – a secure place in the Russian social and economic structure. This change in its circumstances did not cure the political disaffection of the educated elite, however, which by and large remained highly critical of the tsarist system right up to the Revolution.

Initially, Zhivago welcomes the Revolution. Like all his *intelligent* predecessors, he is committed both to individual freedom and fulfillment, and to social justice. That the two are inseparable is illustrated by the very structure of the novel, in which Zhivago's search for peace and personal happiness is inextricably intertwined with the events of his time, the upheavals of his society, and the fate of his native land. Yet, like Zamiatin and Maiakovsky before him, Pasternak raises the question of whether the Revolution can successfully realize those twin goals, or whether it has in fact sacrificed individual liberation to the quest for social transformation. At first, the Revolution had seemed to Zhivago "a god come down to earth from heaven, the god of the summer when everyone had gone crazy in his own way, and when everyone's life had existed in its own right, and not as an illustration for a thesis in support of the rightness of a superior policy."[17] Instead of freeing the individual from the social and political constraints of the old regime, the Revolution is now attempting to imprison him anew within its ideological dogmas. It is trying to impose a rationalist straitjacket on the spontaneous flow of human life, and from such an effort only death can ensue. Zhivago expresses his disillusionment in a discussion with a doctrinaire revolutionary:

But, first, the idea of social betterment as it is understood since the October revolution doesn't fill me with enthusiasm. Second, it is so far from being put into practice, and the mere talk about it has cost such a sea of blood, that I'm not sure that the end justifies the means. And last – and this is the main thing – when I hear people speak of reshaping life it makes me lose my self-control and I fall into despair.

Reshaping life! People who can say that have never understood a thing about life – they have never felt its breath, its heartbeat – however much they have seen or done. They look on it as a lump of raw material that needs to be processed by them, to be ennobled by their touch. But life is never a material, a substance to be molded. If you want to know, life is the principle of self-renewal, it is constantly renewing and remaking and changing and transfiguring itself, it is infinitely beyond your or my obtuse theories about it.[18]

The liberation promised by the Revolution, to Zhivago as to so many other *intelligenty,* was a matter of freeing the individual's spontaneous energies, enabling him to realize at last his true relationship to nature, to his fellow-men, to the very principle of creation – and thereby to transcend death. Instead, in the name of social betterment, it is drying up the wellsprings of human life and destroying the individual for the sake of a rationalistic theory of happiness. The great misfortune of the era, in the words of Zhivago's lover, Lara, is that people have come to imagine "that it was out of date to follow their own moral sense, that they must all sing in chorus, and live by other people's notions, notions that were being crammed down everybody's throat."[19]

Pasternak does not attempt a full resolution of the issue. Instead, he defends the elemental spontaneity of life against all efforts to fetter it and master it. The recurrent theme of the novel is the affirmation of life as a self-renewing force, as rebirth in the midst of destruction and death. Zhivago himself is a symbol: his very name comes from the Russian word for "life"; he is a doctor, a life giver who is called upon at various points in the novel to apply his medical skills to the saving of human life; and he is at the same time a poet, a creator of mankind's collective consciousness through art. The recurrent strands of imagery, which in part replace conventional narrative techniques as the main structural elements of this poet's novel, reiterate the central theme. There is a great deal of nature imagery – storms, blizzards, the changing seasons parallel and dramatize the turning points in Zhivago's life and Russia's. There is a love theme, which runs throughout the novel. Zhivago's affair with Lara is more than a romance, it is an elemental, life-creating force that links them with nature and with the cosmic forces of creation itself.[20] And, finally, in a striking reflection of Russian religious tradition, there is the Christian cycle of death and redemption, a drama overarching all of these other images.

All of the major symbols ultimately meet in the novel's crucial passage. As Zhivago is escaping from captivity in a partisan camp in the forest, he comes across a lone rowan tree, its berries red against the snow.

> The footpath brought the doctor to the foot of the rowan tree, whose name he had just spoken. It was half in snow, half in frozen leaves and berries, and it held out two white branches toward him. He remembered Lara's strong white arms and seized the branches and pulled them to him. As if in answer, the tree shook snow all over him. He muttered without realizing what he was saying, and completely beside himself: "I'll find you, my beauty, my love, my rowan tree, my own flesh and blood."[21]

The rowan tree is an image of Lara, of the Russian motherland, of the resurrection, of the organic forces of life. Nature, love, and religious mystery, the unfathomable forces that so many previous Russian authors had affirmed as the sources of human life and of its spontaneous individuality, here come together in a powerful image of redemption and salvation. *Doctor Zhivago* revived the debate over reason and its relation to the liberation of the individual, a debate that had preoccupied the old intelligentsia and had been forcibly silenced under Stalin, and helped to make it a central theme of post-Stalin dissent.

Yet, there are significant differences between Zhivago and most of the previous *intelligenty* we have discussed. What is particularly striking to a Western reader is Zhivago's passivity. He rarely asserts himself or tries to master his situation; events tend to engulf him, and he resigns himself to his fate. He is not a fighter but a witness to his times, a self-sacrificing sufferer, a figure deeply rooted in Russian religious experience and Russian literature. The "kenotic" element in Russian Orthodoxy gave rise to the ideal of the Christlike individual who voluntarily accepts his suffering in imitation of the humiliated Christ, thereby bearing witness to the faith. The young princes Boris and Gleb, who, according to the eleventh-century Russian chronicle, accepted their own murder at the hands of their older brother without attempting to flee, were considered exemplars of this ideal. The Decembrists in some respects reverted to this tradition: many of them, by their patient submission to suffering in prison and exile, displayed a moral nobility that had a greater impact on their contemporaries than their political activities had ever achieved. The theme recurs again in prison-camp memoirs and fiction about the Stalin period. Zhivago's role, then, is not to struggle, to battle, but to bear witness. This he does both in living his life and enduring its vicissitudes, and, as a true *intelligent*, by distilling his experiences and his consciousness into poetry. It was as a sufferer and a witness rather than as an active battler that he provided a model for one variety of anti-Stalin literature of the Khrushchev period.

The bitter attacks on Pasternak did not prove to signify a permanent retreat from the positions Khrushchev had taken in 1956. The exigencies of external and internal politics impelled him to reaffirm those positions at the Twenty-Second Party Congress in October 1961. In his speeches to the Congress, Khrushchev restated his condemnation of the cult of personality and expressed full approval of the work of the Twentieth Congress. In the course of denouncing the "anti-Party group" once again and associating it with Stalin's repressions, he gave further details on the assassination of

Kirov and the purge of leading government and military figures, and he even suggested erecting a memorial in Moscow to the memory of Stalin's victims. This proposal was not carried out, but as a dramatic and highly visible gesture against the Stalin cult, the Congress did approve a resolution to remove Stalin's remains from the Lenin Mausoleum in Red Square, Moscow. They were subsequently reburied next to the Kremlin Wall. The vast number of place names honoring Stalin throughout the Soviet Union were changed, most notably Stalingrad, the site of one of the major battles of the Second World War, which now became Volgograd. Stalin was well on his way to receiving the treatment he had once meted out to Trotsky, that of becoming a "nonperson," expunged from the annals of Soviet history, his name unmentionable – certainly an ambitious undertaking in regard to a man who had dominated the country's life for more than a quarter-century.

Predictably, the new cycle of liberalization and de-Stalinization initiated by Khrushchev's efforts at the Twenty-Second Congress soon found a major reflection in the realm of literature. Alexander Solzhenitsyn's first novel, *One Day in the Life of Ivan Denisovich,* appeared in *Novy mir* in November 1962, and was then issued in book form. This work – the only novel of Solzhenitsyn's to be published in the Soviet Union – can be considered the highwater mark of the de-Stalinization tide. The first approved work to deal directly with the forced-labor camps, perhaps the most horrifying aspect of the Stalin era, it remains the most searing indictment of the Stalinist past ever to find official publication in the Soviet Union. Like *Doctor Zhivago,* it was partly autobiographical: in 1945, while serving in the Red Army, Solzhenitsyn had been arrested and sentenced to eight years in the camps for criticizing Stalin in private letters to a friend. Remarkably, he treats his subject in a low-keyed, understated manner, a quality not commonly found in Soviet fiction. Short, restricted in scope, and relentlessly down-to-earth in tone, the book's self-imposed limitations serve to underscore the horrors of prison-camp life with devastating impact. It is a deliberately small but exquisitely cut literary gem.

The novel recounts a "typical" day in the life of a labor-camp inmate in the late forties. Ivan Denisovich is one of Stalin's entirely innocent victims. A soldier in the Second World War, he was captured by the Germans, escaped, and made his way back to the Russian lines – only to be arrested, accused of treason, and sentenced to a camp. This was a common fate of Russian prisoners of war upon their return home, another reflection of Stalin's deep suspicion of anyone who had had contact with the West, even the sort of contact experienced in a Nazi concentration camp. Ivan Denisovich Shukhov is a simple, uneducated, honest peasant, and much of the novel's impact derives from the fact that it is narrated from his point of view. The novel merely records his success in getting through one more day in the inhuman conditions of the camp. But he does so with his fundamental decency and his sense of dignity intact. He not only survives but he survives as a human being, thus scoring a shining moral triumph over his brutalizing and dehumanizing environment.

What Solzhenitsyn's novel implied – by subtle omission rather than explicit statement, but nonetheless unmistakably – was that Stalinism was a mass phenomenon. It was not simply the product of individual "excesses" that claimed individual victims, but something that affected the whole of Soviet society and created victims at all levels. Ivan Denisovich is not a Party official or a military commander but a very ordinary, humble citizen, entirely innocent of the absurd charges against him. Nor does the novel offer any excuses for the prison-camp conditions it depicts: no "good" Party member appears to offset the "bad" ones and show how the latter have deviated from the norm, nor does any "positive" official appear to rescue the hero, as in *Not by Bread Alone* and in most other authorized publications. Restrained and understated as it was on the surface, Solzhenitsyn's novel probed more deeply into the injustices of the Stalin era than anything previously allowed to appear in print. For good reason, its publication required authorization from the highest levels of the Party, and apparently received its final clearance from Khrushchev himself.

Around the same time, Evgeny Evtushenko's poem "The Heirs of Stalin" appeared. This poem – the pinnacle of Evtushenko's well-publicized but short-lived career as a dissident – implied that there were still a good many unreconstructed Stalinists in the Soviet Union who were outwardly joining in the denunciations of Stalin but inwardly yearning for the good old days. The poem presented the chilling image of some of Stalin's "heirs" quietly tending roses in their retirement but dreaming of a return to power. It was easy enough to remove Stalin from the Red Square mausoleum, but not so easy to remove him from the habits and instincts of those he left behind him.

The publication of *Ivan Denisovich* and "The Heirs of Stalin" seemed to be the prelude to a new wave of de-Stalinization and a new attack on the conservative diehards. That wave never broke. In October 1962, the Cuban missile crisis occurred, and Khrushchev's withdrawal from Cuba weakened his political position and gave his opponents an opportunity to counterattack. The turning point was a visit at the beginning of December by Khrushchev and other high officials to an exhibit of modernist paintings at the Manezh Gallery in Moscow. Khrushchev greeted the paintings with an outburst of earthy indignation, including abusive and even threatening exchanges with some of the artists present. By early 1963 a campaign against the liberal intellectuals was well under way. Attacks on the younger and more outspoken writers, especially Evtushenko, were becoming ominously shrill. In the summer, however, they ceased, and writers who had recently been denounced were now restored to favor. Khrushchev had evidently managed to restore his position and restrain the conservatives' offensive, and may even have found the chastisement of the writers a useful way of curbing their independence.

Khrushchev's power, however, was now on the wane, and in October 1964 he was abruptly removed from office. As was so often the case in the Khrushchev years, the politics of power remained wrapped in secrecy but found public reflection in the politics of literature. In April 1964, Solzhenitsyn, whose career Khrushchev had personally sponsored, failed to receive the Lenin Prize for literature. This unexpected turn proved to be a portent of what was in store for Khrushchev. Out of a complex mixture of personal and political motivations, he had identified himself with the policy of de-Stalinization and had carefully nurtured it and used it for his own purposes. His successors, feeling less need for such a policy, or fearing that it might escape their control, began cautiously to put the lid back on the Pandora's box Khrushchev had impetuously opened.

To a Western observer, one of the most distinctive features of Soviet dissent, as the preceding discussion demonstrates, is the prominence of literature as its form of expression. Under Khrushchev, the boldest statements of unofficial criticism were embodied in novels, stories, and poetry; greater freedom of artistic expression was one of the demands most frequently made of the authorities and one of the yardsticks used to measure the extent of de-Stalinization; and the rewards and punishments accorded to writers and editors showed which way the political wind was blowing at any given moment. To explain why literature is of central importance in Soviet dissent we must go back into Russian history and examine the role literature has traditionally played in the country's political and social thought.

The conviction that literature must actively fight oppression and injustice, that it bears a heavy burden of social responsibility, is a deeply rooted part of the Russian cultural tradition. It is one of the many elements of

Russian culture that survived the Revolution, and it remains very much alive to this day. It can be traced back to the very origins of modern Russian literature and the didactic poets and playwrights of the latter eighteenth century – Fonvizin is a good example – who felt that they must instruct and civilize their fellow countrymen as well as entertain them. It received its most famous formulation, however, in 1847, in a ringing statement by Vissarion Belinsky, Russia's first outstanding literary critic. In that year Belinsky addressed an open letter to Gogol, mercilessly berating him for his recently published *Selected Passages from a Correspondence with Friends.* In this work Gogol had taken a highly conservative stance, urging his compatriots to submit to the teachings of the church and the guidance of the tsar. To the outraged Belinsky, Gogol had betrayed his calling as a writer, a betrayal made the more unforgivable by the brilliance of his earlier satirical works such as *Dead Souls* and *The Inspector General.* Only literature was in a position to express fresh ideas under Russian conditions, Belinsky wrote, hence the great respect for writers: "The title of poet, the calling of man of letters have long ago acquired a greater luster in our society than the tinsel glitter of epaulettes and motley uniforms." Belinsky maintained that the Russian public had rejected Gogol's book because "it holds the Russian writers to be its only leaders, its only defenders and saviors from the black night of Autocracy, Orthodoxy, and Nationalism, and hence it is always ready to forgive a writer for a bad book, but never for a pernicious one."[22] Even allowing for a degree of overstatement on Belinsky's part, his belief in the social importance of literature and the public function of the writer has remained a permanent feature of Russian literary history.

Just how permanent is suggested by the long series of political persecutions of Soviet writers since the thirties. A number of nonconformist fiction writers and poets perished in the Great Purge along with other categories of the intelligentsia. Few Western political figures would pay much attention to anything from the pen of a poet, but in the Soviet Union literature has always been a very serious matter, sometimes deadly serious. "Why do you complain?" the great poet Osip Mandelstam, who died in one of Stalin's camps, would ask his long-suffering wife. "Poetry is respected only in this country – people are killed for it. There's no place where more people are killed for it."[23] Since Stalin's day, writers are no longer executed for their literature, but, as Pasternak, Solzhenitsyn, Siniavsky, Daniel, and numerous others have learned, they may still be hounded and even brought to trial for it.

The most eloquent spokesman today for the social significance of literature is Solzhenitsyn. In his celebrated open letter to the Fourth Soviet Writers' Congress of 1967, in which he demanded the outright abolition of censorship, Solzhenitsyn declared: "Literature that is not the breath of contemporary society, that dares not transmit the pains and fears of that society, that does not warn in time against threatening moral and social dangers – such literature does not deserve the name of literature; it is only a façade."[24] In his Nobel Prize Lecture he extended the mission of literature even further, from the national to the international plane. Art, in his view, is the distillation and universal expression of all human experience. As such, it is the fullest embodiment of human values and universal ethical standards – transcending individual experiences and national boundaries, it is a unique expression of moral truth. "Who will give the human race one united system of evaluation, for evil deeds and good deeds, for the unendurable and the endurable? How is the line to be drawn between them? . . . It can be done by Art. By literature."[25] No greater tribute could be paid to Solzhenitsyn's claim than the grave concern with which the Soviet authorities came to view Solzhenitsyn himself, investing enormous resources in the effort to control the circulation of his works, to discredit their author, and finally to extrude him from the Soviet body politic as a feared source of ideological contagion.

The reason why Russian literature has played an important political and social role is readily apparent: in an autocratic system of government, where direct expression of all but official political sentiments is prohibited by censorship, fiction and poetry become virtually the only outlets for unorthodox or critical views. Literature, or discussions of literature, with their indirect and figurative modes of discourse, are the most convenient and effective camouflage for ideas or complaints that cannot be stated directly. Hence the rise in imperial Russia, and persistence in the Soviet Union, of a tradition of "Aesopian language," a language of hints and allusions which the writer or literary critic uses to evade censorship and which the initiated reader knows how to translate. In a society where a variety of channels are available for the expression of public opinion, literature takes its rightful place as one of the many ways of commenting on public issues. But in a society where censorship prevails, literature inevitably comes to bear far more of the burden. Russia is not unique in this respect, but its long and remarkably rich literary heritage makes it the most illustrious example.

To bear such a burden, of course, poses a considerable danger to literature itself. It is the danger of politicizing literature, of judging it in terms of its political content or message rather than in aesthetic terms. Belinsky's declaration that a bad book is more forgivable than one that is "pernicious" is clearly a case in point. It is a problem that has been much discussed both in Russian letters and elsewhere, and by no means have Russian writers unanimously accepted the dictum that literature must serve as an expression of political and social conscience.

There is another danger, however, less obvious but perhaps equally important: what are the effects on a country's political and social thinking when it is cast habitually in the form of literature? As Solzhenitsyn noted in his Nobel speech, literature by its very nature deals with the problems of mankind in moral terms, that is, in terms of the clash between good and evil. Indeed, it is the great tradition of moral seeking that has given Russian literature so much of its universal appeal and intensity. The moral force and social commitment of Russian literature have combined to form a powerful and influential literary tradition. Not all political and social issues are moral issues, however, nor are they always susceptible to moral solutions. They may arise not from good or evil intentions but from more impersonal, institutional factors which a change of heart or personnel will not remedy. Often they involve conflicts of interest, each of which has more or less equal validity; in many such cases there is no absolute right or wrong, and the most appropriate resolution is a matter of expedient compromise. Literature, however, seeks moral truth, and moral truth is necessarily absolute and uncompromising. When applied to political and social issues, such an approach may create as many problems as it solves. For instance, it may apply moral criteria to areas where such criteria are not applicable or not useful, turning all conflicts into moral conflicts and viewing them solely in terms of the moral qualities of those involved in them. This was the direction, by and large, of anti-Stalinist literature after 1956. The result was a moving and vigorous, but frequently simplistic body of criticism and protest.

Even further, such an approach may come to regard the resolution of a conflict or a dilemma as primarily a moral concern, to the neglect of the practical exigencies of everyday life. Literary characters such as Doctor Zhivago or Ivan Denisovich by their moral innocence transcend evil and suffering and thereby triumph over it. Yet their victory is a purely spiritual one, for in actuality they experience pain, deprivation, or death. The material world is disdained and conceded to the wicked, while the good conquer in the moral and spiritual realm, which is deemed the more important of the two. In its most extreme form, such an attitude can lead to the acceptance of evil in the real world rather than to an appeal to do battle against it.

Russian literature has a long and honorable history as an opponent of political oppression and social injustice. But it is a form of opposition with inherent limitations, limitations that the prerevolutionary intelligentsia frequently displayed and that have left their mark on Soviet dissent. Having preserved, almost miraculously, a tradition of criticism beneath the frozen surface of enforced conformity during the Stalin era, Russian literature played an indispensable role in the rebirth of independent thought after Stalin's death. But it was a sign of the growing maturity of Soviet dissent that in the late sixties it began, albeit slowly and incompletely, to approach the basic issues of Soviet life in legal, institutional, even political terms, rather than solely from a moral perspective. Literature has continued to serve as an important instrument, but with the Siniavsky–Daniel trial dissent began to outgrow the exclusively literary mold in which it had been cast for the previous decade. At the same time, it outgrew the limits Khrushchev had tried to impose both on criticism of the past and on demands for the future.

6

The Siniavsky–Daniel trial and its aftermath: legal tactics and organizational efforts

A "patient" in a special psychiatric hospital does not even enjoy the meagre rights of camp prisoners. He has no rights at all. The doctors can do what they want with him and no one interferes or comes to his defence. None of his complaints or the complaints of those who are with him will ever leave the hospital. His only hope is for an honest doctor.

. . . Although I have never had cause to regret my faith in the honesty of the doctors, I nevertheless insist – as I always have – that *a system in which your only hope lies in the honesty of the doctors is worthless.*

General Peter Grigorenko.[1]

The intimate relationship between politics and literature continued into the post-Khrushchev period. Not long after Khrushchev's deposition, yet another literary episode touched off a new phase of dissent in the Soviet Union. For several years two writers, Andrei Siniavsky and Iuly Daniel, had been smuggling their writings to the West and publishing them under the pseudonyms of Abram Tertz and Nikolai Arzhak respectively. Finally identified and arrested, they were brought to trial in February 1966.

Even under Khrushchev, however, the complex cross-currents of "de-Stalinization" had generated the trial of Joseph Brodsky, which took place in the early months of 1964. Apparently intended as a warning to the literary community to curb its appetite for independence – although Brodsky's poetry is largely apolitical – the Brodsky trial in retrospect seems to have been a prelude to the more menacing Siniavsky–Daniel trial two years later. Brodsky, one of the finest of the younger Soviet poets, was tried on a charge of "parasitism," that is, of violating the communist (not to mention biblical) injunction against eating without working. Brodsky insisted that he had worked, diligently and arduously, at the task of perfecting himself as a poet and a translator, an effort that could not be measured solely in terms

117

of the meager compensation he had received. The prosecution in effect responded that it was up to the state, not the individual, to determine who was a poet and who was not.

Judge: But in general what is your specialty?
Brodsky: I'm a poet, a poet-translator.
Judge: And who said that you were a poet? Who
    included you among the ranks of the poets?
Brodsky: No one. (Unsolicited) And who in-
    cluded me among the ranks of the human race?[2]

Although expert witnesses testified to Brodsky's abilities and accomplishments, he was sentenced to five years of forced labor in a distant locality (he was quietly released before the expiration of his term and has since emigrated to the United States). In passing sentence on the defendant, the judge stated:

Brodsky systematically does not fulfill the duties of a Soviet citizen with regard to his personal well-being and the production of material wealth, which is apparent from his frequent changes of jobs . . . From the report of the committee on work with young writers it is apparent that Brodsky is not a poet.[3]

The Brodsky trial foreshadowed the broader attack on the autonomy of the arts, and hence on freedom of expression in general, that Khrushchev's successors were soon to launch.

Signs of "re-Stalinization" had been appearing since the removal of Khrushchev from power in the autumn of 1964. Public references to the Stalin era were beginning to play down the negative sides – the purges, the executions, the camps – and to stress the more favorable aspects, such as the heroic efforts of the first Five Year Plans and the war years. Stalin's role as a war leader, which Khrushchev had criticized with particular harshness, was partially refurbished, and articles extolling the victims of Stalin's purges began to disappear from the press. Finally, early in 1966, *Pravda* printed a statement ruling out further use of the term "period of the cult of personality." The rationale was that the phrase exaggerated the historical role of one individual in an un-Marxist fashion. This was belated recognition, perhaps, of the inadequacy of Khrushchev's explanation of the Stalin years, but the primary effect was to eliminate from public discussion the term that had come to stand for everything oppressive and unjust about Stalin's rule.

On the other hand, there appeared to be no concerted effort to turn the clock back and restore Stalin, or his methods, to their pre-Krushchev status. The new leadership seemed to be trying to walk a narrow line between those who wanted to continue and intensify the de-Stalinization process, and those who wanted to reverse it. The government's actions seemed to indicate that there would be no further de-Stalinization, but the full-scale re-Stalinization that many Soviet citizens had begun to fear in the late sixties failed to materialize. The conflicting pressures and forces to which Khrushchev's successors found themselves subject were reflected in the consequences of the Siniavsky–Daniel trial. In some ways the trial seemed an ominous reversion back to the show trials of the thirties; yet it had the unintentional effect of galvanizing the dissidents and giving them a new cause around which to rally.

The embarrassing problem facing the prosecution was that the two writers had not in fact committed an illegal act. There was no law on the Soviet statute books prohibiting an author from sending manuscripts abroad for publication. As a result, Siniavsky and Daniel were charged, under Article 70 of the Criminal Code of the Russian Republic (RSFSR, the largest of the constituent republics of the Soviet Union), with the much vaguer offense of spreading "anti-Soviet propaganda."[4] They were accused of slandering the Soviet government and people, of slandering Lenin, and of enabling some Western commentators to use their works for anti-Soviet purposes – hardly the "especially dangerous crimes against the state" referred to in the law code. In order to prove the subversive nature of the authors' works the prosecution had to subject them to close textual examination, and this lent the trial its bizarre tone. The prosecution was forced to apply a dogged literalism to works of fiction and fantasy, attributing to the authors themselves the views expressed by the characters they had created. The authors, in their defense, insisted that literature could not be taken literally, like a political tract. As fiction uses the artistic devices of satire, hyperbole, and fantasy, it must be judged by its own standards, not those imported from another form of expression. Authors cannot be identified with their fictional characters – especially, as these authors pointed out, when the characters who supposedly expressed anti-Soviet or antisocial views were in fact portrayed in a negative light and were hardly being recommended to the reader. As the trial proceeded, the contradictions inherent in the prosecution's case became more and more glaring. Increasingly, it seemed to be the characters in the stories that were on trial rather than the authors themselves, and the proceedings began to acquire a distinctly Alice-in-Wonderland tinge.

It might well be asked why the Soviet government bothered in the first place to prosecute two fiction writers for a few short stories that were not even available to the Soviet public. The question can be answered, and the trial itself comprehended, only in the light of Russian literature's traditional role as a vehicle of social and political protest. In actuality, the prosecution and the defense were not nearly as far apart as they seemed at first glance, for both sides implicitly accepted that literary tradition. The authors based their defense primarily on the autonomy of literature, the freedom of the artist to choose the literary form that will best express the creative processes of his imagination. Yet, they could not fully reject the political role of literature in the name of "pure art," though this was their strongest line of defense. In fact, their works were deeply concerned with Stalinism and the origins of his despotism. This was particularly evident in Daniel's story *This Is Moscow Speaking,* a chilling satire on the purges in which the government plays on the basest impulses of the population by proclaiming a "public murder day" and allowing citizens to settle personal scores with impunity. In his final plea to the court, Daniel openly admitted that one of his purposes had been to warn of a revival of Stalinist practices: "I was asked all the time why I wrote my story 'This Is Moscow Speaking'. Every time I replied: Because I felt there was a real danger of a resurgence of the cult of personality."[5] This was clearly a political issue, not merely a question of artistic self-expression. Even more forthrightly, Daniel declared: "I have not tried . . . to make out that my only concern is with literature pure and simple. I do not wish to deny the political content of my works."[6] Siniavsky, while maintaining more stoutly, and on the whole justly, that his stories "reflect my feelings about the world, not politics," conceded that one of them, *The Trial Begins,* "is about Stalinism."[7] The two writers were in fact demanding not simply literary freedom but freedom of political expression, at least to the extent of commenting freely on past and present policies of the Soviet government through the medium of literature.

By putting the writers on trial, the authorities tacitly confirmed the political significance of literature and validated the role of the writer as a social critic. Literature is recognized by the Soviet government as such a powerful force that it insists on monopolizing it for its own purposes and on punishing any use of it for unauthorized sentiments – writers, after all, are "engineers of human souls." Hence the demand for literary freedom inevitably turned into a demand not to depoliticize literature but to allow it to fulfill its political and social function without heavy-handed state interference. Confusingly, but in the Russian context appropriately, the demand for political self-expression came to be voiced by two fiction writers on trial for their literary works.

Siniavsky and Daniel were sentenced to seven and five years respectively in labor camps. If the government's intention had been to intimidate out-spoken writers and stifle further expressions of anti-Stalinism, the Siniavsky–Daniel trial proved to have precisely the opposite effect. Instead of discouraging dissent, the trial touched off a series of protests, arrests, and further trials that continued for some two years. Although from a Western perspective the similarities between the writers' trial and the show trials of the thirties may have seemed all too apparent, from a Soviet point of view the differences were even more striking. The verdict was doubtless a foregone conclusion, but the trial was genuine and unrehearsed; the writers did not admit guilt and were given an opportunity, though a limited one, to defend themselves and be represented by counsel; and in their final plea to the court they were able to express some of their thoughts on the function of literature and the duties of a citizen. The last represents one of the many visible links between Soviet dissent and prerevolutionary protest: during the trials of the Populists in the 1870s, the use of the courtroom as a public forum became an established tradition in Russian political practice. Instead of concentrating on their own defense, the accused would issue reasoned statements of their views and ringing denunciations of the political and social system. It was a political device that the purge trials of the 1930s, with their prearranged scenario and abject confessions of guilt, were care-fully designed to eliminate. That tradition was now resumed, as Siniavsky and Daniel maintained their innocence and presented a justification of their actions. Defendants in subsequent political trials were to follow the same course.

The management of the trial reflected the government's general policy toward the issue of Stalinism in the wake of Khrushchev's departure from office. On the one hand, it wished to impose greater restrictions on criti-cism of the Stalinist past, with its inescapable implication of criticism of the post-Stalin present; on the other hand, it showed no desire to revert to the outright terrorism of the previous era. Therefore it sought to manipulate the courts and the legal system, giving a veneer of legality to the curtail-ment of political self-expression. The result was a glaring infringement of legal due process; it shocked many Soviet citizens who felt they had been assured by the Party that such travesties of justice were a thing of the Stalinist past and would not be permitted to recur. This was the main issue on which the various currents of dissent now concentrated.[8]

The wave of indignation elicited by the Siniavsky–Daniel trial advanced two major themes. First, putting writers on trial for the content of their fiction struck many observers as an absurd and shocking violation of the sanctity of literature. A number of prominent writers protested the trial and its outcome in these terms. One of the most eloquent of these protests came from Lydia Chukovskaia, an essayist and author of a novel about the Great Purge, *The Deserted House* (which has been published only in the West). When Nobel Laureate Michael Sholokhov applauded the verdict and seemed to express regret only that the sentences had been so mild, Chukovskaia sternly reprimanded him as a "traitor" to Soviet literature. "Literature," she wrote in an open letter to Sholokhov, "does not come under the jurisdiction of the criminal court. Ideas should be fought with ideas, not with camps and prisons."[9] Others argued similarly for the autonomy of literature, finding it a national embarrassment as well as a threat to cultural development that a powerful state should consider a handful of short stories a danger to its security.

The second major theme, which gave Soviet dissent a new dimension, was a demand for due process of law. Complaints came from many quarters that legality had not been observed in the treatment of Siniavsky and Daniel: the charge against them was false; the standards of evidence and trial procedure had been deplorable; the trial was not truly open to the public, as required by law; and the reports in the press had been scanty and grossly biased against the defendants. Many of those who voiced such complaints stated that they disagreed with the writers' views or with the methods they had used to publish them. Nevertheless, they felt compelled to protest against the arbitrariness and unfairness with which the case had been handled. There were no public complaints about the laws themselves, or about the judicial process or the legal system in general; it was assumed that the law was just but had not been properly applied. The critics therefore demanded that the trial be reviewed and the writers acquitted (because they had obviously not violated the laws under which they had been tried) or, at the very least, that their harsh sentences be reduced. A miscarriage of justice had occurred, the protesters argued, and they called upon the authorities to rectify it.

In making this demand, the critics and protesters were calling for the redemption of one of the promises Khrushchev had made in his 1956 speech. After detailing the arrests and executions of the Stalin period, Khrushchev had assured his audience that "socialist legality" would be restored and violations of it no longer tolerated. But who is to determine what "socialist" legality consists of, and how it is to be applied in specific cases? Soviet courts, to be sure, are guided by legal precedents and the norms of judicial procedure, but, like all other institutions, they are under the ultimate control of the Communist Party as the interpreter of Marxism–Leninism.[10] Therefore the Soviet legal system is under considerable pressure to apply Party policy, that is, to respond to political considerations, in the determination of individual cases. Although most of the critics of the Siniavsky–Daniel trial were unaware of the deeper implications of their complaints, they had moved post-Stalin dissent an important step beyond the appeals for moral reform and personnel changes that had marked the Khrushchev era. They were now beginning to probe into the basic legal issue raised by the Siniavsky–Daniel trial, and, indeed, into the broader problem of the guarantees of civil liberties in the Soviet Union.

At first, the protests against the trial largely took the form of a petition campaign. Addressed to the appropriate judicial and political officials, the petitions called attention to the violations of the two authors' rights as guaranteed by the Soviet constitution, and to the defects in the conduct of the trial. A good many prominent and well-established members of Soviet society signed these respectful requests for official review and redress.

At the same time, some younger individuals decided to adopt bolder, though still technically legal, forms of protest. Even before the trial itself, on December 5, 1965, Soviet Constitution Day, some 200 students from the Gorky Institute of World Literature, where Siniavsky worked, had staged a rally in Moscow's Pushkin Square to demand a fair and open trial for the two writers. (This began something of an annual tradition: silent demonstrations in behalf of dissidents have been held at the same spot on the same day in subsequent years.) The rally was the first public protest by dissidents against an act of injustice, and virtually the first spontaneous street demonstration Moscow had seen since the 1920s. Then Alexander Ginzburg, a young man who had previously edited an underground literary journal called *Syntax*, compiled a "White Book" of documents on the Siniavsky–Daniel case, including an unofficial transcript of the trial surreptitiously taken down by someone who had managed to gain access to the courtroom. Ginzburg made no attempt to keep his compilation clandestine and even sent copies of it to the authorities. Nevertheless, Ginzburg and three others – who, like most of the defendants in the trials of the late sixties, were associated with avant-garde literary and artistic circles – were arrested in January 1967 and brought to trial a year later.

On January 22, 1967, some of their supporters demonstrated in Pushkin Square in Moscow to demand the release of those arrested as well as to protest the addition to the Criminal Code of Articles 190/1 and 190/3, which they saw as new instruments to suppress dissent. Before a small crowd of bewildered onlookers, a tiny handful of young men and women unfurled home-made banners denouncing the illegality of the recent arrests. The main consequence was two further trials, in February and August–September 1967, and the conviction of four of the participants in the demonstration: Vladimir Bukovsky and Victor Khaustov each received three-year camp sentences, while Vadim Delone and Evgeny Kushev were given one-year suspended sentences. Finally, in January 1968, Ginzburg and his associates were brought to trial. Ginzburg and Iury Galanskov received harsh sentences of five and seven years, respectively, in labor camps (where Galanskov subsequently died); Andrei Dobrovolsky, who turned state's evidence, was given two years in a camp; and Vera Lashkova received one year (having already served a year in detention, she was released).

Transcripts of these trials, like that of the Siniavsky–Daniel trial, were taken down by sympathizers in the courtroom and circulated clandestinely. They reveal not only the views of the dissidents but also the attitudes of the authorities as expressed in the statements of the judges and the prosecution. As for the latter, the most frequently recurring theme is an obsessive patriotism, verging on xenophobia, which attempts to brand any critic of the Soviet government or Soviet conditions as an agent of foreign enemies. Again and again, the dissidents are accused of working for, or being duped by, or playing into the hands of, Western governments or anti-Soviet émigré organizations. One of the principal accusations against Siniavsky and Daniel was that their works had supposedly been used for purposes of anti-Soviet propaganda in the West – even though, as the writers reasonably pointed out, this was hardly a crime they had committed or for which they could be tried. Similarly, in the Ginzburg–Galanskov trial, the prosecution emphasized the defendants' alleged involvement with Narodno-trudovoi soiuz (NTS) – The People's Labor League, an émigré organization based in Germany; despite the defense lawyers' heroic efforts to demonstrate the flimsiness of this charge, it was not withdrawn. Through such accusations the government seeks to isolate its critics by exploiting the Russian people's deeply felt fear of foreign subversion and attack. The authorities evidently calculate that the simplest and most effective way of discrediting dissent is to accuse its spokesmen of being in league with the hostile foreigners who allegedly surround the Soviet Union and lie in wait to take advantage of any weakening of its defenses. Anti-Semitism and anti-Chinese sentiment, both of which have been used by the regime for the same purpose, are variations on this device.

But along with strident patriotism and the deliberate effort to turn it against the defendants, the trial transcripts reveal another side of the Soviet regime's attitude toward its home-grown critics: a somewhat perplexed paternalism. At times the dissidents are treated less as dangerous and subversive criminals than as children who have misbehaved. In the Siniavsky–Daniel trial, for instance, the prosecution expressed considerable pain at the racy language and erotic themes in the writers' stories, as though Siniavsky and Daniel were two little boys who had been caught chalking naughty words on a fence. (The images and vocabulary of their writings were mild enough by present-day Western standards but, particularly in Siniavsky's case, went far beyond what is permissible in officially sanctioned Soviet literature. Similar charges of "pornography" had been made against Brodsky at his trial.) To be sure, this is a reflection of the extreme prudishness that reigns over Soviet art and literature – and from which underground writers and artists often consciously attempt to escape – but it is symptomatic of a broader attitude toward the citizenry on the part of the government.

In all the trials there is an undercurrent of surprise expressed by the judges and prosecutors that ordinary citizens should have meddled in affairs that did not personally concern them: namely, public affairs and government policies. These are matters on which the individual citizen must trust entirely to the higher wisdom of the state and the Party. Time and again, the defendants explained their actions in terms of a sense of civic duty. Iuly Daniel, for example, stated that he had written one of his anti-Stalinist stories "because I think that all the members of a society, each of us individually and all of us collectively, are responsible for what happens."[11] Ginzburg's defense lawyer tried to argue that his client's activities on behalf of Siniavsky and Daniel reflected a commendable sense of social involvement, the mark of a good Soviet citizen.[12] The feeling of individual responsibility for public affairs was most clearly stated by Anatoly Levitin-Krasnov, a dissident religious writer, in a letter of protest against the Ginzburg–Galanskov trial: "People's consciousness has altered [since 1956]: we all of us feel we are adults, and it only irritates us when we are watched over like babies and spoon-fed on pap."[13] These expressions of civic initiative, public duty, and social conscience were consistently brushed aside by the court as outlandish, unheard-of notions. Quite possibly, the inability of the guardians of this highly paternalistic political system to understand such impulses is unfeigned. For this reason they find it necessary to attribute to the dissidents more sinister but more comprehensible motivations of subversion and treason.

The trials of 1967 and 1968, like the Siniavsky–Daniel trial, generated a series of petitions and open letters to the authorities protesting these new violations of due process and calling for review of the convictions and sentences. Neither the petition campaign nor the more public demonstrations of support for the defendants accomplished their original purpose: the convictions were upheld, the harsh sentences were not reduced, and the prospects for fair treatment of political offenders in the courts did not improve. As a result, the dissidents were forced to confront head-on the basic issue that underlay all of the trials: the lack of firm protection of individual civil liberties. The defiant statement to the court by Vladimir Bukovsky, one of the participants in the Pushkin Square demonstration, defined the issue clearly: "I absolutely don't repent of having organized the demonstration. I believe it has done its job and, when I am free again, I shall organize other demonstrations – always, of course, like this one, in perfect conformity with the law."[14] Bukovsky made no effort to mask the issue behind a plea for artistic freedom or for the correction of judicial errors. He boldly demanded protection of the individual's right to formulate and express his own opinion on public affairs. Herein lies the most significant difference between Soviet dissent and many of the currents of protest that burst forth in the West in the late sixties and early seventies. In the Soviet case the conflict is less concerned with substantive issues of political and social reorganization or development (although such concern is certainly not absent) than with the question of civil liberties. The Soviet dissidents are still battling to achieve the fundamental personal and political rights long since taken for granted – and sometimes even belittled – in most Western nations. At the Ginzburg–Galanskov trial, Levitin-Krasnov summarized the objectives of the defendants quite simply: "Like many people I have met, they were dissatisfied with the very severe censorship, with the lack of enough religious liberty (here of course, I'm speaking from my pulpit) – in a word, they all wanted greater freedom of expression and nothing else."[15] It was in these terms that the dissidents confronted the authorities in the wake of the trials, when it became clear that respectful petitions to the authorities for the redress of injustices would have little effect.

The most conspicuous effort in behalf of freedom of expression – and, in retrospect, the highwater mark of the tide of dissent in the late sixties, at least in terms of public assertiveness – was the demonstration in Moscow's Red Square on August 25, 1968. The purpose of the demonstration was to protest the Soviet invasion of Czechoslovakia, which had just taken place. Two of the participants, Larisa Daniel (then the wife of the exiled writer, later married to another dissident, Anatoly Marchenko) and Pavel Litvinov (a physicist, the grandson of the distinguished early Soviet diplomat Maxim Litvinov), were already prominent dissident activists, and they were joined by five other people, one of whom, Vadim Delone, had participated in the Pushkin Square demonstration of January 22, 1967. The word "demonstration" somewhat magnifies what actually occurred: seven individuals gathered at noon at the ancient Execution Place in Red Square and unfurled a few hand-lettered banners protesting the invasion. They were immediately set upon by agents of the secret police, beaten, and taken away to a police station. Nevertheless, in the Soviet context such organized public criticism of government policy, especially in foreign affairs, was a totally unprecedented assertion of independent opinion, the significance of which far exceeded its size or effectiveness.

What was so unique about this event was that, for the first time in the history of Soviet dissent, the demonstrators were not protesting a specific case of injustice in the Soviet Union or even an issue that directly concerned them (although in the crushing of the Czech experiment in "democratic socialism" they perceived a real threat to their aspirations for their own country). The demonstration in Red Square was purely an act of civic duty ✓ and individual conscience. This is amply confirmed by the statements of the defendants at their subsequent trial. Larisa Daniel gave voice to a sentiment widely held among the dissidents: only by speaking out now could they atone for society's silence in the Stalin era.

I was faced by the choice of protesting or staying silent. Staying silent would have meant for me sharing in the general approval of actions which I did not approve. Staying silent would have meant lying. I do not consider mine the only right action, but to me it was the only action *possible*.

. . . Had I not done this, I would have considered myself responsible for these actions of the government, just as all adult citizens of our country bear the responsibility for all the actions of our government, just as our whole people bears the responsibility for the Stalin–Beria camps, the death sentences, for . . . [cut off by the prosecutor].[16]

Vladimir Dremliuga summed up their position most poignantly: "All my conscious life I have wanted to be a citizen – that is, a person who proudly and calmly speaks his mind. For ten minutes, I was a citizen."[17] The demonstration on Red Square was of considerable importance for the development of Soviet dissent, aside from its display of support for liberalization in Czechoslovakia. In the clearest and most unmistakable terms it presented a demand for an autonomous public opinion, for the recognition of the citizen as an "adult," capable of making up his own mind on public issues and sharing responsibility for their resolution.

It was in this period that the dissidents began to perfect the techniques of communication, often ingenious, which have characterized their activities. Even literature, which had proved so useful in the past, could no longer serve as an effective expression of dissent. The late sixties saw a steady constriction of the permissible boundaries in literature. Solzhenitsyn's *The First Circle* and *Cancer Ward* were refused publication; Alexander Tvardovsky, who had been Solzhenitsyn's chief patron and sponsored other literary voices of de-Stalinization, was forced out as editor of *Novy mir* at the beginning of 1970; and in general it was made clear that no further literary bombshells like *Ivan Denisovich* or "The Heirs of Stalin" would be tolerated. In a political system where the mass media and all other public forms of expression are controlled by the government and subject to censorship, those who wish to propagate unofficial views must create unofficial channels for their transmission. An entirely new communications vocabulary has arisen to describe these channels in the Soviet Union, a vocabulary which, with its wit and playfulness, is itself a commentary on the sterility of official Soviet culture. In the wake of the Siniavsky–Daniel trial, the West became aware of the phenomenon of *samizdat,* as large quantities of material disseminated by this method began to cross the Soviet frontiers. *Samizdat* refers to the hand-to-hand circulation of manuscripts – stories, poetry, petitions, documents of various sorts – which for censorship reasons are unpublishable by regular means. The word stands for "self-publishing house," an ironic play on the acronym *gosizdat,* or "state publishing house." The device has historical precedents stretching back to the eighteenth century. Most of the copies of Alexander Radishchev's *Journey from St. Petersburg to Moscow,* for instance, were confiscated and destroyed immediately after the book's appearance. Nonetheless, the work circulated in manuscript copies throughout the nineteenth century and was well known in Russia. It was joined by masses of literary and political works that could not pass the tsarist censorship.

Usually a work enters *samizdat* circulation as the result of a deliberate decision by the author, but it can also involve a work that was not intended for circulation but which someone else decided to make available to a wider audience. Copies of novels under consideration by publishing houses, for example, have often multiplied in this fashion. The first reader makes as many typewritten carbon copies as he can – sometimes ten or twelve, using the thinnest paper available – and distributes them to trustworthy readers. Each recipient then makes an additional number of copies and passes them on to his friends, and so on. The process has the same pyramid effect as a chain letter, and can produce an "edition" of a work, even a lengthy novel like *First Circle* or *Cancer Ward,* numbering in the thousands. For Soviet citizens who wish to express independent thoughts, these are, in the poet Anna Akhmatova's phrase, "pre-Gutenberg times."

It is often pointed out that modern technology enables the Soviet government to exercise surveillance and control over its citizens to a degree far beyond the capacity of the tsarist government. The establishment of underground printing presses, a favorite and effective instrument of the nineteenth-century revolutionaries, is now exceedingly difficult. (It is not impossible, however: according to a report in No. 34 of *A Chronicle of Current Events,* a clandestine printing press created by a Baptist group in Latvia was seized by the police in October 1974 – along with nine tons of paper and 15,000 copies of the Bible!) Even simpler duplicating devices such as mimeographs and xerography machines are tightly controlled or too easily traced. In other respects, however, modern technology works against government controls. Photography has frequently been used to reproduce uncensored material, although this method is relatively cumbersome. The widespread ownership of typewriters provides a communications device which the government cannot effectively curtail. Similarly, the tape-recorder (in Russian, *magnitofon*), easily obtainable in the Soviet Union, has been put to use by dissidents, giving rise to a phenomenon called *magizdat* (or *magnitizdat*). Critical or nonconformist songs of various sorts – prison-camp songs from the Stalin era, the satirical songs and ballads of poets Bulat Okudzhava, Vladimir Vysotsky, and the late Alexander Galich – circulate hand-to-hand on home-made tapes and, like *samizdat,* are duplicated in large numbers.

Finally, publication in the West has become an important tool in the hands of the dissidents. Copies of documents circulated in *samizdat* often make their way to the West, sometimes carried out by travelers, sometimes through the open mails (in several copies mailed separately, on the chance that at least one will get through), sometimes by clandestine means. In some cases a statement may be sent directly to the West for publication, even before circulating in *samizdat,* in the hope that it will in some way be brought back into the Soviet Union. This technique has contributed another term to the vocabulary of Soviet dissent: *tamizdat,* from the Russian word for "there" (i.e., abroad). In recent years, especially with the emigration of a number of important writers, a new Russian émigré press has arisen in Western Europe and the United States. Some of these publications, like Herzen's *The Bell* in the nineteenth century, concentrate on the efforts of the dissidents within the Soviet Union (e.g., *A Chronicle of Human Rights in the USSR,* issued by Khronika Press in New York). Others, like the periodical *Kontinent,* are more literary in orientation. Older émigré publishing enterprises, such as Possev in Frankfurt and the YMCA-Press in Paris, and newer establishments such as the Alexander Herzen Foundation in Amsterdam have become important outlets for *samizdat* works by writers still within the Soviet Union. These publications, which are often issued in Western translations as well as in Russian, provide both dissidents and émigrés with a forum of expression while at the same time serving to inform public opinion in the West.[18]

A variant of *tamizdat* is the use of foreign radio stations that beam Russian-language programs to the Soviet Union, such as Radio Liberty, to broadcast protest documents and other materials. These materials, known as *radizdat,* may reach a sizable audience, and then, in the form of *magizdat* tape recordings, circulate still further. Yet another technique is the use of ham radios, both legal and illegal. Although the extent and influence of this method is difficult to determine, it has been used to disseminate unofficial information – and hence has come to be called *samefir,* "self-broadcasting," from "ether," or airwaves. Through devices such as these, the resourceful dissidents have established an alternative set of communications media, which enable them to maintain firm links among themselves and to reach a sizable audience both at home and in the West. Although the government has prosecuted many individuals for possession of unauthorized publications, it seems unlikely to be able to stop the flow of such materials without resorting to a crackdown of Stalinist proportions.

The outcome of the trial of the Red Square demonstrators was not such as to encourage further public protest: two of the defendants were sentenced to camps and three (including Litvinov and Daniel) to terms of exile in remote regions of the country, while two other participants in the demonstration were confined for periods in psychiatric hospitals. It was clear that the authorities would not tolerate such open displays of nonconformist opinion, and that efforts to repeat them would result only in decimating the already thin ranks of the dissidents. Small public manifestations continued to be held from time to time, but Soviet dissent now moved, tentatively and with a number of false starts, into a third stage. Instead of head-on confrontations

with the authorities over specific cases, efforts now began to create permanent citizens' associations that would exert persistent pressure on the government to widen the sphere of civil liberties and political self-expression.
Until now, dissidents had formed only *ad hoc* groups, coming together to
sign petitions, to express support for particular individuals who were being
victimized by the authorities, or to participate in demonstrations. The
composition of these groups was accidental, and they dispersed once their
specific purpose had been accomplished. The only unifying element in these
manifestations of dissent had been the recurrent participation in them of a
small core of individuals. Some of those already mentioned in connection
with the trials of the late sixties belong in this category, along with such
figures as Peter Iakir, Andrei Sakharov, and Peter Grigorenko. Many of
these individuals had become personally acquainted in the course of their
dissident activities and could call upon each other for mutual support in
time of need.

Such personal ties were not enough, however. Some kind of permanent,
cohesive organization was essential in order to mount a sustained campaign
for civil liberties instead of merely responding to the government's acts of
repression; it was also essential if such a campaign were to survive the arrest
of individual dissidents by the police. With an organizational base, the
scattered and highly vulnerable individuals and circles that had emerged in
the late sixties might be able to transform their expressions of criticism and
protest into a real "movement" on behalf of civil liberties.

One of the first, and most successful, of these organizing efforts was *A
Chronicle of Current Events*. The *Chronicle* is a journal, published by the
samizdat method, which serves as an information clearing-house on infringe-
ments of rights throughout the Soviet Union. A number of other underground journals have made their appearance in the last two decades, some of
a literary nature and others devoted to political and social themes.[19] Like
the intelligentsia's "thick journals" of the nineteenth century, they have
served as vehicles for the expression of a variety of nonconformist ideas,
though most of these publications have been of brief duration. The *Chronicle,* however, was the first one devoted exclusively to dissent itself. The first
issue appeared in April 1968. (It subsequently inspired the rise of several
more specialized counterparts reporting the activities of dissident Jews,
Ukrainians, Baptists, and Lithuanian Catholics.) It provides news of political arrests and trials, information on prisoners in camps and psychiatric
institutions, accounts of national and religious protest currents, and lists of
samizdat publications. Originally it was intended merely to acquaint the

various currents of dissent with each other's efforts; the official news media do not report the activities of the dissidents except to denounce or discredit them. Ultimately, however, the *Chronicle* has itself become one of the principal factors in the civil rights campaign.

The most remarkable aspect of the *Chronicle* is the nationwide information network it created. The fifth issue provided a glimpse into its method of operation:

anybody who is interested in seeing that the Soviet public is informed about what goes on in the country, may easily pass on information to the editors of the *Chronicle*. Simply tell it to the person from whom you received the *Chronicle*, and he will tell the person from whom *he* received the *Chronicle*, and so on. But do not try to trace back the whole chain of communication yourself, or else you will be taken for a police informer.[20]

Through this extensive chain of communication it receives correspondence and reports from all over the Soviet Union, and it has been able to cover events in small towns and provincial areas as well as the major cities. It has doubtless contributed greatly to the morale of the various dissidents by reassuring them that they were not completely isolated, that their objectives were shared by others and could continue to be pursued even if they themselves were arrested. Furthermore, the *Chronicle* offered an important example of an autonomous civic association of a sort hitherto nonexistent in the Soviet Union. Outside the framework of Party or state domination, it linked in its pages a number of people who did not know each other personally but cooperated on the basis of a common set of principles and objectives. It suggested the possibility of a broader organizational basis for the civil liberties campaign than had hitherto existed, and hence the prospect of surmounting the atomization of Soviet society that Stalin had achieved in the Great Purge of the thirties.

In the first years of the *Chronicle's* publication, Western observers in Moscow were uncertain whether the secret police were in fact unable to suppress it or whether they tolerated it for their own purposes, perhaps as a relatively harmless safety valve for the expression of nonconformist sentiments or even as a useful source of information on the activities of the dissidents. In 1972, after the arrest of Victor Krasin and Peter Iakir (who later publicly repented their dissident activities), publication was suspended. Iakir was a particularly prominent dissident who was believed to be one of the leading spirits behind the *Chronicle*,[21] and his removal from the dissidents' ranks was a heavy blow. The *Chronicle* resumed publication in the spring of 1974, however, and has continued to appear ever since.

A second attempt to create an organizational base was the Initiative

Group (or Action Group) for the Defense of Human Rights, founded early in 1969. Unlike the *Chronicle,* the Initiative Group set out to be entirely open and public in its activities. Its first action was an appeal to the United Nations Commission on Human Rights protesting violations of civil liberties in the Soviet Union. The fifteen members who signed the appeal (along with thirty-nine sympathizers) included some familiar figures from the central core of dissidents in Moscow, but also some lesser-known residents of provincial towns and representatives of religious and national-minority groups. The Initiative Group was rapidly depleted by arrests and repressions (by the end of 1977 only two of its members still in the USSR were at liberty), but it continued to issue periodic protest statements. Its composition seemed to reflect a growing recognition by the various protest currents that despite the many differences among them they had an interest in transcending their fragmentation and pooling their efforts to press for civil freedoms for all Soviet citizens.

The end of 1970 saw the formation of the Human Rights Committee in Moscow. The three founders of this small group were physicists: Andrei Sakharov, Valery Chalidze, and Andrei Tverdokhlebov. In November 1970, the committee distributed a statement of its principles to Western newsmen. It asserted that its objective was not to attack the government but to assist it in safeguarding civil liberties through analysis of problems in this area, dissemination of information and documents, and constructive criticism of Soviet practices. Guided by the principles of the United Nations and of Soviet law, the committee would offer "advisory assistance to state agencies in creating and applying safeguards for human rights."[22] The most noteworthy feature of this organization was its stipulation that membership be limited to those individuals "not members of political parties." As the Communist Party is the only political party allowed in the Soviet Union, this provision deliberately excluded Party members. In the Soviet context, this was a significant step, for the Communist Party is expected to be the guiding force in every Soviet institution or organization; the nucleus of Party members in each place of work, study, or cultural activity is supposed to provide ideological direction and ensure conformity with Party policy. The committee denied that it had any political purposes. As a deliberate attempt to form a non-Party association, however, the Human Rights Committee represented the first modest step on the road to true political activity: the formation of an organ of public opinion independent enough of the authorities to scrutinize and criticize on a continuing basis government policy in respect to civil liberties.

Shortly after its foundation the committee was joined by Solzhenitsyn and several other writers and scientists. In 1971 it established a link with the International League for the Rights of Man in New York and the International Institute for Human Rights in Strasbourg. Although the committee has spoken out in defense of individuals, much of its work has been of a theoretical and scholarly nature. Perhaps because of its less militant character, the Human Rights Committee has in general been treated less harshly than the Initiative Group. Once again, however, arrests and emigration deprived it of most of its active figures, leaving Sakharov as virtually its sole spokesman.

In September 1973 the formation of an organization called Group-73 was announced, its purpose being to offer assistance to "prisoners of conscience" and their families. Among its initiators was Andrei Tverdokhlebov, one of the founders of the Human Rights Committee. In 1974, Group-73 affiliated with the International Human Rights Federation in Paris. Also in 1974, a Soviet chapter of Amnesty International was founded, with Tverdokhlebov as secretary, Valentin Turchin, also a physicist, as chairman, and a membership of about twenty. Like the Human Rights Committee and Group-73, this was an effort to form a non-Party, nongovernmental civil liberties organization with the support, and protection, of an international affiliation.

The latest link in the chain of organizational efforts by dissidents is the committee, or group of committees, formed to monitor Soviet compliance with the humanitarian provisions of the Helsinki agreement (the Final Act of the Conference on European Security and Cooperation). In May 1976, eleven Soviet citizens announced in Moscow the formation of the Public Group to Promote Observance of the Helsinki Accords in the USSR, also known as the Helsinki Watch Group. Its chairman was Iury Orlov, yet another physicist, and among its members were some of the veteran dissidents of the late sixties and early seventies (e.g., Alexander Ginzburg, Peter Grigorenko, Anatoly Marchenko, and Elena Bonner, the wife of Andrei Sakharov). There is a central organization in Moscow and local committees in several of the non-Russian republics. These committees have been particular objects of government repression, however, and their future remains uncertain. By the end of 1978 Orlov, Ginzburg, and members of the Helsinki Watch Groups in Georgia, Armenia, Lithuania, and the Ukraine had all been put on trial and in most cases sentenced to terms in prison camp.

The organizations that have been mentioned by no means exhaust the types or scope of dissident activity in the sixties and seventies. A number of underground study circles and even some clandestine political groups have risen and fallen over the years. In some cases they have managed to issue manifestoes or other literature, but often their principles, activities, and membership remain shrouded in obscurity.[23] Perhaps the most significant of these was the All-Russian Social-Christian Union for the Liberation of the People, organized in 1964. An underground organization centered in Leningrad, the Union aimed at the armed overthrow of the Soviet regime and its replacement by a new order combining elements of Russian Orthodoxy, socialism, and democracy. When it was broken up by the police in 1967, it had close to sixty actual or prospective members. Other dissidents have preferred to speak out individually and have not identified themselves with any particular group or association. Although Moscow remains the center of dissident activities, there are many dissidents outside the capital as well, as indicated by the number of political trials and other repressive actions the *Chronicle of Current Events* has reported in Russian provincial centers and in the Ukraine and other non-Russian areas.

As a reflection of the evolution of dissident thought and strategy at the center of the civil liberties campaign, the organizational attempts discussed here are of greater significance than their few tangible accomplishments would suggest. First, they indicate that it may be possible for the dissidents to surmount the social atomization that has prevented organized public pressure from being an effective force in Soviet life. The Soviet authorities prefer to deal with isolated individuals or specific interest groups, which can more easily be bought off or played off against one another. For the most part, they have been successful until now in keeping criticism of government policies within these manageable bounds. Therefore the appearance of organizations that attempt to transcend the interests of any particular group and seek to defend the rights of *all* citizens on a sustained, day-to-day basis represents a step forward in Soviet civic consciousness.

More broadly, the rise of autonomous public associations represents a new stage of political consciousness on the part of at least some Soviet dissidents. Post-Stalin dissent in its initial phase was limited to moral appeals to the authorities for more humane treatment, and in its second phase to petitions and protests against violations of Soviet law and judicial procedure. It did not challenge the authorities' right to rule, nor did it question their legitimacy or demand that they be held accountable for their actions except in a moral sense. But the attempt to create citizens' organizations independent of Party and state represents a significant break with the paternalistic principle of authority comparable to that achieved by the early intelligentsia at the end of the eighteenth and beginning of the nineteenth centuries.

Here is at least a glimmer of the notion that the state exists for the benefit of society, not vice versa, and that the public has the right to judge the policies of the government and to hold their executors accountable for their actions. The state, or Party, does not embody a higher wisdom in the name of which it has the right to demand childlike obedience from its citizens. The Soviet dissidents, as represented by the civil liberties movement, have reached a stage of development similar to that of Radishchev and the early Decembrists: a realization that protection of the individual citizen from governmental arbitrariness requires fundamental institutional, legal, and even political reforms, and not just humanistic appeals to the authorities; but at the same time, a desire to work for such changes gradually and legally, rather than to attack the system from without as the later revolutionaries were to do.

The behavior of the Soviet authorities in regard to these organizations offers some confirmation of their significance, despite their meager membership lists. Of course, one must always be wary of judging the importance of an event or development by the government's reaction to it – the Soviet authorities are just as prone to errors of judgment, overreaction, or political blindness as government authorities elsewhere. But their unremitting effort to crush these relatively ineffectual organizations does seem to bespeak an awareness that such groups call into question the very bases of Party political control. By insisting that an educated, concerned citizenry is capable of exercising adult judgment on public issues, and that public opinion should influence policy making, these organizations serve to undermine the paternalistic relationship between state and society that has dominated Russia for so many centuries. The principle they represent offers a sufficiently fundamental challenge to the Soviet system that its spread must (in the view of the authorities) be checked by every means available.

By the late seventies, the prospects for the success of the dissidents' efforts in the near future seemed dimmer than at any time since the fall of Khrushchev. The trials of 1966–8, like those of the tsarist regime in the 1870s, had tended to backfire on the government. The defendants were convicted and removed from circulation, but the travesties of judicial procedure required to achieve this objective discredited the legal system, provided unwelcome publicity for the dissidents and their views, and generated new sources of protest. As a result more subtle, or at least less public, methods of dealing with outspoken critics began to be employed with considerable success. These measures included dismissal from jobs and blacklisting from further employment – a procedure which, among other penalties, exposes an individual to prosecution on the charge of "social parasitism," that is, refusal to work, as in the trial of Joseph Brodsky in 1964; denial or revocation of residence permits, which are required for domicile in the large cities (a device used, for instance, to keep Solzhenitsyn out of Moscow); incarceration in psychiatric hospitals (among the many subjected to this method have been Zhores Medvedev, Vladimir Bukovsky, Peter Grigorenko, and Victor Fainberg and Natalia Gorbanevskaia, two of the participants in the Red Square demonstration); and, most recently, forced emigration to the West (Zhores Medvedev, Solzhenitsyn, Bukovsky, Chalidze, Litvinov, and numerous others). These methods have been effective, at least temporarily, in removing most of the leading activists from the scene and in isolating those who are left.

For the moment, the opportunities for outspoken criticism of the government are narrower, and the risks greater, than they were a decade or so earlier. Active dissent remains a very limited fragmented phenomenon, the property of a lonely handful of individuals. It shows no signs of drying up entirely, however, for these individuals are not mere aberrations or social misfits, much as the government would wish this to be believed. At least to some degree, they reflect the sentiments of sizable and influential groups and serve as spokesmen for broader aspirations within Soviet society. The discontent they represent has important social roots, and that is what gives Soviet dissent an underlying vitality and dynamic force, which the silencing of particular individuals cannot fully suppress.

7

The Soviet dissidents

In periods of violence and terror people retreat into themselves and hide their
feelings, but their feelings are ineradicable and cannot be destroyed by any amount
of indoctrination. Even if they are wiped out in one generation, as happened here to
a considerable extent, they will burst forth again in the next one.

Nadezhda Mandelstam, *Hope against Hope.* [1]

Who are the Soviet dissidents? What is their background, what segments of
Soviet society are they drawn from, what are their personal characteristics?
To answer these questions, we must look not only at the small group of
prominent activists but at the larger number of individuals who have in
some way expressed support for them, particularly by putting their names
to various petitions and open letters on behalf of the dissidents and their
causes. The first and most striking feature most of these people have in
common is their education. Nearly all are university educated, or the equivalent, and work in the professions, or are fringe members of the educated
elite, such as aspiring poets and university dropouts. The rare petition
signers who identify themselves as "workers" stand out vividly as exceptions to the rule. Andrei Amalrik, examining the social background of his
fellow dissidents, found that of the 738 people who signed petitions and
protests against the Ginzburg–Galanskov trial in 1968, workers numbered
6 percent; the rest were academics, people in the arts, professionals, or
students.[2] Even Ivan Iakhimovich, the collective-farm chairman who
joined the dissidents, and was committed for a time to a mental hospital,
was a university graduate in philology. The demand for human rights and
for civil liberties and political self-expression is very much a demand
emanating from the educated segment of Soviet society.

The parallel with the intelligentsia of tsarist Russia is obvious and raises

138

the same question: why does Soviet dissent issue from those whose income and status would seem to place them among the more privileged members of their society? The answer is virtually the same in both cases, because the contemporary Soviet educated elite is in many respects the counterpart of the Western-educated nobility of imperial Russia. Despite the obvious differences in property ownership and social origins, the Soviet educated elite occupies a position relative to the state, on the one hand, and the rest of society on the other, remarkably similar to that of the service nobles of Radishchev's time. It enjoys a relatively privileged material position, a high degree of self-consciousness and social awareness thanks to superior education, and a strong sense of service to its society. In at least some of its members these characteristics have generated the desire for personal autonomy and freedom of self-expression so evident in the statements of the dissidents. Yet, like their predecessors in the imperial period, they find themselves unable to defend their self-esteem and independence of mind against the arbitrariness of an overbearing state.

The Soviet educated elite, like the educated nobility of the eighteenth and nineteenth centuries, is itself a product of the Russian state. Stalin, while decimating the old educated elite in the purges of the thirties, at the same time greatly expanded educational facilities and promoted the training of a vast new educated elite to implement his plans for industrializing the country.[3] Like the modernizing tsars of the past, Stalin was wary and mistrustful of his educated subjects but could not dispense with their services. Therefore he provided considerable incentives to education in terms of economic benefits and social prestige, while seeking to keep the educated elite within narrow technical bounds by means of strict cultural and political controls. Under Stalin the members of that new elite, like Peter the Great's nobility, were too cowed, or too satisfied with their recent rise in society, to question the state's treatment of them. Since Stalin's death, however, some of them, as well as their children, who have grown up in relatively more secure times, have become increasingly resentful of a paternalistic state that continues to insist on guiding the thought and behavior of each of its citizens. As before, the conflict remains one between a strong state, bent on mobilizing all of Russia's energies for development purposes, and an educated elite, essential to the state's modernization efforts but increasingly restive under the state's strong hand. Thus, for all the vast social, economic, and political changes that have swept over Russia since 1917, the social sources of Soviet dissent are strikingly similar to those that had begun to generate the Russian intelligentsia at the end of the eighteenth century.

Like the old intelligentsia, the spokesmen for contemporary dissent constitute only a narrow section of the educated elite from which they are drawn. They are the small minority who, as a result of independent thinking about the existing political and social order, have come to question, however tentatively, some of its fundamental principles and institutions. There would be considerable justification in speaking of them as a continuation of the intelligentsia, or as a "neo-intelligentsia," and many commentators today, both Soviet and Western, do apply the term intelligentsia to them. In view of the much broader official Soviet definition of the intelligentsia as those who engage in "mental work," including all professionals and most white-collar workers, a usage adopted also by some Western scholars, it seems best to avoid the word altogether in speaking of contemporary Soviet developments and to use, as we have been doing, the term dissidents instead.

While the relationship of the educated elite to the state displays a considerable historical continuity, the composition of that elite has changed drastically. As the previous two chapters have indicated, the Soviet dissidents and their supporters are drawn predominantly from two specific occupational groups: writers and scientists. Other individuals appear in the dissidents' ranks, of course, but none with the frequency of these two elements. Solzhenitsyn and Sakharov, the two best-known dissidents in the West, one a novelist and the other a physicist, are not merely outstanding individuals but are representative of the two main pillars of Soviet dissent. These two groups figure so prominently in post-Stalin dissent because their members experience more acutely than any others the general conflict between the educated elite and the state. In the Soviet context writers and scientists, though for somewhat different reasons, have the greatest opportunity to develop the heightened sense of self that throws them into conflict with the autocratic state. At the same time, they are in the best position to articulate their resentment. Hence it is primarily from these two groups that the latter-day counterparts of Radishchev, the Decembrists, or Herzen have emerged.

Unquestionably, the names of Soviet dissidents most familiar to Westerners have been those of writers: Solzhenitsyn, Pasternak, Siniavsky, Daniel, Evtushenko, Voznesensky, more recently Vladimir Voinovich, and numerous others. These individuals, along with a host of less prominent novelists and poets, have played a much more significant role in Soviet dissent than have their literary counterparts in any Western protest movement. Given the traditional role of literature as the "conscience" of Russia, and the high moral calling that many writers consequently feel, it is not surprising that literature and nonconformity show a marked affinity for one another. Because of its social commitment and its frequent use as a vehicle of critical ideas, literature naturally attracts the restless, the questioning, the individualistic spirits. Nor can the government impose quite the same controls on literature as on such closely watched fields as history or philosophy. Because the regime needs literature to pursue its own educative and political functions, it must give writers a certain amount of creative autonomy; literature, after all, cannot educate if the public refuses to buy books or come to the theaters. The authorities need the writers and must grant them at least a minimum of freedom to exercise their imagination. (By the same token, the more abstruse and theoretical scientific disciplines also enjoy a relatively high degree of creative freedom, and this may have something to do with the kinds of personnel they attract.) Not only writers and poets but critics and historians of literature have figured prominently among the personnel of dissent. One of the most frequent professional identifications among the petition signers, as well as among the activists themselves, is "Candidate of Philological Sciences," the Soviet equivalent of a Ph.D. in literature or languages. The composition or study of literature represents a highly congenial career for a dissident or a potential dissident.

Under Soviet conditions, however, literature does not merely attract dissidents, it generates them; for the amount of creative liberty granted to it, though greater than in some other endeavors, has strict limits. The very nature of his work propels the writer into a head-on confrontation with the control apparatus of the state through the latter's exercise of censorship. Not only may the writer's art be subjected to mutilation or outright suppression but it is at the mercy of people whose literary judgment he cannot accept, namely, bureaucrats. Censorship thwarts his creative impulses – and hence his very personality – and at the same time humiliates him by subjecting him to the dictates of individuals who are less knowledgeable, less imaginative, less sensitive than he feels himself to be. Solzhenitsyn referred bitterly to this situation in his outspoken letter to the Fourth Congress of Soviet Writers in 1967. He called for the complete abolition of censorship, which "imposes a yoke on our literature and gives people unversed in literature arbitrary control over writers."[4] The sense of humiliation a writer can experience under these circumstances is vividly reflected in the open letter that the poet Andrei Voznesensky addressed to the newspaper *Pravda* on June 22, 1967. Voznesensky's scheduled visit to the United States for a poetry reading had been canceled by the Soviet authorities for political reasons, but the official explanation referred to the poet's "illness." Voznesensky declared that he was not ill at all, that everyone knew he was not ill, and that this transparent lie embarrassed and humiliated him. "It is an insult to elementary human dignity," he wrote. "I am a Soviet writer, a human being made of flesh and blood, not a puppet to be pulled on a string."[5]

One of the most dramatic and illustrative clashes between artistic self-expression and bureaucratic arbitrariness took place in the realm of painting, but the conflict it reflected applies equally to literature. As mentioned in Chapter 5, in December of 1962, Khrushchev visited an exhibition at the Manezh Gallery in Moscow. The result was a tragicomic collision between the forms and principles of modern art, on the one hand, and the aesthetic sensibilities of the First Secretary, on the other. One room of the exhibition was devoted to abstract art by contemporary Russian artists, virtually the first time such work, which violates the official canons of "socialist realism," had been put on public display. According to one theory, it was the liberals who arranged the display, hoping that Khrushchev would react favorably and thus register official approval of this type of art; another theory holds that the inclusion of abstractions was a deliberate provocation on the part of the conservatives, who anticipated Khrushchev's negative reaction. Whatever the case, Khrushchev harshly condemned most of the works he viewed. What is particularly striking is the language he used to express his disapproval – salty and irreverent, as one would have expected from Khrushchev, but also scolding and offensively paternalistic. He suggested, for instance, that such works must have been done by "pederasts," and that they represented a waste of state educational funds. Turning to one of the artists, he said: "You're a nice-looking lad, but how could you paint something like this? We should take down your pants and set you down in a clump of nettles until you understand your mistakes. You should be ashamed." And twice he asked offending painters, "Who are your parents?", implying that they were wayward children whose naughtiness stemmed from a lack of parental guidance.[6] It is revealing that Khrushchev's first reaction – a spontaneous, instinctive one, perhaps – to art that he did not understand or appreciate was to address its practitioners as juvenile delinquents, or, in the Russian term, "hooligans," rather than as responsible adults or serious artists.

The notion that the proper attitude of the state to the creative artist must be one of paternalistic discipline was not unique to Khrushchev. As noted earlier, he same attitude dominated the Siniavsky–Daniel trial, which took place after Khrushchev's departure from the political scene. The prosecution attempted to demonstrate that the writers' works contained subversive, "anti-Soviet" sentiments, but many of the negative comments that the prosecutor and the judge made on those works in the attempt to discredit them had little to do with political views. Siniavsky's prose, particularly, is quite experimental in places; it employs surrealistic devices and a good deal of erotic imagery. Judging from the transcript of the trial, the court was hopelessly baffled by the literary significance of such language. The result was a good deal of tongue-clicking and numerous expressions of dismay at the "unmentionable" words, the unspeakable acts, the parodies of sacrosanct figures such as Lenin – and the writers were denied even the dignity of recognition as serious practitioners of their craft.

Censorship of literature and the arts reflects not merely the political sensitivities of the authorities but their level of taste. Khrushchev's reaction to the Manezh exhibit may have been politically calculated, but in addition it was probably the heartfelt cry of a man of minimal formal education and cultural refinement faced with examples of avant-garde art. Given his age and background, his standard of taste was predictably limited to the realistic, strictly representational style enshrined in "socialist realism." Since Soviet censorship on the whole is exercised not by artists or professional critics but by bureaucrats, their standards, too, are bound to be conventional, routine, and safe. Such individuals find it difficult to understand abstract art, with all its indirectness, suggestiveness, and playfulness. They not only dislike it but fear that it might harbor subversive sentiments they may not be able to discern. Their reasoning is like that of the official in a nineteenth-century satire by Saltykov-Shchedrin: "What I do not understand is dangerous for the State."[7] One of the reasons for the stubborn persistence of "socialist realism" in dogmatically rigid form may simply be that it conforms to the limited aesthetic taste and comprehension of those who exercise control over art and literature in the Soviet Union. Politicians and bureaucrats in Western countries rarely display more highly developed aesthetic sensibilities, to be sure, but they lack the power to impose their limitations on the rest of society.

The social significance of literature in the Russian tradition develops in writers a strong sense of their own worth, of their value as guardians of the public conscience. Their self-esteem receives further confirmation from the considerable material rewards and public prestige that the state, in its effort to utilize that literary tradition for its own purposes, confers on officially approved writers. At every step of his career the Soviet writer is told that he is an important individual performing a valuable service to his society. Yet, through censorship, the state frustrates the self-expression that is essential to him and, with its heavy-handed bureaucratic controls, reveals to him just how vulnerable he really is, both as an artist and as an individual. Thus the Soviet writer is sufficiently privileged to develop a strong consciousness of self-worth and human dignity, yet sufficiently powerless to prevent gross violations of his basic human rights. He is therefore likely to be particularly sensitive to the kind of humiliation – widespread in the paternalistic Soviet system – described by the writer Victor Nekrasov (now in emigration in the West) on a group trip to New York. The Russian tour guide herded Nekrasov and his fellow tourists about, lecturing and scolding them: "Like schoolchildren, we stood along the wall of the enormous building listening to him in silence, and then the accused began to justify themselves . . ."[8] Under pressure of the contradictions in their situation, writers, as well as other creative artists, may prove willing to jeopardize their material benefits and secure place in the system in order to pursue their creative impulses freely. In some cases they may even become outspoken defenders of civil liberties and human rights for all citizens.

At first glance, the striking number of natural scientists in the ranks of the dissidents seems harder to explain than the presence of writers. Like writers (or at least the successful ones), the scientists are part of the Soviet professional elite, and probably the most privileged part: thanks to the state's commitment to economic, military, and technological development, their material rewards are high and their social status considerable. The social function and moral tradition of literature, however, with its inherent potential for conflict with the state, would seem to have no counterpart in the sciences. On the contrary, official Soviet ideology, itself claiming a basis in scientific principles, virtually worships science and technology as the foundation of material production and the road to communism. To claim that there is something in the intellectual activity of scientific inquiry itself that breeds critical thought and a demand for freedom is an inadequate explanation of the Soviet scientists' behavior, for their counterparts in the West have not been nearly as conspicuous for their nonconformist political thought. The answer appears to lie as much in the social position of the Soviet scientist as in the nature of his work. Despite his status and the respect accorded to his professional activity – and in fact partly because of it – the scientist may experience many of the same injuries at the hands of the paternalistic bureaucracy as the writer, and may react in much the same way.[9]

One problem afflicting science is the ever-present danger of the politicization of scientific research in a system where all resources are government controlled and are allocated by a centralized bureaucracy. The novel *Not by Bread Alone* is a detailed fictional treatment of this issue. Here, the inventor-hero's creative individualism threatens the mediocrities and vested interests within the bureaucracy, which reacts by marshaling political influence to try to crush him. A real-life example on a much wider scale was the infamous Lysenko affair. Trofim Lysenko was a biologist and animal breeder who upheld a version of the theory, contrary to modern genetics, that acquired characteristics can be inherited. Winning the support first of Stalin and then of Khrushchev, he was able to impose his views on broad areas of Soviet biological research, severely hampering the progress of biology in general and nearly destroying genetic research in the Soviet Union. Zhores Medvedev, a biologist himself, in the *Rise and Fall of T. D. Lysenko* (published only in the West) describes the valiant efforts of the geneticists to survive: hounded out of the biology laboratories, they would sometimes find refuge in an obscure corner of a sympathetic physicist's or chemist's laboratory and covertly carry on their research. In this case, political leaders rejected the best scientific advice available to them and supported scientifically unsound schemes. Although on the whole the natural sciences enjoy considerably more autonomy than the social sciences, even within the scientist's strictly professional sphere of competence far-reaching decisions may be made by scientifically ignorant politicians and bureaucrats. It is perhaps more likely to occur in fields with direct practical application, such as, in this case, animal husbandry and crop development: both Stalin and Khrushchev doubtless felt that their peasant descent made them better qualified than laboratory scientists to judge such matters. But no scientific sphere, however esoteric, is fully immune to such interference. A few years before his death, for instance, Stalin made a similar foray into the field of linguistics. Medvedev ends his book with words of praise for the pluralistic Western system of scientific research. With a variety of independent academic institutions and funding available from foundations, institutes, and universities as well as government, it is more difficult for a single school of thought to predominate than under the highly centralized Soviet system.

Professional contacts and working conditions are a second area of potential conflict between the scientist and the ubiquitous bureaucracy. In general, there is a greater need for international communication in the natural sciences than in the humanities or the social sciences. Scientific information becomes obsolete very quickly and must be communicated rapidly if it is to be useful; otherwise, research can end up in a blind alley or be forced into enormously wasteful and time-consuming duplications of effort. Therefore the scientist has a compelling professional interest in the free exchange of scientific information through access to the printed word, correspondence with counterparts abroad, and attendance at international meetings. That interest, however, conflicts with the bureaucratic controls that the Soviet authorities insist on exercising over all citizens. The scientist may find himself harassed and thwarted in his purely professional communication with scientists in other countries.

The most detailed examination of this problem has been supplied, once again, by Zhores Medvedev. In *The Medvedev Papers* he describes in great detail how he was refused permission to attend an international scientific congress; how his correspondence from abroad was censored, resulting in the delay or confiscation of scientific materials; and other examples of political and administrative interference in a scientist's professional life. Beneath the scientifically detached and at times ironical tone in which he narrates his ordeals with the bureaucracy can be detected the frustration of a dedicated scientist unable to obtain the information essential to his work. In addition, however, and even more important, one can sense the humiliation felt by a trained scientist, with a considerable degree of pride in his abilities and accomplishments, who must submit to the supervision of untrained, semieducated officials. For instance, Medvedev was informed by a minor official of the Central Committee that he would not be allowed to attend a scientific congress in the United States, and in response to his protests he received "the standard demagogic answers," such as the following: "You ought to know that they're sending U-2 planes over, and dropping spies by parachute. And you've been getting ready to go and visit them!"[10] Furthermore, although this official was in charge of the administration of scientific affairs, Medvedev concluded that she was incompetent to deal with them. "From further conversation it became clear, however, that, although Filippova had on her desk a neat pile of books on physiology and medicine, she was completely uninformed on the questions we were discussing. She knew nothing of the problems of gerontology and had not even read the whole of my memorandum."[11] Medvedev discovered that foreign travel is not a right of Soviet citizens but a privilege granted by the Soviet government for good behavior – and granted sparingly, in view of its historical association with critical thought.[12] What infuriated him as much as the withholding of the privilege was the behavior of the officials he had to deal with: he was treated like a child who must accept without question the authority of his elders, even when it is clearly arbitrary and unjustified.

There is yet a third area of potential confrontation between the scientists and the state. Even when allowed to pursue their work freely, scientists may discover that the respect and social prestige they have come to regard as their due has very narrow limits. Andrei Sakharov, in the course of his work on thermonuclear development, "noticed that the control levers were in the hands of people who, though talented in their own way, were cynical."[13] In other words, he began to realize that although he could pursue his research freely, and was handsomely rewarded and honored for it, he had no say at all in the way the forces he was developing were to be utilized. In 1961, when he made an effort to prevent Soviet resumption of nuclear tests, Khrushchev crudely rebuffed him. "He said more or less the following: Sakharov is a good scientist. But leave it to us, who are specialists in this tricky business, to make foreign policy."[14] When he failed to persuade Khrushchev to call off a specific test in 1962, he experienced a sense of "impotence and fright" to which he attributes much of his later dissident activity.[15] The disparity between the respect and privileges granted him for his scientific accomplishments and his utter powerlessness outside that sphere must have come as a profound shock to Sakharov. Even the "father of the Soviet H-bomb" was not expected to have an independent opinion on public issues, much less offer advice to the authorities. When he attempted to do so, he was, on the one hand, treated as a state resource who should unquestioningly perform his assigned function, and on the other humiliatingly brushed off as unqualified to meddle in political affairs.

Both writers and scientists, then, inevitably encounter arbitrary treatment at the hands of the state, for, much more than the ordinary citizen, they are drawn by the nature of their work into direct conflict with the bureaucratic controls over the means of communication and expression. In important respects they are part of the privileged elite: they are well educated, well paid, and have a considerable degree of social prestige, and they enjoy a certain amount of creative autonomy in their work – more, in fact, than most other professionals. In addition, they are instilled with a particularly strong sense of responsibility for their country's progress. Just as the writers derive a sense of social service from the long-standing role of Russian literature as the moral spokesman of society, the scientists feel that they are serving their country as the vanguard of its development efforts. Yet, they may on occasion be forced to recognize that they have no greater measure of personal freedom than a common laborer, and that they too are subject to arbitrariness, bureaucratic heavy-handedness, and even police action.[16] They are particularly humiliated and embittered by such treatment because their relative privilege has given them a sense of individual self-respect that makes the conduct of the authorities intolerably painful.

Thus the writers and scientists occupy a position in Soviet society analogous to that of the educated nobility in imperial Russia of the eighteenth and nineteenth centuries. In both cases, a relatively privileged position permitted the rise of a new consciousness of individual worth, generating a demand for greater autonomy from state controls; education enabled such individuals to articulate their grievances; and a strong sense of service to their society impelled them to speak out despite the obvious risks of such behavior. Both groups were privileged enough to be provoked by the treatment they received at the hands of the state, instead of merely acquiescing in it, as most citizens would do, but not privileged enough to defend themselves effectively against it. It is for these reasons that Soviet poets, biologists, chemists, novelists, mathematicians, and physicists have begun to express the same demands for independence of thought and the protection of elemental human and civil rights that Radishchev and his fellow nobles began to voice more than a century and a half ago.

These considerations help to explain the social origins of Soviet dissent. They do not, however, account for the decision of particular individuals to become dissidents. Like the Western-educated stratum of imperial Russian society from which the intelligentsia was drawn, the professionally trained elements of Soviet society form the broad social base from which the active dissidents originate and to which their pronouncements are usually addressed. It is easier to understand, however, why most remain satisfied with their position than why some prove willing to jeopardize it. The great majority of the Russian service gentry of an earlier age were content with their place in the imperial order and accepted the institutions that made it possible; similarly, it is to be expected that most members of the Soviet educated elite are generally content with their situation and that few experience profound resentment at the price they may have to pay for it. Either they do not feel that their self-esteem is seriously challenged by the state's actions, or they prefer to ignore or tolerate such challenges. Only a small minority – and this is hardly unique to the Soviet Union – prove sensitive enough or courageous enough to protest the arbitrariness of the state and its violations of rights, especially when the risks entailed are as great as they are in the Soviet case. Just why they choose to do so is a matter of individual psychology and personality structure that can rarely be traced in detail, especially as we lack the wealth of biographical and autobiographical material that is available for prerevolutionary figures. Few Soviet dissidents have had the leisure, or perspective, to scrutinize their thoughts and motivations in the manner of a Herzen or a Gorky or a Trotsky. Nonetheless, certain general patterns do emerge from the information at hand, particularly when we compare today's activists with their predecessors in the tsarist era.

It would be a mistake to think that all the dissidents are spotless heroes or selfless idealists, as Westerners (more generously than the dissidents themselves) often assume. Like the intelligentsia before them, today's dissidents exhibit the various weaknesses, failings, and temptations to which real people, as distinct from fictional characters, are subject. Some have been unable to withstand the pressures brought to bear on them and have publicly recanted to one degree or another; others have turned state's evidence against erstwhile colleagues; still others have exhibited erratic or reckless behavior or a lack of deep commitment. What is remarkable, however, is not that such episodes have occurred but that they have occurred so infrequently, even though dissent has involved hundreds, possibly thousands of people in the last two decades. It would be equally mistaken to believe, as the Soviet authorities would have it, that the dissidents on the whole are unstable individuals whose minds are unbalanced or who harbor private grudges against society. The impulses that move Soviet dissidents, as well as the sources of the staying power they have demonstrated, are far more complex and difficult to fathom than either of the above characterizations would suggest.

A number of Western commentators have stressed the role of a "generation gap" in the rise of Soviet dissent. According to this theory, dissent is largely the work of the postwar generation. This younger generation was shocked and repelled by the revelations of its parents' complicity, whether active or passive, in Stalin's repressions; having grown up in relative security and prosperity, it is more willing to assume the risks of outspoken criticism than its elders, who cherish the peace and stability they have at last achieved. From this perspective, Soviet dissent may appear to be a local branch of the worldwide youth rebellion of the late sixties and early seventies, rejecting, like its foreign counterparts, "bourgeois" materialism, social conformity, and political hypocrisy – an example, perhaps, of the "convergence" of industrial societies, whether socialist or capitalist.

This interpretation seemed particularly plausible during the series of political trials in the late sixties that followed the prosecution of Siniavsky and Daniel. Many of the defendants were indeed relatively young, and, in Soviet terms, were rebels: unpublished poets, university dropouts, marginally employed individuals. That situation has not persisted. It may be true that the postwar generation on the whole is more critical and less intimidated than its elders; on the other hand, it may also be more cynical and politically apathetic. In any case, Soviet dissent has not followed clearly defined generational lines. One of its distinguishing characteristics, for instance, by comparison with contemporary Western experience, is the relatively minor role played by students. To refer again to Amalrik's analysis of the 1968 petition signers, he found that only 5 percent were students. The institutions of higher learning are too tightly controlled by the state, and the consequences of expulsion in terms of career, status, and earning power too great, for most students to risk the open expression of dissident opinions. Although youthful rebels have been one element among the active spokesmen for dissent, they have not predominated. Siniavsky, Solzhenitsyn, Lydia Chukovskaia, Grigorenko, and Sakharov, to mention just a few, were all older and more or less established figures when they added their voices to the chorus of dissent. Despite some external similarities to contemporary currents in the West, the character of Soviet dissent has been determined by specific Russian historical and political circumstances and is a response to local Russian events. Those who have displayed the most intense commitment to it have included not only the young but the middle-aged and even senior citizens.

One of the themes the dissidents voice most frequently when asked to explain their actions is a strong sense of personal guilt over the repressions of the Stalin era, and a determination to redeem that guilt by combating injustice in the present. Even when they themselves in no way participated in the repressions, the silent acquiescence, the passivity, and the unquestioned faith in the authorities that Soviet society displayed under Stalin torment them and compel them to speak out. The theme of collective complicity appears frequently in underground poetry, as in Iury Galanskov's angry "Manifesto of Man":

> This is me
> calling to truth and revolt
> willing no more to serve
> I break your black tethers
> woven of lies.

In more ironic form, it is the message of Alexander Galich's "Silence Is Gold," which includes the refrain:

> Mum's the word – and you'll get preferred.
> Mum's the word, mum's the word, mum's the word.[17]

When Larisa Daniel was asked why she assumed the risks inherent in her political protest activities, she "shrugged her shoulders and answered very quietly: 'I cannot do otherwise.'"[18] Similarly, Sakharov told a Western reporter in 1973: "[A man] may hope for nothing but nonetheless speak because he cannot, simply cannot remain silent."[19] Natalia Gorbanevskaia, summing up the motivations of those who participated in the Red Square demonstration against the invasion of Czechoslovakia, reiterated the sense of deep personal guilt at the thought of participating, however involuntarily, in lies and repression: "The purpose of our demonstration was, so it seems to me, not merely to give expression to our own remorse, but also to redeem at least a fraction of our people's guilt before history."[20]

What awakened this new sense of individual conscience, and why did it begin to find expression in the late 1950s and the 1960s? The shattering impact that Khrushchev's revelations had on thoughtful Soviet citizens was crucial, and the dissidents almost universally acknowledge the enormous role it played in their lives. Stalin had been so glorified as the supreme leader and all-wise guardian of the Soviet Union that at first it was difficult for many citizens to conceive of national existence without him. Evtushenko has vividly described the widespread reaction to Stalin's death: "Trained to believe that they were all in Stalin's care, people were lost and bewildered without him. All Russia wept. And so did I. We wept sincerely, tears of grief – and perhaps also tears of fear for the future."[21] The abrupt transition from the unrestrained adulation of Stalin, so carefully cultivated for more than two decades, to Khrushchev's revelations just three years later, inevitably had a traumatic effect on many people, shattering their whole conception of life. To quote Evtushenko again:

Although I had some idea of Stalin's guilt, I could not imagine, until Khrushchev made his speech, how tremendous it was. Most people had the same experience. After the text was read to them at Party meetings they went away, their eyes on the ground. Probably many among the older people tortured themselves with the question: had they lived their lives in vain?[22]

Many, probably most, found ways of rationalizing their past beliefs and behavior and managed to paper over the chasm between ideal and reality that suddenly yawned beneath their feet. For others, however, the dramatic realization of what they had until now passively accepted proved a painful but decisive turning point in their lives. It was not so much that Khrushchev *created* uncertainties about the past where none had existed before. Stalin had victimized too many Soviet citizens to pass from the scene without leaving a deep residue of anguished questions, suspicions, and reservations. What Khrushchev did, by showing that Stalin's deeds were not inevitable or unavoidable, was to articulate hitherto unspoken doubts, to bring them to the forefront of people's consciousness, and to give them the sanction of the highest state authority.

The corrosive examination of past and present that Khrushchev initiated played a role in the awakening of Soviet dissent very much like that played by Enlightenment thought in eighteenth-century Russia. In unmistakable terms he provided a new standard for measuring the gulf between the inherent worth of the individual as an end in himself and the despotic disregard with which the political order treated him. In an effort to strengthen and modernize the existing system, Khrushchev, like Peter the Great and Catherine the Great, introduced a new principle of criticism for judging the system's faults. In the eighteenth and nineteenth centuries the impact of that new principle, Western thought, was social and cultural as well as ultimately political, for the notion of the freedom and dignity of the individual conflicted with virtually every aspect of Russian life. Its effects, therefore, were often felt first in personality development and family life, and it was only on the basis of a prolonged change within the educated elite's way of life that the new ideals could begin to affect political and social thought. Under Stalin, who deliberately curtailed contacts with Westerners and fostered an atmosphere of xenophobic fear and suspicion of outside cultural influences, most Russians were too effectively isolated from the West for direct knowledge of it to play a significant critical role in their lives. (In the post-Stalin era, however, contacts with the West have played an increasingly important role in the development of dissent.) But such immediate experience was now less crucial, for the ideals of Western life had already been officially accepted: they were the explicit principles behind the Russian Revolution, and they were enshrined in the Soviet Constitution, the legal system, and the ultimate goals of communism. Unlike Peter the Great, Khrushchev did not implant in his society a wholly new set of human values which would require decades to take root. Instead, he exposed the disparity that had developed between the stated values of the Soviet system and its actual practice. For this reason Soviet dissent has been able to develop much more rapidly than did the intelligentsia in the past. The effect, however, has been much the same: a "revolution from above," in which a progress-minded but authoritarian state introduced a far-reaching element of self-criticism which began to go beyond the bounds the state had set for it.

As a group experience, the impact of Khrushchev's secret speech on the educated elite of Soviet society was as decisive as the impact of the wholesale importation of Western culture had been on the Russian nobility in the eighteenth century. In both cases, established Russian institutions and practices were called into question and people were forced to reassess their own contribution, active or passive, to them, be it serfdom, lawlessness, or forced-labor camps. Those who engage in such a reassessment are predominantly members of the educated elite, because they have a more precise consciousness of the gap between ideal and reality, the leisure and comfort to brood about it, and the articulateness with which to protest against it. But in order to thrust a particular individual onto the path of outspoken dissent, group experiences must be refracted in personal experience, they must be brought home to the individual in his own personal life. Otherwise they are likely to remain theoretical, abstract issues to which he may pay lip service but which do not move him, almost uncontrollably, to action.

A major difference from the intelligentsia in tsarist Russia is that today we do not generally find that refraction occurring in family conflict (although, as we shall see, family experiences can be significant). Thanks to social and economic change, neither the personal values nor the educational and occupational expectations of a Soviet individual today clash with his family's outlook in the manner or degree of a Herzen, a Kropotkin, or a Gorky, nor do the clashes that may occur have the same cultural significance. In addition, the Soviet family is considerably less patriarchal than it was in the nineteenth century, particularly in the urban areas from which most of the dissidents originate. Under Soviet conditions the family is more likely to be a refuge, a haven, than a trap or a constricting force. Rebellion thus comes later in life than it did for many *intelligenty* and it is political from the start, arising from a direct encounter with the government.[23]

In some cases individuals have become dissidents because they took Khrushchev too seriously: a modest effort to contribute personally to the "de-Stalinization" of Soviet life led to a harsh rebuff from the authorities and a radicalization of protest. One of the most important examples is Andrei Sakharov, who has testified to the profound impression Khrushchev's action made on him: "in the ideological atmosphere that came into being

after the death of Stalin and the Twentieth Congress of the CPSU," he
recalls, he began "to reflect in general terms on the problems of peace and
mankind, and in particular on the problems of a thermonuclear war and its
aftermath."[24] The effect of the exposure of Stalin's injustices was to make
him examine his own relation to the forces of good and evil in the world and
to arouse within him a latent sense of guilt over his contribution to the
forces of nuclear destruction. With a new sense of civic responsibility bred
of this guilt, Sakharov began to urge the Soviet government to cease atomic
tests. One of the results was that Khrushchev ordered his officials to find
some compromising materials on him.[25] In an autobiographical statement
Iury Orlov, later to be chairman of the Helsinki Watch Committee in
Moscow, traces his dissident activity also to Khrushchev's speech. In April
1956, he spoke at a meeting in criticism of the policies the Party had followed prior to the Twentieth Congress. According to Orlov, he spoke of the
loss of honesty and morality, and of the need for democratic changes; for
this, he was expelled from the Party, dismissed from his job, and prevented
from defending his thesis.[26] The effect on such individuals of the denunciation of Stalin's policies was to make them look with new eyes at their own
relationship to the balance of justice and injustice in the world and to
awaken in them a new feeling of personal responsibility for the well-being of
their society.

More frequently, however, a deeply affecting personal taste of Stalinism
helps to explain the feelings and determination of the dissidents. A large
number of the most prominent among them are individuals whose lives
were touched directly by Stalin's persecutions. Solzhenitsyn, of course, is
the most prominent of the dissidents who were themselves imprisoned or
sent to camps under Stalin. There are others as well. Anatoly Levitin-
Krasnov, the Orthodox religious writer and civil rights activist, spent seven
years in Stalin's camps. Peter Iakir, one of the leading dissidents until his
trial and recantation in 1973, is the son of a Red Army general who was
executed in 1937, and he himself spent most of his youth in camps. Eugenia
Ginzburg, though not herself active in the currents of criticism and protest,
provided one of the literary monuments of post-Stalin dissent – her
memoirs of her years in prison and camp; her son, Vasily Aksyonov, was one
of the more outspoken young writers under Khrushchev.

We should not, however, expect to find a predominance of Stalin's
victims in the ranks of the dissidents, for many of those who survived
emerged from the camps too old or too broken to seek anything more than
well-earned peace and quiet. Solzhenitsyn, who survived prison, labor

camps, and exile (as well as near-fatal cancer) with enough strength of will and moral fervor to become a militant crusader against the kind of treatment he had received, is scarcely a representative figure. Much more frequent among the dissidents are those who themselves emerged unscathed from the purges but saw loved ones disappear. Again, a few examples will have to suffice. Evtushenko's grandfather was arrested and taken away in 1938. The husband of Lydia Chukovskaia and the father of the Medvedev brothers died in the camps. The latter was arrested in 1938, when his twin sons, Roy and Zhores, were twelve years old; the family was then evicted from its apartment, its belongings literally flung out into the snow while the neighbors stood by and watched.[27] Amalrik's father was arrested during the war and sent to a camp for criticizing Stalin. Several of those who protested the Ginzburg–Galanskov trial called attention to their loss of family members under Stalin. Boris and Iury Vakhtin, one a China specialist and the other a cytologist, "lost our father during the mass repressions of the Stalin period," while Peter Grigorenko's wife stated that she lost her first husband, her sister, and her brother-in-law, and was herself arrested.[28] Although Sakharov himself was not affected by the purges, his second wife, Elena Bonner, is the daughter of a woman who spent long years in Stalin's labor camps.

Andrei Siniavsky provides a particularly striking example of the impact of such experiences. He was apparently a fully orthodox young citizen until his father was arrested in 1951. This event seems to have shattered his faith in the Soviet system, for his father had been an active revolutionary and symbolized the ideals of the Revolution for Siniavsky. A foreign friend has described the effect of this episode on him: "The arrest of his father in 1951, on some absurd pretext, was a deep shock to him. For the first time, the problem of injustice, of lawlessness, of the suffering of the innocent, confronted him in his intimate family life."[29] It also made him brutally aware of his own vulnerability, as he indicated in the course of his trial in 1966. "During the [house] search one of the MGB [secret police] people had said that I too should be arrested together with my father. This staggered me, and I kept telling people that my father had always been a loyal Soviet citizen."[30] Interestingly, however, he did not begin writing the unorthodox works that were to lead to his arrest until 1956.

Given the unpredictability of human nature, such experiences are not a guarantee of a particular course of behavior: people who themselves were victims of Stalin's repressions have on occasion participated in denunciations of the dissidents. In many cases, however, it was the loss or persecution of a close relative that planted the first seeds of dissent. The lack of individual rights in the face of the arbitrary power of the state ceased to be an abstract problem and became a concrete fact with the force of immediate personal experience. The guilt that many of the dissidents express about the events of the past is, at least in part, the guilt of the survivor. When those close to them – no more innocent or blameworthy than they themselves – were arbitrarily annihilated, they perceived how fragile their own personal security was; this opened their eyes to the vulnerability of others and gave them a sense of identification with all victims of injustice. For some of the younger activists, who have no memory of the Stalin years, the treatment of contemporary dissidents, many of them friends and relatives, has had the same effect. The demonstrations and trials of the late sixties produced a chain reaction of criticism and protest, as each instance of injustice and persecution radicalized some of the onlookers.

Thus the psychological roots of Soviet dissent, no less than the psychological roots of the old intelligentsia, lie in personal experience of arbitrariness and injustice at the hands of the state. For most dissidents Stalin's "excesses" were no abstraction but a grim reality, just as autocratic despotism was a reality for the *intelligenty* of the late eighteenth and early nineteenth centuries. The sense of personal injury and insecurity generates the first shocks to an individual's unquestioning acceptance of the prevailing social and political order. Without Khrushchev's forthright criticism of Stalin, however, it is unlikely that unspoken questions would have been voiced and private doubts made public, at least to the extent shown in the last twenty years. Just as the potential Russian *intelligent* found confirmation of his resentment at the restrictions on his life in Western literature and philosophy, with its strong humanistic and individualistic tendencies, the potential Soviet dissident found his doubts and suspicions about the Stalin era decisively validated in Khrushchev's denunciation of the dictator's despotism. The social conscience displayed in contemporary Soviet dissent owes much of its intensity to the reform-minded First Secretary, just as the Russian intelligentsia was in many respects the unplanned child of the Westernizing monarchs of the eighteenth and nineteenth centuries.

8

Programs and prospects

A world has collapsed . . . a new one will be born.

Boris Pasternak, 1956.[1]

I shall not live to see the future, but I am haunted by the fear that it may be only a slightly modified version of the past.

Nadezhda Mandelstam.[2]

In the nineteenth century, frustrated by the imperial government's unwillingness or inability to implement timely reform, Russian dissidents ultimately turned to revolution. In view of the steady repression of dissent by the Soviet authorities since 1966, is such a development likely to recur? Unless circumstances change drastically, today's dissidents seem certain to remain committed, as, with few exceptions, they have been hitherto, to peaceful improvement. Unlike the nineteenth-century intelligentsia, the Soviet dissidents have not produced an inner core of activists consistently advocating violent overthrow of the existing regime, although a few individuals or groups may have expressed themselves in favor of such a course to one degree or another. Even if it were a practical possibility under Soviet conditions, a revolutionary upheaval could appeal only to the most incorrigible romantics. Russian history contains persuasive arguments against revolution as the road to civil liberties and the rule of law. The Revolution of 1917 and the three-year civil war that followed it unleashed deep-rooted social tensions and bitter ideological fanaticism, which not only caused unimaginable destruction and loss of life but helped to generate the methods of rule that Stalin was later to perfect. Many of the dissidents display a keen awareness of this historical lesson. Andrei Sakharov undoubtedly speaks for the vast majority of them when he characterizes himself as "a confirmed evolutionist and reformist" and an opponent of revolutionary

157

upheavals, "which always lead to the destruction of the economic and legal systems, as well as to mass suffering, lawlessness, and horrors."[3]

What, then, are the prospects for attainment of the dissidents' goals? Given the steadfast opposition to most of those goals by the present Soviet leaders (who, of course, are subject to change in the course of time), the prospects seem, at best, very limited. Not only do the dissidents face increasingly effective repressive measures but they are hampered both by internal divisions and by the limited appeal of their views to the rest of Soviet society.

The dissidents are in considerable disagreement over the specific kinds of change they feel the Soviet system must introduce in order to secure civil liberties and provide guarantees against a recurrence of Stalinism. Any comprehensive attempt to catalogue their diverse ideas for regenerating Soviet political and social life would go far beyond the scope of this book. The extreme ideological fragmentation of Soviet dissent is hardly surprising. Through *samizdat,* the dissidents at last have the opportunity to say precisely what is on their minds, and they are indulging in the unfamiliar luxury of free expression. Nor is this entirely unhealthy, even though it may contribute to the scattering of the already thin ranks of dissent. The "democratic" character of *samizdat,* which functions without censorship or any kind of central direction, and the toleration of diverse opinions practiced by such enterprises as *A Chronicle of Current Events,* make them highly educational. They are working models of the kinds of liberties the dissidents advocate, a concrete embodiment of their fundamental principles.

Most dissidents have not had the opportunity, or inclination, to draw up reform programs. The great majority of their writings are confined to individual cases or specific complaints. Those who have addressed themselves to more probing inquiries into Russia's problems and to proposals for solving them tend to fall into three broad categories: those who advocate a return to "pure" Marxism-Leninism, cleansed of its Stalinist accretions; those who propound some form of religious humanism and urge the restoration of Christian, often specifically Russian Orthodox, moral principles (the commitment to Russian Orthodoxy sometimes entails an element of Russian nationalism); and those who wish the introduction of Western-style liberal and pluralistic practices, usually combined with significant elements of socialism. In no way do these three viewpoints represent "parties" or even coherent schools of thought, however. Each of them is capable of yielding a variety of practical proposals, and individual dissidents have interpreted and combined their basic elements with great inventiveness.

These positions – Marxism, Christianity, Western liberalism – represent the most significant cultural influences that have shaped modern Russian thought, and it is not surprising to see them reflected or revived in current dissent. (The effort to recapture a cultural past that has been withheld is one of the elements distinguishing Soviet dissent from radical Western currents of protest, which often are rebellions against cultural tradition.) At the same time, they point to an even deeper intellectual continuity between the principal representatives of Soviet dissent and the intelligentsia of imperial Russia. The revelations concerning the Stalin era focused the attention of Soviet dissidents on the need for assuring the security and autonomy of the individual, and this remains their first priority. Their disagreements arise over how the social and political arrangements individual freedom requires are to be attained. Essentially, the dissidents are pursuing in contemporary terms the debate that preoccupied the intelligentsia into the 1930s: the role that reason can, and should, play in liberating the individual.

The dialogue within the Russian intelligentsia on this issue, which we have followed from Chernyshevsky and Turgenev to Pasternak, recurs in Solzhenitsyn's novel *First Circle*. Here it is embodied in the divergent outlooks of Gleb Nerzhin and Lev Rubin, both inmates in the late forties of a special political prison devoted to scientific research. It is significant that the two men are friends and that Rubin, although he does not reflect the author's point of view, is portrayed sympathetically – they are in effect *alter egos* of the divided *intelligent*.

Rubin is the true believer, a communist who remains unshakably devoted to the principles of Marxism and to the Party that claims to speak for them, even while perceiving the failings of its present leaders and suffering at their hands. He is faithful to Marxism's vision of history as inexorable progress toward mankind's liberation, and, though personally a man of integrity, he accepts the necessity of sacrificing certain individuals, including himself, along the way to that goal. Nerzhin is a seeker after truth in the time-honored Russian tradition; he has rejected the comforting certainties that sustain Rubin and is searching for moral guidance and for the meaning of his existence. Rubin is a Jew who is steeped in German philosophy and culture – not, as sometimes alleged, an example of anti-Semitism (although in other hands the alleged "foreignness" of Russia's Jews can be used for this purpose), but an indication of Solzhenitsyn's view of Marxism as a Western importation not indigenous to Russia. Nerzhin, by contrast, bears the ancient Russian name of Gleb, the young prince of eleventh-century Kiev who died a voluntary, Christlike death at the hands of his murderous older brother. In the end, Rubin's adherence to the rationalistic ideology of Marxism, with its notion of a morality created by the objective forces of history, betrays him into collaborating with his captors in a morally reprehensible act.[4] Nerzhin, assuming the agonizing responsibility of moral choice, withholds his cooperation. In normal life, before being plunged into the world of prisons and camps, he "had no idea what good and evil were," but now, "the lower I sink into this inhumanly cruel world, the more I respond to those who, even in such a world, speak to my conscience."[5] The price he must pay is to be shipped back to the labor camps, to an almost certain doom. To a considerable degree *The First Circle* depicts the thought world of Soviet dissent in microcosm, for the positions taken by the protagonists of Solzhenitsyn's novel parallel the views advanced by some of the leading real-life dissidents.

Roy Medvedev is the most active spokesman today for those who regard the Soviet Union's primary task as one of restoring the ideals and values of Marxism-Leninism distorted by Stalin. (Peter Grigorenko, now in emigration, also declared his objective to be the revival of Leninism.) An educator, historian, and member of the Party until he was expelled in 1969 for his critical views, Medvedev sees the source of the Soviet system's problems in the Communist Party's deviation from the standards set by Lenin. His *Let History Judge* is a massive study of the purges, which steadfastly condemns Stalinism. Rejecting the official view that Stalin's policies, harsh though they may have been, did facilitate the timely construction of socialism, Medvedev argues that Stalin's methods were highly wasteful and counter-productive. If the Soviet economy grew rapidly during those years, it was in spite of, not because of, Stalin's leadership. For thirty years Stalin was "the helmsman of the ship of state. . . . Dozens of times he steered it onto reefs and shoals and far off course. Shall we be grateful to him because he did not manage to sink it altogether?"[6]

At the same time, however, *Let History Judge* shares the official ideology's glorification of the Revolution of 1917 and the principles and policies of Lenin. The Revolution, in Medvedev's view, was an entirely positive historical event which opened the door to socialism and world progress; therefore whatever contributed to the success of the Revolution was historically necessary and justifiable. There is no acknowledgment of the possibility that revolution – as Pasternak, among others, pointed out – besides inspiring heroic deeds, also accustoms people to resolving their differences by violent means, or that it may contribute to a cheapening of human life by justifying its sacrifice in the name of ideological principles. Medvedev's viewpoint, like the official cult of the Revolution, sees it as a wholly constructive, invigorating phenomenon, which bears no relationship to the events of the thirties.

Similarly, Medvedev makes no sustained attempt at a critical evaluation of Lenin's years in power. He accepts Lenin's policies virtually *in toto,* thus begging the question of how the system established by him could have degenerated into Stalinism less than ten years after his death. Medvedev does take Lenin to task for continuing to use political terror against his opponents even after the end of the civil war, conceding that "various abuses of revolutionary legality were possible during Lenin's lifetime."[7] Nevertheless, he upholds single-party rule by the Bolsheviks as a historical necessity.

Although the Bolsheviks' treatment of the other democratic parties was not beyond reproach, it should be pointed out that the Communist Party's monopoly of political activity was a product of history; in a certain period it was an important condition for the realization of the dictatorship of the proletariat.[8]

If Khrushchev refused to date the "crimes" of Stalin earlier than 1934 and the onset of the purges, Medvedev's analysis in *Let History Judge* refuses to trace the roots of Stalinism any earlier than Lenin's death in 1924.

Medvedev wrote *Let History Judge* hoping (in vain) to have it legally published, and for that reason he may have felt constrained to make concessions to official orthodoxy. In addition, his own views appear to have evolved in the years since he wrote this work. In any case, his more recent *samizdat* writings display a greater flexibility. *On Socialist Democracy* spells out a detailed set of proposals for the democratization of the Communist Party and of Soviet life in general, including even the rise of opposition parties. In *Let History Judge* he had termed the introduction of a multiparty system "not possible or feasible,"[9] but *On Socialist Democracy* allows for "the possibility of forming independent social and political associations."[10] Even if these reforms were implemented, however, he sees little possibility that they would jeopardize "the socialist system as such or the leading role of the CPSU."[11] Given "conditions of real socialist democracy," non-Marxist parties "will be deprived of a mass base"; the introduction of normal political debate and a dialogue with dissidents "will only promote the development of Marxist–Leninist ideology and the formation of a new, more capable generation of communist leaders."[12] The position of the "party–democrats," as he terms those who share his views, is that "Marxism–Leninism should still be the basis of our ideology and social science."[13] In recent works, Medvedev has shown a greater willingness to challenge some of Lenin's actions, criticizing him more sharply for excessive violence and acts of terror after coming to power, and for pursuing an agricultural policy that, initially at least, was misguided and unnecessarily alienated the peasantry. Despite the increasing flexibility of his historical perspective, however, he refrains from calling into question in any fundamental sense either the Revolution itself or Lenin's role in it. Stalinism, he insists, was not a continuation of Leninism, and it preserved "only a veneer of so-called Leninist norms, only the terminology of Marxism–Leninism."[14]

Despite Medvedev's undoubted personal commitment to the reform of Soviet life, it is difficult to see how his advocacy of political pluralism can be reconciled with his continued belief in Marxism–Leninism as a *scientific* theory. He claims that Marxism–Leninism is comparable to Darwinism: it contains some inadequacies, to be sure, but, like any scientific theory, it needs only further development in order to overcome them.[15] But if Marxism–Leninism is scientifically correct as a theory of historical development and social analysis, then opposing views must be wrong. On what grounds, then, can the decisions of the Communist Party (or the decisions of those who claim to speak for the Party), the guardian of Marxist–Leninist wisdom, be called into question? Political opposition might be tolerated to a degree, but it could not be allowed to pose a fundamental challenge to Party rule, much less to contend for power. The degree to which it was allowed would ultimately depend on the Party leaders' sense of moderation and self-restraint – an unreliable safeguard, to say the least, against arbitrary action by the government. There is no doubt that Medvedev's proposals would introduce a welcome degree of liberalization into Soviet political life, particularly within the Communist Party. To the extent, however, that Medvedev is representative of those who advocate a "purified" Marxism–Leninism as a safeguard for individual liberty and a bulwark against a recurrence of Stalinism, this position – like that of the advocates of a reformed autocracy in a previous age – seems to be trapped within its own contradictions.

While the Marxist–Leninists remain within the framework of the official ideology, the spokesmen for a religio–moral regeneration of Russian life have cut themselves off from it entirely. They attribute the repressions of the Stalin era to blind adherence to secular rationalistic ideologies, be it "humanism" in general or its Marxist variant in particular, and they believe that change must begin with a repudiation of Marxism and a religious affirmation of the absolute value of individual life. Rationalistic humanism, one such spokesman has written, by rejecting the belief that "*every* human being bears the form and likeness of God," rejected the only unshakable basis for the dignity and rights of the individual. "Rationalism, positivism and materialism, developing in opposition to religion, successively destroyed the memory of this absolute source of human rights."[16] Advocates of this point of view regard the sufferings of the past as an opportunity for spiritual purification, and they hope not so much for reform as for redemption. Just as much as the Marxist reformers, who seek liberation and fulfillment of the individual in terms of a rationalistic ideological system, those who seek individual freedom in spiritual and religious terms are deeply rooted in Russian intellectual history. Alexander Solzhenitsyn and his collaborators on *From under the Rubble,* the book of essays that forms one of the major expressions of this tendency, are representatives of a current of Russian thought that stretches back to the Slavophiles of the 1840s. Their direct source of inspiration is the *Signposts* collection of 1909, which served them to a degree as a model for their own volume. In much the same terms that *Signposts* used to criticize the Russian intelligentsia of its day, *From under the Rubble* censures the Soviet educated elite for succumbing to secular, rationalistic, ultimately antiindividualistic forms of thought.

To the adherents of this current of Soviet dissent, liberation consists first of all, and above all, of inner change. A spiritual transformation must take place within the individual, for it is impossible "to liberate anyone who has not first become liberated in his own soul."[17] To Solzhenitsyn, who is the most prominent representative of this tendency, such liberation is most likely to occur through trial and sacrifice. The moral strength of his fictional characters – Ivan Denisovich, Gleb Nerzhin, the heroine of *Matryona's House* and the hero of *Cancer Ward* – derives from their capacity to endure, with courage and human dignity, the ordeals they must undergo. This point of view also pervades his mammoth work on the purges, *The Gulag Archipelago.* He remarks, for example, of a general whose arrogance persisted even into the labor camps: "The way was not closed for him to become a fully good person. But – only through suffering. Through suffering."[18] Asceticism, the renunciation of physical or material gratification, plays a significant role in Solzhenitsyn's thinking. Love in the labor camps, he tells us, often remained unconsummated because of lack of privacy, interference by the authorities, and physical exhaustion. "But from its unfleshly character, as the women remember today, the spirituality of camp love became even more profound. And it was particularly because of the absence of the flesh that this love became more poignant than out in freedom!"[19] Sometimes prisoners would even "marry" without ever having seen one another. In such marriages, Solzhenitsyn comments, "I hear a choir of angels. It is like the unselfish, pure contemplation of the heavenly bodies. It is too lofty for this age of self-interested calculation and hopping-up-and-down jazz."[20]

The conviction that the things of the flesh are merely excess baggage on the journey to spiritual growth considerably reduces the importance of the external conditions of life. Asceticism becomes a way of morally transcending worldly reality, while physically submitting to it, rather than struggling to improve it. This is a problem that has always confronted advocates of religio–moral reform, both today and in the past. A notable exception was the *Signposts* collection, which firmly maintained that the moral freedom and spiritual development of the individual find their true fulfillment only when embodied in the social, political, and cultural institutions of everyday life, and are inseparable from them. By contrast Solzhenitsyn, while drawing many lessons from *Signposts,* minimizes the significance of political freedom. "We can firmly assert our inner freedom even in external conditions of unfreedom," he writes; "the absolutely essential task is not political liberation, but the liberation of our souls from participation in the lie forced upon us," a task that "requires no physical, revolutionary, social, organizational measures, no meetings, strikes, trade unions," only a moral decision within the individual.[21]

The clear distinction between external, material life and inner spiritual existence underlies Solzhenitsyn's controversial *Letter to Soviet Leaders,* the closest he has come to outlining a program for the reform of Soviet life. He urges the rulers of the Soviet Union to renounce their threadbare Marxism, with its crushing burden of international commitments, and to adopt a policy that truly conforms to national interests. He declares his willingness to accept their continued monopoly on political power in return for a shifting of national priorities away from the polluted, overindustrialized, depersonalized cities and toward balanced development, on a more human scale, of the country's northeastern wilderness region. The ultimate goal of his program is national spiritual regeneration, to be attained through abstinence, simplicity, material renunciation, and a life close to nature, and political democratization is deemed irrelevant to that overriding objective. As Solzhenitsyn puts it elsewhere, there is no reason to regret having to "render unto Caesar what is Caesar's," for what is Caesar's is of secondary importance.[22]

To conclude that the sanctity of individual life can be securely grounded only in religious faith, in the vision of God-created man dwelling in a divinely ordained universe, is an understandable response to the moral expediency of the Stalin era. As a program for preventing a repetition of Stalinism, however, the religio–moral approach has serious weaknesses. At least in Solzhenitsyn's formulation it regards political activity as a trivial, even unseemly aspect of human existence. It accepts continued political control by a self-selected state leadership so that society can get on with the important task of inner development. Solzhenitsyn's *Letter to Soviet Leaders* has perhaps been taken too literally, as a set of concrete expectations rather than a set of ethical prescriptions. Elsewhere in his writings he has shown himself immune from the belief that all that is needed is the replacement of wicked rulers by benevolent ones: "If only it were all so simple! If only there were evil people somewhere insidiously committing evil deeds, and it were necessary only to separate them from the rest of us and destroy them. But the line dividing good and evil cuts through the heart of every human being."[23] But renunciation of political activity by the citizenry provides no concrete means of exerting pressure on the leadership to alter the priorities it has set for Russian development; there remains only reliance on the leadership's goodwill to grant society the autonomy it needs to cultivate its own spiritual growth. Paradoxically, then, the religio–moral reformers lean on the same weak reed as the Marxist–Leninist purists, who in other respects are at the opposite end of the ideological spectrum: moral restraint on the part of the rulers. They have a noble vision of human betterment, but from the perspective of Russian history it would seem to offer little prospect of realization.

Andrei Sakharov represents a third approach to the regeneration of Soviet life. Early in his dissident career, Sakharov remained largely within the framework of official ideology. In his first major statement, *Thoughts on Progress, Peaceful Coexistence, and Intellectual Freedom,* he upheld "the vitality of the socialist course," although he conceded the vitality of the nonsocialist world as well. A scientist himself, he saw the solution to mankind's ills in "an all-encompassing scientific and technological revolution" including "effective control and direction of all life processes at the levels of biochemistry and of the cell, organism, ecology, and society."[24] He regarded scientific and material progress as the paramount task, although he insisted that such progress must be achieved in conformity with "human values."

In recent years Sakharov has become the foremost leader of the campaign for legal and civil rights. He has attended the trials of other dissidents as a public observer, protested violations of the law and judicial procedure, and in general tried to persuade the authorities to uphold their own laws. He has sought to exert pressure on them not only through individual activity but also by the establishment of autonomous civic organizations, such as the Human Rights Committee, which are free of Party control and represent independent expressions of public opinion. Finally, he has come to advocate significant political reforms: "The total nationalization of all means of production, the one-party system, and the repression of honest convictions – all must be avoided or totalitarianism will prevail."[25] His concrete proposals for domestic reform include encouragement of a greater degree of private initiative in the economy, the guarantee of civil liberties and the right of workers to strike, and, most of all, a multiparty political system.[26] In an interview in October 1972, he said: "I would no longer label myself a socialist. I am not a Marxist–Leninist or a Communist. I would call myself a liberal."[27]

Sakharov acknowledges the need for institutional safeguards of individual freedom and takes a pragmatic approach to creating them. Unlike the religio–moral reformers, he believes that not merely ideological renunciation and moral betterment but specific improvements in the legal, economic, and political environment are the prerequisites for the kind of individual self-expression and self-development all the dissidents seek. In a reply to Solzhenitsyn's *Letter to Soviet Leaders* he advocates "a scientific and rational approach to social and natural phenomena," one that would not oppose technology and material progress. He also insists that Russia needs more democracy, not more authoritarianism.[28] Only by establishing an effective mechanism for calling political leaders to public account for their actions can the individual find the security and opportunity for shaping his own life that Stalinism so grievously denied him. Unlike the Marxist–Leninist reformers, Sakharov is genuinely committed to a pluralistic economic and political structure as the foundation for such a mechanism. Society can hope to exert effective influence on the state only through an independent public opinion generated and expressed in a variety of civic, economic, cultural, and even political associations.

Sakharov's approach seems to avoid the major pitfalls of the two other dominant currents of dissent, though it is thereby no more assured of success. He shares the deep belief in the absolute value of the individual that endows Alexander Solzhenitsyn's writings with such moral authority, but he recognizes the importance of external conditions for safeguarding the individual's integrity. He shares the healthy concern for institutional change that Roy Medvedev displays, but he avoids the dogmatism and intolerance that may ensue from a belief that certain institutions are repositories of incontrovertible truth. In general, Sakharov has confidence in the usefulness of reason as a tool to liberate man from ignorance, prejudice, and want, but he is wary lest that tool become a new source of subjugation. His pragmatic, gradualist, pluralistic view of social and political affairs is very close in spirit to traditional Western liberalism, and his unshakable adherence to the rule of law, the central principle of the entire civil liberties campaign, is a hopeful development in a country where legal consciousness and due process have never been firmly rooted. To many Western observers Sakharov's position will appear the most attractive and the most promising of the various currents of Soviet dissent. It must be kept in mind, however, that such an approach to change has few precedents in Russian history, and Soviet society has very little experience of it. Liberalism on the Western model was always a frail political growth in Russia, and the Revolution and civil war plowed up the social and institutional roots it had begun to put down in the last years of the empire. As Russian history has amply demonstrated, what seems sensible and plausible to most Westerners is not necessarily what will seem sensible and plausible to most Russians. Sakharov's position, nonetheless, whatever its ultimate prospects may be, at the very least demonstrates the fertility and creativity of Soviet dissident thought, its ability to break out of the rigid framework of official ideology as well as the traditional patterns of critical thought and to generate new ideas for discussion and debate.

Like the intelligentsia of imperial Russia, today's dissidents universalize their protest and express concern for *all* the victims of injustice in the Soviet Union and the rights of *all* their fellow citizens. In part, the dissidents' sense of their own oppression gives them a natural sense of affinity with others who are similarly afflicted. In part, also, there is the fear that limiting their protest to their own grievances might make them appear to be merely self-interested, a pressure group seeking greater privileges for itself rather than liberation of the individual for its own sake. Soviet society contains many such interest groups (including writers and scientists) who lobby the government in one way or another for their own benefit. As we have seen, however, the fundamental motivation of the dissidents is an offended sense of personal dignity, and the only sure solution to that problem is recognition of the principle of the inviolability of all individuals, regardless of their status or occupation. Inevitably, therefore, the dissidents reach beyond their own stratum of the educated elite to defend the rights of other groups they perceive as unjustly harassed or persecuted by the government. The groups whose cause they choose to champion, however, and the terms in which they express their support, reflect the psychological sources of their own dissent.

In the eighteenth and nineteenth centuries, critics of the imperial regime turned naturally toward the serfs. Here was not only the largest reservoir of social distress in Russia but a clear-cut case of the denial of human rights. The educated nobleman could empathize with the serf despite the vast social gulf between them, because he saw reflected in the serf's condition of subservience his own helplessness at the hands of the autocratic state and its officials. Even after the abolition of serfdom, the continued economic distress of the peasants and then the sufferings of the new industrial workers made them the chief objects of the intelligentsia's concern: human beings who, guilty of no wrongdoing, were degraded and robbed of their humanity. It was to enable all men to develop their individual personalities freely and fully that the intelligentsia sought to create a new world out of the old imperial political and social order.

Similarly, the Soviet dissidents have looked for and found victims of oppression and injustice whose cause strikingly epitomizes the dissidents' own concerns. These are groups that serve as glaring examples, as highly visible social enlargements, of the general lack of individual rights and denial of human dignity. Russian society has changed drastically since the Revolution, however, and as a result the groups to whom the Soviet dissidents have turned their attention are quite different from the workers and peasants whom the prerevolutionary intelligentsia defended.

One such group, particularly in the initial phases of post-Stalin dissent, has been the Jews. In the fifties and early sixties, unofficial criticism and protest contained many denunciations of anti-Semitism. Hostility to Jews continues to exist to a considerable degree on a popular level in the Soviet Union, and it has been exploited from time to time by the authorities in official policies. The most extreme episode of officially sponsored anti-Semitism in Soviet history was the so-called anticosmopolitan campaign of the late forties. A by-product of the general postwar effort to purge Soviet culture of the Western elements it had been allowed to acquire during the war, as well as of changing Soviet policy in the Middle East, this campaign resulted in the closing of Jewish cultural institutions and the execution of a number of Jewish intellectuals, and culminated in the "doctors' plot" of 1953. It is believed that the latter episode may have been intended as a prelude to a much broader action against the Soviet Jewish population as a whole, a move averted only by Stalin's death. Since the Six-Day War of 1967 in the Middle East, pressures on the Jews appear to have become a permanent fixture of internal policy, as official "anti-Zionism" at times becomes virtually indistinguishable from anti-Semitism and Jewish citizens find their educational and occupational opportunities restricted.

Anti-Semitism as a government policy represents a particularly stark example of arbitrariness and injustice toward the individual. The budding forces of dissent were quick to call attention to it. The most notable literary example of "pro-Semitism" was Evtushenko's celebrated poem "Babi Iar." Babi Iar was the site of a Nazi massacre of the Jews of Kiev, and the central point of the poem is a complaint that no monument has been erected to memorialize the event and repudiate the sentiments that gave rise to it. From the first lines of the poem, the poet identifies himself with the innocent victims of anti-Semitism through the ages: "Today I am as old in years as all the Jewish people./I seem to be a Jew." "I seem to be Dreyfus," he continues, a young boy in Belostok witnessing a pogrom, Anne Frank. Gazing at the remains of Babi Iar, he feels that "I am each old man here shot dead/I am every child here shot dead./Nothing in me shall ever forget!"[29]

Although Evtushenko's own commitment to dissent proved to be fragile, his poem illustrates the psychological process by which the dissidents select their social causes. Feeling themselves to be the impotent victims of despotism, they are drawn to those larger groups in the society which, through no fault of their own, are prevented from leading a fully human existence. It is notable that Evtushenko's poem contains no mention of specifically Jewish grievances or problems, such as religious discrimination or cultural restrictions. Instead, the Jews are presented as a universal symbol of injustice and degradation. As Jewish protest began to put forth specific interests and objectives, especially the desire for free emigration to Israel, the Jews began to resemble more closely the other national minorities who have been making their demands heard, and their image as the archetypal symbol of persecution necessarily altered. The best of the dissidents have remained irreconcilably hostile to anti-Semitism and quick to denounce its manifestations (like the tsarist government, the Soviet authorities often seek to discredit dissent in the popular mind by branding it a subversive Jewish activity), but this theme no longer plays the same role in Soviet dissent that it did earlier.

On a smaller scale, the Crimean Tatars have served the same function as the Jews. A small nation numbering about 200,000, the Tatars were accused by Stalin of wholesale collaboration with the Germans during the war and brutally resettled in Central Asia in 1944, with great loss of life. Since Stalin's death they have been cleared of the treason charges previously leveled against them, but they have not been allowed to resettle *en masse* in their ancestral homeland in the Crimea. Their cause has been championed by some of the leading dissidents, most notably General Grigorenko, and the *Chronicle of Current Events* devoted the whole of its thirty-first issue (1974) to them. Here again is a group that could be seen as helpless martyrs, whose injury symbolized the plight of all victims of despotism. The Meskhetians, a smaller, Turkic people from southern Georgia who suffered the same fate as the Tatars and, like them, are agitating for permission to return to their original homes, have also found a sympathetic place in dissident literature.

Another type of victim that has figured prominently in post-Stalin dissent is the prison-camp returnee. Here is a moral symbol *par excellence:* an individual falsely accused and then degraded and abused beyond measure, who yet endures and survives as a human being. The image of martyrdom that the Decembrist exiles acquired at the hands of Nicholas I, and which did so much to create sympathy for their cause, comes to mind in this connection. In dissident literature, the prison-camp survivor is presented as a triumph of the human spirit over those who have sought to crush it, an affirmation of life over death. Three of Solzhenitsyn's novels – *Ivan Denisovich, First Circle,* and *Cancer Ward* – center around such figures, and Solzhenitsyn himself owes much of his moral stature as a spokesman of dissent to his own history as a survivor of the camps. Vasily Grossman's *Forever Flowing* is another novel on the same subject. The prison and camp memoirs of purge victims, which, like most of the novels on the subject, circulate in *samizdat,* have supplemented fictional accounts in developing this theme. Finally, Solzhenitsyn's *Gulag Archipelago* has added a significant documentary dimension. The preservation of human dignity in the face of brutal humiliation, and the attainment of spiritual purity through suffering, recur throughout these works and link them to the great traditions of Russian literature.

The dissidents' sense of identification with the victims of the purges, and the latter's role as a focus for the dissidents' social conscience, finds its supreme expression in Anna Akhmatova's cycle of poems "Requiem," the greatest monument in poetry to Stalin's victims. Akhmatova, whose own son was arrested in the purges, begins with a prose introduction entitled "Instead of a Preface":

In the terrible years of the Yezhov terror I spent seventeen months waiting in line outside the prison in Leningrad. One day somebody in the crowd identified me.

Standing behind me was a woman, with lips blue from the cold, who had, of course, never heard me called by name before. Now she started out of the torpor common to us all and asked me in a whisper (everyone whispered there):

"Can you describe this?"

And I said: "I can."

Then something like a smile passed fleetingly over what had once been her face.[30]

In the labor-camp survivors the dissidents see an inescapable reminder of their own sense of helplessness and vulnerability, especially as so many of those sentenced to the camps were well-educated professionals whose behavior had in no way merited the treatment they received at the hands of the authorities. Thus the dissidents, with their concern for fundamental human and civil rights, have regarded the returning prisoners as one of the most forceful arguments for their position, as living proof of the consequences of unrestrained state power. As a result, they have made the rehabilitation of the survivors and the exposure of their tormentors one of their foremost objectives.

Such groups as the victims of anti-Semitism or survivors of the labor camps, despite their great appeal as moral symbols, do not provide the dissidents with much of a social base from which to exert mass pressure on the government. Nor have they been very successful in appealing to the three broad socioeconomic groupings of Soviet society: the workers, the peasants, or even the educated stratum from which most of the dissidents themselves originate. Estimates of the numbers of dissidents are necessarily highly conjectural, given Soviet conditions, but informed observers place them at no more than a few thousand. Iury Glazov, a dissident now in emigration, in the mid-seventies estimated the number of "those who have signed letters" at about 1,100 people, while behind each of those he saw five or six moral supporters. One of the leading Western students of Soviet dissent, Peter Reddaway, writing in 1970–1, found that about 2,000 dissidents had thus far identified themselves by name, although they had "many thousands of sympathizers." Another Western analyst guesses that among the educated perhaps one in 300 or 400 will risk open support of protest activities.[31] In any case, it is clear that active dissent attracts no more than a very small minority of the educated urban segment of Soviet society.

As Andrei Amalrik points out in his essay *Will the Soviet Union Survive until 1984?*, in the Soviet Union's state-controlled economy *everyone* is in effect a government employee, a state servant. When all are mere cogs in the giant state machine, it is difficult to break out of the cautious, routinized "bureaucratic" mentality of the functionary and achieve a critical perspective. Even if ideological detachment is achieved – and obviously a number of individuals, including Amalrik himself, have managed to achieve independence of thought despite the enormous obstacles – the lack of material independence inhibits its expression. Unlike imperial Russia, there are no economically or occupationally autonomous social groups (noble landowners, members of the free professions) with a material base of their own from which to launch views unwelcome to the government. The pressures to conform under such conditions have been described with characteristic bluntness by Nadezhda Mandelstam. "It may seem a small thing, but a private income apparently makes for a certain freedom of thought. If you receive every morsel of your daily bread from the hands of the powers-that-be, then you are wise, if you want to be sure of getting a little extra, to give up thinking altogether."[32]

Capitalizing on this situation, the government is able to exert economic pressures that discourage dissent within the educated elite without resort to arrest and imprisonment. Individuals have been fired from their jobs and blacklisted from getting another. Younger people have been expelled from institutions of higher education, the primary avenue of socioeconomic advancement in the Soviet Union and one completely dominated by the government. Soviet society is far more tightly controlled by the state than imperial society ever was, not just by police methods such as surveillance, residency restrictions, and the passport system, but economically and even psychologically by the government's exclusive "ownership" of the economy, the educational system, and virtually all occupations. An individual who no longer wishes to "serve the state" finds it extremely difficult to withdraw; he literally has nowhere to go.

Industrial workers in the Soviet Union are, in theory and in some respects in practice, the favored class in this officially "proletarian" state. Skilled workers, particularly, have considerable social status, and the material conditions of urban workers in general have visibly improved in the last decade or two. Access to free higher education for their children gives them opportunity for social and occupational mobility. Many inadequacies continue to exist in the provision of housing, goods, and services to the cities, but the expectation of most urban workers is that things will continue to improve gradually in the future, as they have in the recent past. Few have shown themselves willing to jeopardize their share in that improvement by supporting the dissidents in a hazardous and uncertain campaign against the government. Dissatisfaction both with living standards and with the high-handedness of the "bosses" certainly exists among the workers, and a sharp economic crisis could bring their grievances to the foreground. For the most part, however, they seem willing to accept the paternalism of the state and to wait patiently, though with much grumbling, for the authorities to grant further benefits.[33] At the same time, it is difficult for the dissidents to idealize the workers, largely complacent and already officially idealized, as prerevolutionary *intelligenty* could when the workers were a downtrodden, underdog group.

The attitude of the dissidents toward the peasants is more complex. Considerably less privileged and with less official status than the industrial workers, and the victims of one of Stalin's most brutal policies – the collectivization of agriculture – the peasants are not undeserving of the dissidents' sympathies. But the cultural gulf between the peasantry and the dissidents is as great as it ever was in the nineteenth century; even greater, perhaps, because much of the prerevolutionary intelligentsia at least came from a rural environment. One of the most unsentimental of the dissidents, Andrei Amalrik, was at one point exiled to a collective farm where for the first time he found himself in direct contact with the peasants. In his *Involuntary Journey to Siberia* he describes with dismay the ignorance, squalor, and apathy he found among the peasants, a way of life unimaginably primitive and remote from any understanding of the aspirations of the dissidents.

On the other hand, a new romanticism concerning the peasantry has arisen in Soviet letters among the "village prose" writers, who stress the durability and "rootedness" of rural life as the repository of Russian traditions and Russian virtues. The glorification of rural virtue is, of course, a hoary theme that goes all the way back to Radishchev and other eighteenth-century Russian writers, reappearing in nineteenth-century Slavophilism and then later in revolutionary Populism. Village prose emphasizes the victimization of the peasants both by the impersonal forces of modern life and by the unfeeling Soviet bureaucracy. Many of the stories depict the stoical endurance and simple dignity of humble peasant folk in the face of these pressures. Works in this vein have a fresh, faintly subversive appeal in a society whose official ideology is so thoroughly committed to urban-industrial development. As the stepchildren of the Soviet economy, the peasants have paid much of the price of industrialization, as well as bearing the brunt of Stalinism, and glorification of their traditional way of life implies some questioning of the state's policies and priorities. More broadly, such writing tends to attribute the positive features of the Russian national spirit less to the influence of Marxism–Leninism than to the people's relationship to their land, to nature, and to ancient folkways. Some of Solzhenitsyn's writings – *Ivan Denisovich,* and especially the glowing *Matryona's House* – reflect these themes, but most of the "village prose" writers are not dissidents and their works have been published legally. In any case, the peasants have played virtually no role in Soviet dissent. One would search the ranks of the dissidents in vain for peasants, and except, perhaps, for those dissidents interested in nationalist or religious protest, the plight of the peasantry seems unlikely to play a major role as a rallying cry for Soviet dissent.

Cutting across the large socioeconomic divisions of contemporary Soviet society are two significant groups that do represent possible allies of the dissidents in sizable numbers: the national and the religious minorities.[34] The dissidents have become increasingly conscious of their grievances, and some have sought to link the campaign for civil liberties with the demands of the minority nationalities and persecuted religious groups.

The resurgence of national consciousness among the minorities and even among the Great Russians themselves (who constitute a bare majority of the Soviet population), and of religious consciousness among the young, has been one of the most remarkable social developments in the post-Stalin Soviet Union. The need for group identity in mass industrial societies, which has generated a revival of communal and ethnic awareness in the West, appears to be at work among the Soviet Union's various nationalities as well. At the same time, the arid dogmas of Marxism–Leninism have failed to satisfy the moral and spiritual needs of many individuals, and religious thought (not necessarily accompanied by denominational practice) is a familiar and easily available alternative. The official ideology, however, considers both national and religious consciousness to be retrograde, mere relics of the "bourgeois" past, which will gradually fade away under socialism. In recent years, many of the national and religious minorities have been persecuted to one degree or another and have been victims of administrative and police harassment.

We have already mentioned the Jews and the Crimean Tatars, two national minorities that have received considerable attention from the dissidents. By far the largest national minority in the Soviet Union, and because of its numbers the most worrisome to the Soviet government, is the Ukrainians. The primary concern of those motivated by Ukrainian national sentiment is the creeping Russification of the Ukraine, and they have been waging a persistent campaign for the preservation of the Ukrainian language, educational system, and culture. Numerous trials of Ukrainians accused of nationalist activity have been held, and those convicted have received particularly severe sentences. To one degree or another, fears for the preservation of national identity in the face of Russification pressures affect many of the national minorities who inhabit the great arc of territory along the western and southern frontiers of the Soviet Union, from the Baltic to the Caucasus, and have begun to arouse some of the peoples of Central Asia as well. The long-term significance of national-minority discontent is difficult to predict, but many Western observers, as well as Soviet dissidents, see it looming as the most serious internal threat to the future of the Soviet system.

Even among the Great Russians, national sentiment has begun to find growing expression, from the neo-Slavophile nationalism of the *samizdat* journal *Veche* ("Assembly": significantly, a term borrowed from the medieval Russian past) to underground manifestoes of a more chauvinistic or xenophobic character. In a multinational state where the Great Russians are the dominant ethnic group, however, Russian nationalism necessarily differs in its implications from the nationalism of the minorities. The rediscovery of Russian cultural traditions and folkways, as in the case of the "village prose" writers of the Society for the Preservation of Historical and Cultural Monuments, founded in 1966 and particularly interested in the preservation of old churches, can serve as a way of criticizing the Marxist dogmas and international ambitions of the Soviet government and urging a greater concentration on popular welfare. But a more intense form of Russian nationalism may pose a threat to the identity of the national minority groups. The desire of the national minorities for greater cultural recognition and self-development is one form of opposition to political centralization and bureaucratic despotism (although the minorities may not themselves be immune from chauvinistic impulses), and thus provides some basis for cooperation with the civil liberties dissidents. Great Russian nationalism, however, risks turning into an instrument of political control and cultural conformity. Some observers have expressed concern over an apparent rise of nationalist sentiment within the ranks of the dissidents themselves, or of former dissidents. Others consider it a distinct possibility that as Marxism wears increasingly thin as an ideological justification for the Communist Party's monopoly on political power, the Party will move in the direction of chauvinism and base its support more and more on an overtly nationalistic appeal to the Great Russians, as occurred in the reigns of Alexander III and Nicholas II. Reportedly there are important elements within the Party, the armed forces, and the secret police that favor such a reorientation. A policy of this sort, however, could be carried out only at the price of considerable repression, both of the national minorities and of dissent in general. Like other right-wing ideologies, such as neo-Stalinism, a strident Russian nationalism may be critical of the existing leadership but it is deeply unsympathetic to the goals of the civil liberties dissidents. It may perhaps prove significant for the future evolution of the Soviet Union, but it contradicts the basic principles Soviet dissent has espoused since the death of Stalin.

Religious protest movements have involved groups that are in essence outlawed – for example, Uniates (Greek Catholics, or Eastern Rite Catholics), Jehovah's Witnesses – and those that are officially recognized by the state but have spawned dissenting movements seeking greater freedom from state control. Among the latter, the Baptists have been the focus of particular attention. A significant number of Baptists, the so-called *Initsiativniki* (Action Group), broke away from the official Baptist organization in an effort to gain a greater measure of autonomy from government restrictions on their activity, and they have been the objects of considerable repression. They are exceptionally well organized, have established a network of secret printing presses, and issue their own periodicals as well as religious literature. Dissatisfied Orthodox have spoken out against the restrictive religious policies of the government and the acquiescence of the church's leadership in them. (In fact, the fiercest antireligious campaign since the death of Stalin took place under Khrushchev, whose liberalism did not extend to this sphere. The situation improved somewhat after his removal from power, though not for all groups.) In some areas, religious and national sentiment are intertwined and reinforce each other. This is true to some extent of the Uniates, who are particularly strong in the Western Ukraine, and especially in Lithuania, where a significant movement has arisen among Lithuanian Catholics for greater religious autonomy. The Lithuanian Catholics, like the Baptists, are well organized and have produced a sizable *samizdat* literature, including regular periodicals. A petition by Lithuanian Catholics addressed to Leonid Brezhnev and the Secretary-General of the United Nations in 1972 received 17,000 signatures; in the following year another letter of protest was signed by over 30,000 people. Unlike the civil liberties campaign, the national and religious currents are in many cases mass movements, drawing support from strata of the population that the dissidents rarely penetrate.

There have been a number of points of contact and instances of interaction between the dissidents and the national and religious protesters. Sol-zhenitsyn, for example, has spoken out on a number of occasions to de-nounce state control of the Orthodox Church and has complained of what he sees as suppression of the Russian cultural heritage. Levitin-Krasnov, an Orthodox believer whose primary concern is religious freedom, was also active in civil rights protest. He was a member of the Initiative Group for the Defense of Human Rights, and when he was arrested in 1969 an open letter was circulated in his defense that described him as believing that "freedom is indivisible and there can be no religious freedom if basic human rights are being trampled upon."[35] Peter Grigorenko, a "Leninist" and one of the most active defenders of those prosecuted in the trials of the late sixties, became also a determined advocate of the Crimean Tatars' cause, while Mustafa Dzhemilev, a Crimean Tatar activist, was, like Levitin-Krasnov, a member of the Initiative Group for the Defense of Human Rights. There have been close links between the Jewish emigration move-ment and the civil rights activists, particularly among Jews residing in Moscow, such as Vladimir Slepak.

Despite these examples of mutual support, and the continuing possibil-ity of tactical alliances, relations between the civil rights dissidents on the one hand and the national and religious groups on the other harbor at least as much potential for tension and conflict as they do for cooperation. In the first place, while equally unhappy with their treatment by the authorities, the various protesters do not necessarily have the same objectives. The Soviet Union's dissatisfied national minorities, including many of the Jews who do not wish to emigrate, are seeking not merely freedom from dis-crimination but greater recognition of their national identity, with all the linguistic and cultural autonomy and opportunity for development that such recognition implies. Similarly, the religious groups want not only fair treatment under the law but freedom of worship, religious education, and proselytization. Just how far the urbane, cosmopolitan intellectuals of Moscow and Leningrad – especially those who remain committed to the principles of Marxism – might go in supporting such demands is at least open to question. Co   sted on the whole are the Crimean Tatars, for e: ng to their ancestral home-land in the Crimea, in   hors to publish experimen-tal prose, or the freed   international conferences? Such individuals as   Krasnov are eloquent tes-timony to the ability   extend understanding and support to each othei   ility of discord remains.

A second problem is that the demands of the civil rights proponents are inherently universalistic: they demand rights for all men as human beings, regardless of their origins or affiliations. The demands of the national minorities and religious groups are necessarily particularistic, concentrating on winning greater freedom and recognition for themselves; they may not always be willing to extend the same freedom and recognition to other groups, especially when they find themselves in competition with them. Ukrainian nationalists, for instance, demand more cultural autonomy for Ukrainians, but what is their attitude toward the large Russian and Jewish minorities in the Ukraine? Will Orthodox believers, Baptists, or Jehovah's Witnesses be willing to make sacrifices in order to secure each other's freedom to spread their doctrines? The national and religious movements, for understandable reasons, are seeking freedom and security first and foremost for their own group. Their interests may often coincide with the humanistic demands of the dissidents, but they are intrinsically more narrow.

The existence of such tensions gives the authorities the opportunity to play off discontented groups against each other. The most conspicuous example of such a policy is anti-Semitism, which has been used to provoke popular antipathy to the dissidents and their cause and, especially in the Ukraine, to deflect anti-Russian sentiment. Once again, there are impressive examples of the possibility of transcending such discords, such as the eloquent condemnation of anti-Semitism by the Ukrainian dissident Ivan Dziuba in his Babi Iar address of 1966.[36] To date, however, the national-minority and religious groups have tended to remain isolated from each other, in separate confrontation with the authorities. They remain the most promising source of popular pressure on the Soviet authorities to liberalize their policies, but it remains to be seen whether they can effectively make common cause with the dissidents and with each other.

For all these reasons – internal fragmentation, enormous government leverage, the difficulty of recruiting mass support – Soviet dissent is likely to remain confined for the foreseeable future to relatively isolated individuals and circles within the urban educated elite. (Again, "dissent" here is distinguished from broader forms of mass discontent, be it economic, religious, or national.) Paucity of numbers, however, does not necessarily mean absence of influence. Public opinion in the Soviet Union does not have to manifest itself on a mass scale in order to make an impression on the authorities. In many ways the Soviet Union is a caste society – this is, in fact, one of the most frequent complaints voiced by the dissidents in their analyses of Soviet society. As a result, relatively small groups with high prestige can have a considerable impact behind the scenes. This is particularly true of the higher-ranking scientists, whose services are so necessary to the state. The most outstanding example is Andrei Sakharov. Though subjected to countless harassments and even physical threats, he was able to function openly for several years as the dean of Soviet dissidents in Moscow. In January 1980, Sakharov was arrested and exiled to Gorky, a large industrial city on the Volga River. As Gorky is closed to foreigners, the intention, apparently, was to sever his extensive contacts with the West and prevent him from serving any longer as a spokesman for the dissidents. Yet, from a Soviet perspective, his treatment has been relatively mild, at least to date. Though stripped of his various awards and removed from Moscow, he has not been imprisoned or subjected to the harsh conditions of banishment to Siberia or a similarly remote area. Nor, evidently, has the Academy of Sciences expelled him from its ranks. A number of reasons have been suggested for the government's unusual tolerance in this instance: Sakharov's past services as one of the leading inventors of the Soviet hydrogen bomb; sympathetic friends in high places; fear of offending the Soviet scientific community by persecuting a prominent member of the prestigious – and often independent-minded – Academy of Sciences. In any case, it is questionable whether a member of any other occupational group would have been able to engage in dissident activity as long or as freely as this eminent physicist.

Two other examples involve dissident scientists who were freed from detention as a result of concerted pressure by their professional colleagues. In 1968, Alexander Esenin-Volpin, a brilliant mathematician and long-time dissident, was placed in a psychiatric ward for his protest against the Ginzburg–Galanskov trial. Ninety-five academics, including some of the most prominent mathematicians in the Soviet Union, signed an appeal on his behalf, and he was soon released. He remained active in dissident circles until his emigration to the United States.

The better-known case of Zhores Medvedev is similar. A biologist with a long history of dissident activity, Medvedev was arrested and incarcerated in a mental hospital in 1970. In their book *A Question of Madness,* Zhores and his twin brother Roy describe in detail how his release was secured. Roy Medvedev energetically deployed an impressive array of important scientists, including the physicists Peter Kapitsa and Andrei Sakharov, and well-known literary figures such as Alexander Tvardovsky, the editor of *Novy mir.* The methods they employed included telephone calls to highly

placed individuals, visits to the provincial authorities who had custody of
Zhores (and who seem to have been thoroughly cowed by the procession of
famous authors and Academicians coming from the capital to remonstrate
with them), and discreet meetings with responsible officials of the appropriate ministries. The pressure they brought to bear on the authorities was
successful, but it was entirely private and personal.

Thus a small number of well-placed individuals have on occasion proved
sufficiently influential to "pull strings" and defend one of their colleagues
against arbitrary government action. It need hardly be pointed out, however, that there are severe limits to what can be accomplished by behind-
the-scenes caste pressure. For dissidents less well connected than Zhores
Medvedev, influential sources of aid may not be available. In addition, the
support Medvedev elicited from the scientific community was, at least to
some degree, self-interested. Medvedev was a leading critic of restraints on
scientific freedom, and he was being victimized for, among other things,
his outspoken advocacy of scientific integrity and autonomy. In rallying to
his defense, his fellow scientists were helping to defend their own professional freedom, not necessarily civil rights *per se*. Personal action by strate-
gically placed members of the educated elite can be an effective source of
pressure in specific cases, but it is inadequate for the defense of individual
liberties for all Soviet citizens, which is the ultimate objective of the dissidents.

Except in special cases, then, Soviet dissidents remain isolated in their
own society and highly vulnerable to government pressures and repressions.
Since the early seventies the authorities, by means of imprisonment, commitment to psychiatric institutions, exile, and forced emigration, have dispersed the leaders of the civil rights campaign and cowed most of its supporters.[37] At least for the moment, dissent is less visible and less vocal than it
has been at any time since the Khrushchev years. As this book has sought to
demonstrate, however, Soviet dissent is not just the product of a particular
moment of Soviet history that is now passing. It has deep historical roots in
the relationship between a modernizing but paternalistic and authoritarian
state, and the educated class on which modernization depends. The Soviet
state, like the imperial state before it, must give its educated elite some
measure of prestige, sense of responsibility, and privilege in order to ensure
its intellectual creativity and its incentive to work. But the self-respect and
self-esteem that the educated elite develops, as a result both of its education
and of its elite position, generates within it a growing demand for individual autonomy and self-expression, not only in matters relating to its

work but on broader public issues as well. Individuals whose talents and achievements the state acknowledges to be vital for their society's development grow increasingly irritated when that same state continues to treat them like children rather than responsible citizens in all but the narrowest areas of their professional activity.

The state can accede to these individualistic demands only to a limited degree, not because it is inherently "totalitarian" or insatiably power-hungry (although its leaders obviously enjoy their power and have no wish to dilute it), but because the Russian state historically – and not without reason – has regarded itself as the country's sole source of initiative and progress. Russian political traditions ineluctably lead those in charge of the state to regard a demand for greater individual freedom not just as a challenge to their own monopoly of political power but as an anarchic and intolerable threat to the country's welfare. And it is a major part of the dissidents' problem that the great majority of their fellow countrymen, themselves products of this long political tradition, still share the state's attitude. In suppressing the disaffected minority, however, the state runs the risk of stifling, or alienating, the segment of society on which its program of modernization depends most – and on the success of which the government will ultimately be judged and its political monopoly justified. Zhores Medvedev's friends and scientific colleagues were able to secure his release from a mental hospital not because they had any real political power, or because they had any mass public opinion behind them, but because they represented a professional community on which the government is heavily dependent for the fulfillment of its own aspirations.

To be sure, the authorities have shown themselves willing to sacrifice some of the services of that community to political objectives: aside from arrests, dissident scientists have frequently been fired from their jobs and prevented from getting another one in their field, thus depriving the economy of their talents. There are serious restraints, however, on the government's use of traditional instruments of control and punishment. In the post-Stalin era neither charismatic leadership nor ideological fervor nor large-scale terror are available, and even if they were, it is unlikely that they would be as economically effective as they were in the thirties and the forties. The very nature of economic activity in the computer age may require a greater degree of individual autonomy than in the past. In March 1970 Andrei Sakharov, Roy Medvedev, and Valentin Turchin, a physicist, addressed a letter to the top Soviet leaders urging the introduction of a broad program of liberal reforms. They argued that the "second industrial revolution," as they termed the age of automation and computer technology, is heavily dependent on free exchange of information, critical thought, and creative freedom. Therefore a substantial degree of democratization is essential in order to guarantee industrial progress and avoid economic stagnation.[38] Western scholars, it should be noted, are less certain that an authoritarian political structure is incompatible with the economic processes of the "postindustrial" age; as some have pointed out, there are ways in which computer technology may foster rather than erode political controls. Nevertheless, the connection Sakharov, Medvedev, and Turchin draw between continued economic development and the necessity of democratization goes to the heart of the Soviet leadership's deepest interests and concerns.

By themselves, the dissidents are too weak to force any major liberalization of the Soviet system. If the Russian past, from Peter the Great to Khrushchev, is any guide to its future, fundamental reforms will come not from below, from inexorable popular pressure, but from above, on the initiative of the state. A major external crisis, an economic catastrophe, a succession struggle when the aging leaders currently in power leave the scene – such are the events that could impel the Soviet rulers to implement far-reaching changes for the sake of the country's (and their own) survival. (There is no guarantee, of course, that they would in fact respond effectively to such a challenge. Russian history has its Alexander II's and its Khrushchevs, but it also has its Nicholas I's and Nicholas II's.) Should such a crisis occur, however, the existence of a body of public opinion dedicated to the introduction of civil freedoms for all citizens could be a highly significant factor in shaping the outcome. Meanwhile, the dissidents are at least capable of mitigating the government's arbitrariness in specific cases, both through their own efforts and with the help of the West, by exposing the authorities to the embarrassing glare of international publicity; they perform a function the value of which should not be underestimated.

While the dissidents for the time being have been reduced to a painful but manageable thorn in the government's side, they have stubbornly refused to disappear entirely. The Soviet authorities are no more likely to succeed in eliminating dissent by removing its leading spokesmen than were the tsarist authorities. The importance of outstanding individuals endowed with moral strength and tactical resourcefulness cannot be denied, and their removal must necessarily have a serious impact. But Soviet dissent has not arisen solely from the personal qualities of such individuals. It is a structural phenomenon, inherent in the peculiarities of Russian historical development in modern times and intensified by the rapid economic development of the Soviet period. At root, as in the eighteenth and nineteenth centuries, it is a drive for personal security, self-expression, and a degree of civic responsibility – in short, for greater individual freedom – led by some of Russia's most thoughtful, conscious, and economically and culturally vital citizens. It is no small part of the dilemma facing the Soviet rulers that the most outspoken critics of the paternalistic political system over which they preside are themselves one of the system's main pillars and cannot be removed without placing the whole structure in serious jeopardy. As they have been ever since the reign of Catherine the Great, the Russian state and Russia's dissidents are locked in a troubled but inextricable relationship.

Notes

Chapter 1. Introduction

1. Vasily Maikov, "Derevenskii prazdnik" (A Village Holiday), *Rossiiskii featr, ili polnoe sobranie vsekh rossiiskikh featralnykh sochinenii* (Russian Theater, or a Complete Collection of All Russian Dramatic Works), 43 vols. (St. Petersburg: Pri Imperatorskoi Akademii Nauk, 1786–94), XVIII, 156.

2. I have used the term "dissent" to refer in general to expressions of unofficial – i.e., unauthorized by the government – criticism of public policy. But I have preferred to call the agents of dissent "dissidents," since the term "dissenters" is so closely identified with religious movements, especially in English history. The Russians themselves seem to find the word dissidents a useful one, and the term *dissidenty* has recently begun to appear in the documents of Soviet dissent.

Russian terminology before 1917 distinguished clearly between the Russian Empire, a multinational state, and the Russian (technically, Great Russian) people, the largest of the many ethnic groups within the empire's boundaries. The terms "Soviet" and "Russian" contain the same distinction today: Ukrainians, Georgians, Lithuanians, and so on, are all Soviet citizens, as are the Russians. In conventional English usage, however, the words Soviet and Russian are often used interchangeably, and the distinction is as difficult to preserve as that between "British" and "English." In some cases the reader must rely on context to determine precisely who is meant by the term "Russian."

It is often argued that to draw a line of demarcation between "Russia" and "the West" can be artificial and misleading, because the West is neither a monolithic unity nor clearly set off from Russia. This is perfectly true, but the fact remains that the Russians themselves have always drawn such a line, and the contrast between "Russian" and "Western" continues to form an important element of their thinking. Therefore the distinction cannot be avoided, but it must be kept in mind that "the West" has meant different things to different Russians (and "Westerners") at different times.

3. The term "patrimonial," suggesting the tsar's hereditary "ownership" of the country, is frequently applied to the Russian political system, as in the following: "In a patrimonial state there exist no formal limitations on political authority, nor rule of law, nor individual liberties. There can be, however, a highly efficient system of political, economic and military organization derived from the fact that the same man or men – kings or bureaucracies – dispose of the country's entire human and material resources." Richard Pipes, *Russia under the Old Regime* (New York: Scribner, 1974), p. 23.

The classic Russian historian Sergei Platonov put it another way: "Muscovites were unable to think of their country otherwise than as a 'house' which had its owner and master . . . " S. F. Platonov, *The Time of Troubles,* translated by John T. Alexander (Lawrence, Kan.: University Press of Kansas, 1970), p. 170. Platonov was referring to the sixteenth century, but the political outlook he described persisted long afterward.

Chapter 2. The genesis of the Russian intelligentsia

1. M. A. Bakunin, *Sobranie sochinenii i pisem, 1828–1876* (Collected Works and Letters, 1828–1876), edited by Iu. M. Steklov, 4 vols. (Moscow: Izdatelstvo vsesoiuznogo obshchestva politkatorzhan i ssylno-poselentsev, 1934–5), I, 189–90.

2. Robert G. Kaiser, *Russia: The People and the Power* (New York: Atheneum, 1976), p. 197n.

3. This is an adaptation and extension of an idea suggested by Paul Miliukov in his essay "Intelligentsiia i istoricheskaia traditsiia" (The Intelligentsia and Historical Tradition), in *Intelligentsiia v Rossii: Sbornik statei* (The Intelligentsia in Russia: A collection of Articles) (St. Petersburg: Knigoizdatelstvo "Zemlia", 1910), p. 94.

4. Sergei Bulgakov, "Heroism and Asceticism," *Vekhi (Signposts): A Collection of Articles on the Russian Intelligentsia,* translated and edited by Marshall S. Shatz and Judith Zimmerman, *Canadian Slavic Studies* (Fall 1968), p. 293.

5. V. O. Kliuchevsky, *Sochineniia v vosmi tomakh* (Works in Eight Volumes) (Moscow: Gosudarstvennoe Izdatelstvo Politicheskoi Literatury, 1956–9), III, 274.

6. Kliuchevsky, "Evgeny Onegin i ego predki" (Eugene Onegin and His Forebears), *ibid.,* VII, 417.

7. Nikolai Ivanovich Novikov, "[On Man's High Estate]," translated by Valentine Snow, in Marc Raeff, ed., *Russian Intellectual History: An Anthology* (New York: Harcourt Brace Jovanovich, 1966), p. 64.

8. Novikov, "On the Upbringing and Instruction of Children," translated by Valentine Snow, *ibid.,* p. 70 (translation revised).

9. P. N. Berkov, ed., *Satiricheskie zhurnaly N. I. Novikova* (The Satirical Journals of N. I. Novikov) (Moscow: Izdatelstvo Akademii nauk SSSR, 1951), p. 328.

10. Denis Ivanovich Fonvizin, "The Minor," in F. D. Reeve, ed. and trans., *An Anthology of Russian Plays,* 2 vols. (New York: Random House, Vintage Books, 1961), I, 78–9.

11. *Ibid.,* p. 47.

12. *Ibid.,* p. 79.

13. Aleksandr Nikolaevich Radishchev, *A Journey from St. Petersburg to Moscow,* translated by Leo Wiener and edited by Roderick Page Thaler (Cambridge, Mass.: Harvard University Press, 1958), p. 209.

14. *Ibid.,* p. 208.

15. Catherine, by contrast, commented on one of the episodes in Radishchev's book: "he continues to bewail the sad fate of the peasants, although it cannot be denied that our peasants who have good masters are better off than any in the world." *Ibid.,* p. 243.

16. Nor could anything better illustrate the response of the autocracy to the expression of independent views on public affairs than Catherine's reaction to Radishchev's book. She conceded that "he has learning enough, and has read many books." But she preferred to regard him either as a subversive who, "full of French madness, is trying in every possible way to break down respect for authority and for the authorities," or as a man of "unbounded ambition nursing a grudge because he had not attained high office – anything but a responsible citizen concerned about the welfare of his countrymen. *Ibid.,* pp. 239–40, 244.

17. Radishchev, "Zhitie Fyodora Vasilevicha Ushakova" (The Life of Fyodor Vasilevich Ushakov), *Polnoe sobranie sochinenii* (Complete Collected Works), 3 vols. (Moscow: Izdatelstvo Akademii nauk SSSR, 1938–52), I, 161.

18. Radishchev, *Journey,* p. 40 (translation revised); Nicolas Berdyaev [Nicholas Berdiaev], *The Russian Idea,* translated by R. M. French (Boston: Beacon Press, 1962; first published 1947), p. 28.

19. I. D. Iakushkin, *Zapiski, stati, pisma* (Memoirs, Articles, Letters), edited by S. Ia. Shtraikh (Moscow: Izdatelstvo Akademii nauk SSSR, 1951), pp. 8–11.

20. L. Ia. Lure, "Nekotorye osobennosti vozrastnogo sostava uchastnikov osvoboditel-nogo dvizheniia v Rossii (dekabristy i revoliutsionery-narodniki)" (Some Features of the Age Structure of Participants in the Liberation Movement in Russia: The Decembrists and the Revolutionary Populists), *Osvoboditelnoe dvizhenie v Rossii,* No. 7 (1978), pp. 64–71.

21. Aleksandr Sergeyevich Griboyedov [Griboedov], "The Trouble with Reason" (*Woe from Wit* is a more literal translation of the title), in Reeve, ed. and trans., *Anthology of Russian Plays,* 1, 108–10.

22. Quoted in Michael Gershenzon, *A History of Young Russia,* translated and edited by James P. Scanlan, *Russian History,* 1 (1974), Part 1, p. 76.

23. Some have attributed this trait to the peculiarities of Russian religious culture. The Slavophile Alexis Khomiakov, for instance, identified a strong sense of community, or *sobornost,* as one of the outstanding characteristics of Orthodox worship. Whatever its origins, this characteristic may help to explain not only some of the distinctive features of the intelligentsia's thought, such as its attraction to socialism, but also one of the distinctive features of Russian literature. The classic Russian novel, from Dostoevsky and Tolstoi to Pasternak and Solzhenitsyn, teems with characters – as so many Western readers, finding themselves drowning in a sea of Russian names, have discovered. All of these characters, it turns out, are linked with each other in complex but inextricable patterns. Is this possibly a reflection of a distinctive Russian communal sense, a conviction that the fate of the individual, while an end in itself, is inseparable from a myriad other individual fates, and that one can be resolved only in terms of the others? Both in the history of the intelligentsia's dissent and in the literature that so often expressed it, individual liberation and social justice are treated as mutually complementary rather than mutually exclusive ideals.

24. It should be noted that the correspondence between Kurbsky and Ivan is the subject of considerable controversy, its authenticity having been challenged by Edward L. Keenan in his *The Kurbskii–Groznyi Apocrypha* (Cambridge, Mass.: Harvard University Press, 1971).

25. "The ideal of Pugachev's followers was essentially a static, simple society where a just ruler guaranteed the welfare of all within the framework of a universal obligation to the sovereign. The ruler ought to be a father to his people, his children; and power should be personal and direct, not institutionalized and mediated by land- or serf owner." Marc Raeff, "Pugachev's Rebellion," in Robert Forster and Jack P. Greene, eds., *Preconditions of Revolution in Early Modern Europe* (Baltimore: Johns Hopkins Press, 1970), p. 198.

Chapter 3. The formation of a Russian *intelligent*

1. Michael Bakunin, "Nauka i nasushchnoe revoliutsionnoe delo" (Science and the Vital Question of Revolution), in Arthur Lehning, ed., *Michel Bakounine et ses relations slaves, 1870–1875* (Leyden: E. J. Brill, 1974), p. 41.

2. Alexander Herzen, *My Past and Thoughts: The Memoirs of Alexander Herzen,* translated by Constance Garnett and revised by Humphrey Higgins, 4 vols. (New York: Knopf, 1968), 1, 75.

3. *Ibid.,* p. 23.

4. This theme figures prominently in Herzen's major work of fiction, the novel *Kto vinovat?* (Who Is to Blame?).

5. A Soviet scholar, M. M. Shtrange, has recorded one such case – but only one. *De-*

mokraticheskaia intelligentsiia Rossii v XVIII veke (The Democratic Intelligentsia of Russia in the Eighteenth Century) (Moscow: Izdatelstvo "Nauka," 1965), pp. 205–7.

6. In the words of Martin Malia, whose biography of Herzen I have drawn on in this discussion, "the ideals which animate [the *intelligent's*] opposition are derived by universalizing and absolutizing the values of independence and human dignity appropriate to the benefits of his greater or lesser privilege . . . In Russia during the first half of the nineteenth century such individuals on the whole could come only from the gentry, since only that group had the privileges necessary to arrive at such ideals." Herzen "came to a realization of the humiliation of others only through the wounds dealt his own ego." *Alexander Herzen and the Birth of Russian Socialism, 1812–1855* (Cambridge, Mass.: Harvard University Press, 1961), pp. 5, 19.

7. Herzen, *My Past and Thoughts*, II, 434.

8. *Ibid.*, pp. 426–7.

9. "Contributions à la biographie de Michel Bakounine," *La Société nouvelle* (September 1896), p. 312.

10. M. A. Bakunin, *Sobranie sochinenii i pisem, 1828–1876* (Collected Works and Letters, 1828–1876), edited by Iu. M. Steklov, 4 vols. (Moscow: Izdatelstvo vsesoiuznogo obshchestva politkatorzhan i ssylno-poselentsev, 1934–5), I, 57.

11. A. A. Kornilov, *Molodye gody Mikhaila Bakunina: Iz istorii russkogo romantizma* (The Youth of Michael Bakunin: From the History of Russian Romanticism) (Moscow: Izdanie M. i S. Sabashnikovykh, 1915), p. 141 n. 2.

12. Quoted from the Russian version of Kropotkin's memoirs in Martin A. Miller, *Kropotkin* (University of Chicago Press, 1976), p. 51. In the separately composed English version – P. Kropotkin, *Memoirs of a Revolutionist* (Boston: Houghton Mifflin, 1899) – Kropotkin does not refer specifically to his father.

13. Kropotkin, *Memoirs of a Revolutionist*, pp. 215, 217.

14. As one recent study suggests, "the tension between individual pride and institutional humiliation" in the country's elite educational institutions was itself a fertile source of radicalism. Daniel R. Brower, *Training the Nihilists: Education and Radicalism in Tsarist Russia* (Ithaca, N.Y.: Cornell University Press, 1975), p. 138. Like Herzen and Kropotkin, Leon Trotsky was also to participate in a classroom rebellion against a despised teacher. See Leon Trotsky, *My Life: An Attempt at an Autobiography* (New York: Scribner, 1930), pp. 66–72.

15. Priests in the Russian Orthodox Church are allowed to marry. Their sons were normally expected to follow in their fathers' footsteps, for which they received an appropriate education. If unwilling or unable to pursue an ecclesiastical career, priests' sons frequently put their education to use by entering government service – or, in some cases, the intelligentsia.

16. N. G. Chernyshevsky, *What Is to Be Done? Tales about New People*, translated by Benjamin R. Tucker, revised and abridged by Ludmilla B. Turkevich (New York: Random House, Vintage Books, 1961), pp. 41–2 (translation revised).

17. *Ibid.*, p. 40.

18. *Ibid.*, p. 109.

19. *Ibid.*, p. 73 (translation revised).

20. Maxim Gorky, *The Autobiography of Maxim Gorky* (New York: Collier Books, 1962), p. 117.

21. *Ibid.*, p. 47.

22. Gorky describes the impression foreign literature made on him in these words: "I became aware of a fact of vast importance to me; I glimpsed the contours of another sort of life with other relationships. It was clear to me that in Paris the cabbies, workmen, soldiers, and

all the 'rabble' were not like those in Nizhni-Novgorod, Kazan, and Perm . . .In general, life abroad as depicted in the books was better, easier, and more interesting than the life I knew. In foreign countries people did not fight so often and so brutally, did not make the vicious sport of a man the passengers had made of that soldier on the steamer, and did not pray to God as vindictively as my old mistress." *Ibid.*, p. 342.

23. *Ibid.*, p. 33.

24. *Ibid.*, p. 90.

25. *Ibid.*, p. 94.

26. *Ibid.*, p. 109.

27. Erik H. Erikson, *Childhood and Society*, 2nd edition, revised and enlarged (New York: Norton, 1963), pp. 366, 399–400. Gorky himself says of his grandmother: "Sometimes I was touched by the blind way in which she forgave everything, but at other times I wanted to hear her cry out harsh words of protest." *Autobiography*, p. 164.

28. Trotsky, *My Life*, pp. 1–2.

29. *Ibid.*, p. 43. Like every other *intelligent*, Trotsky pays tribute to the influence of literature on his consciousness: "The forbidden world of human relations burst into my consciousness fitfully from books and much that I had heard spoken of in a casual, and usually coarse and gross manner, now through literature became generalized and ennobled, rising to some higher plane." *Ibid.*, p. 62.

30. *Ibid.*, p. 96.

31. Chernyshevsky, *What Is to Be Done?*, p. 229 (translation revised).

32. Trotsky, *My Life*, p. 87; see also pp. 340–1.

33. *Ibid.*, pp. 96–7.

Chapter 4. Reason and revolution

1. Stephen Spender, in Richard Crossman, ed., *The God That Failed* (New York: Harper & Row, 1949), p. 261.

2. As a Soviet scholar has remarked, "Progressive individuals [in the latter eighteenth century] believed in the power of reason; they regarded the dissemination of knowledge as the means to profound social changes." M. M. Shtrange, *Demokraticheskaia intelligentsiia Rossii v XVIII veke* (The Democratic Intelligentsia of Russia in the Eighteenth Century) (Moscow: Izdatelstvo "Nauka," 1965), p. 174. In this, they were following the personal example that Peter the Great had set for them earlier: "What gave direction to the sovereign in his work, what lent him confidence and furnished him the moral strength he needed, was the discovery of reason, the alliance with reason." Reinhard Wittram, *Peter I: Czar und Kaiser*, 2 vols. (Göttingen: Vandenhoeck & Ruprecht, 1964), II, 212.

3. Ivan Turgenev, *Fathers and Sons*, translated by Bernard Isaacs, edited by Neal Burroughs (New York: Washington Square Press, 1962), p. 23.

4. *Ibid.*, p. 45.

5. *Ibid.*, p. 35.

6. N. G. Chernyshevsky, *What Is to Be Done? Tales about New People*, translated by Benjamin R. Tucker, revised and abridged by Ludmilla B. Turkevich (New York: Random House, Vintage Books, 1961), p. 60.

7. *Ibid.*, p. 229.

8. *Ibid.*, p. 238.

9. *Ibid.*, p. 241.

10. *Ibid.*, p. 294.

11. *Ibid.*, p. 240.

12. Nikolay Valentinov [N. V. Volsky], *Encounters with Lenin*, translated by Paul Rosta

and Brian Pearce (London: Oxford University Press, 1968), pp. 67–8. The quotation is Valentinov's reconstruction of Lenin's words.

13. V. I. Lenin, *What Is to Be Done? Burning Questions of Our Movement* (New York: International Publishers, 1943), p. 116.

14. *Ibid.*, p. 119.

15. Leon Trotsky, *My Life: An Attempt at an Autobiography* (New York: Scribner, 1930), p. 90.

16. *Ibid.*, p. 87 (emphasis added).

17. Leon Trotsky, *The Young Lenin*, translated by Max Eastman, edited by Maurice Friedberg (Garden City, N.Y.: Doubleday, 1972), p. 111 (emphasis added).

18. Fydor Dostoyevsky [Dostoevsky], *Notes from the Underground*, in *Three Short Novels by Fyodor Dostoyevsky*, translated by Constance Garnett (New York: Dell, 1960), pp. 52–3.

19. Nicholas Berdiaev, "Philosophical Verity and Intelligentsia Truth," *Vekhi (Signposts): A Collection of Articles on the Russian Intelligentsia*, translated and edited by Marshall S. Shatz and Judith Zimmerman, *Canadian Slavic Studies* (Summer 1968), p. 163.

20. Semyon Frank, "The Ethic of Nihilism: A Characterization of the Russian Intelligentsia's Moral Outlook," *ibid.* (Fall 1971), pp. 340–1.

21. Berdiaev, "Philosophical Verity and Intelligentsia Truth," *ibid.* (Summer 1968), p. 172.

22. Frank, for instance, defined "culture" in the following terms: "The objective, inherently valuable development of the external and internal conditions of life, increased material and spiritual productivity, the perfection of the political, social and domestic forms of intercourse, progress in morality, religion, science and art, in a word, the multifarious labor of raising collective existence to an objectively higher level." Frank, "The Ethic of Nihilism," *ibid.* (Fall 1971), p. 336.

23. Konstantin Paustovsky, *The Story of a Life*, translated by Joseph Barnes (New York: Pantheon Books, 1964), p. 615. Trotsky also ran into difficulties when, having acquired glasses as a schoolboy in Odessa, he wore them on a visit home: "I was taken to an eye-specialist, who supplied me with glasses. This did not hurt my pride at all, for the glasses gave me a sense of added importance . . . For my father, however, the glasses were a great blow. He held that it was affectation and swank on my part, and peremptorily demanded that I remove them. In vain did I protest that I could not read the writing on the blackboard and the signs on the streets. In Yanovka I wore the glasses only secretly." *My Life*, p. 56. The most famous illustration of the intelligentsia's alienation from the peasantry was the "to the people" movement of 1874, when hundreds of young Populists streamed out to the countryside to preach socialism and revolution to the peasants and were met with bewilderment, suspicion, and in some cases hostility. The history of the industrial labor movement and of the Social–Democratic Party also was punctuated with instances of friction between *intelligenty* and workers.

24. Alexandra Kollontai, "Communism and the Family," in Thornton Anderson, ed., *Masters of Russian Marxism* (New York: Prentice-Hall, 1963), pp. 176–7.

25. Klara Zetkin, *Reminiscences of Lenin* (London: Modern Books, 1929), p. 58.

26. Leon Trotsky, *Literature and Revolution*, translated by Rose Strunsky (Ann Arbor: University of Michigan Press, 1960), p. 252 (translation revised).

27. *Ibid.*, p. 254.

28. *Ibid.*

29. *Ibid.*, p. 256.

30. Yevgeny Zamyatin [Evgeny Zamiatin], *We*, translated by Mirra Ginsburg (New York: Viking Press, 1972), pp. 12–13.

31. In *We*, where "the once wild element of poetry" has been tamed and turned into "state

service," D-503 admires a sonnet called "Happiness" in praise of the "eternal bliss of the multiplication table." It teaches that "there is only one truth, and only one true way; this truth is two times two, and the true way – four." *Ibid.*, p. 59.

32. *Ibid.*, p. 204.

33. Technology-worship in the Russian radical movement predated the rise of Marxism, however. The non-Marxist socialist Chernyshevsky paints a picture of the future in *What Is to Be Done?* Vera Pavlovna has a dream of a world filled with vast glass and aluminum structures – unlike Zamiatin's image, however, it is a world of freedom and happiness. This passage, entitled "Vera Pavlovna's Fourth Dream," was for some reason omitted in Tucker's translation.

34. One memoirist, comparing his interrogator in 1937 with those assigned to his case in 1933, found the former culturally inferior: "He had no knowledge whatever of the books of a writer whom he was accusing of all the seven deadly sins with which a writer (and, for that matter, a non-writer) could be charged. I could not but recall with regret the recent era of the Buznikovs and Kogans: the latter had been equally unpleasant individuals but at least they were literate . . . there was a distinct contrast between the breed of GPU interrogators and that which appeared in the 'Yezhov period' of the NKVD." [R. V. Ivanov-Razumnik], *The Memoirs of Ivanov-Razumnik,* translated by P. S. Squire (London: Oxford University Press, 1965), pp. 149–50.

The social change occurring within the Party finds reflection in Arthur Koestler's *Darkness at Noon,* the classic novel about the purges. Rubashov, an Old Bolshevik who has faithfully served the Party for decades, comes from a well-to-do family, is well educated, and has traveled abroad. His interrogator when he is arrested, a younger man named Gletkin, is of peasant origin; he is a tougher, more ruthless individual totally lacking in the humanistic scruples Rubashov's background has enabled him to acquire. Gletkin has never been exposed to a set of values different from those of the system in which he now finds himself – a system which is elevating him to a position of power – and he has neither the capacity nor the motivation to question them.

35. Khrushchev's memoirs are strewn with such remarkable statements as the following: "A list was put together of the people who should be exiled from the city. I don't know where these people were sent. I never asked. We always followed the rule that if you weren't told something, that meant it didn't concern you; it was the State's business, and the less you knew about it the better." Or: "When Stalin proposed something, there were no questions, no comments. A 'proposal' from Stalin was a God-given command, and you don't haggle about what God tells you to do – you just offer thanks and obey." [Nikita Khrushchev], *Khrushchev Remembers,* translated and edited by Strobe Talbott (Boston: Little, Brown, 1970), pp. 79, 279.

36. *Memoirs of Ivanov-Razumnik,* p. 210.

37. "Prisoners recognized, in most cases of arrest, that there was an 'objective characteristic' basic to the case. This might be social origins, past or present posts, relationship or friendship with someone, nationality or connexion with a foreign country, or activity in specific Soviet organizations. This probable 'real' cause of arrest was at once plain to cellmates, though it was never mentioned by the interrogators." Robert Conquest, *The Great Terror: Stalin's Purge of the Thirties,* revised edition (New York: Collier Books, 1973), p. 403.

38. "O postanovke partiinoi propagandy v sviazi s vypuskom 'Kratkogo kursa istorii VKP (b)'" (On the Formulation of Party Propaganda in Connection with the Publication of the *Short Course on the History of the All-Union Communist Party (Bolsheviks), Pravda,* November 15, 1938, p. 2. The term intelligentsia is used here in the official Soviet sense of a professional-technical class. Several months later, Stalin himself hailed the creation of a new "Soviet intelligentsia": "Hundreds of thousands of young people, offspring of the working

class, the peasantry, and the toiling intelligentsia, went to higher schools and *tekhnikums* and, returning from the schools, filled the depleted ranks of the intelligentsia. They poured new blood into the intelligentsia and revitalized it in a new Soviet way . . . The remnants of the old intelligentsia were dissolved in the body of a new, Soviet, people's intelligentsia. Thus was created a new Soviet intelligentsia, firmly linked with the people and ready en masse to give it true and faithful service." Quoted in Sheila Fitzpatrick, "Stalin and the Making of a New Elite, 1928–1939," *Slavic Review* (September 1979), p. 399.

39. As one Party member said to Eugenia Ginzburg of the other prisoners in their Moscow cell: "Who knows which of them really is an enemy, and which are the victims of a mistake, like you and me?" Eugenia Semyonovna Ginzburg, *Journey into the Whirlwind*, translated by Paul Stevenson and Max Hayward (New York: Harcourt Brace Jovanovich, 1967), pp. 154–5. See also pp. 283–4.

40. *Ibid.*, p. 3.

41. *Ibid.*, p. 74.

42. *Ibid.*, p. 113.

43. *Ibid.*, p. 145.

44. *Ibid.*, p. 151. Vasily Grossman, a Soviet writer who died in 1964, includes in his novel *Forever Flowing* an account by a peasant woman, a Party activist, of her participation in the collectivization of agriculture: "And nowadays I look back on the liquidation of the kulaks in a quite different light – I am no longer under a spell, and I can see the human beings there. But why had I been so benumbed? After all, I could see then how people were being tortured and how badly they were being treated! But what I said to myself at the time was 'They are not human beings, they are kulaks.' . . . But that is a lie. They are people! They are human beings! That's what I have finally come to understand. They are all human beings!" Vasily Grossman, *Forever Flowing*, translated by Thomas P. Whitney (New York: Harper & Row, 1972), p. 144.

45. The demise of the intelligentsia is graphically depicted in *Darkness at Noon*. At the end of the novel Rubashov, having stifled the promptings of his conscience over his past deeds and rationalized his surrender to the Party's demands, goes peacefully to his execution. On his way to the cellar where he is to be shot, he accidentally drops his pince-nez, and they splinter. The eyeglasses, in an association we have come across on other occasions, symbolize Rubashov's identity as an *intelligent*. They represent the education and culture that have enabled him to view his surroundings with "new eyes" and formulate an independent judgment on them. Their shattering marks his renunciation of that independent judgment and his submission to the Party's judgment of good and evil, guilt and innocence.

Chapter 5. Khrushchev and the de-Stalinization campaign

1. [Nikita Khrushchev], *Khrushchev Remembers: The Last Testament*, translated and edited by Strobe Talbott (Boston: Little, Brown, 1974), p. 79.

2. According to Roy and Zhores Medvedev, one million copies of the speech were printed for public sale, but then second thoughts prevailed and all but a few copies were destroyed. Roy A. Medvedev and Zhores A. Medvedev, *Khrushchev: The Years in Power*, translated by Andrew R. Durkin (New York: Columbia University Press, 1976), p. 70n.

3. *The Crimes of the Stalin Era: Special Report to the 20th Congress of the Communist Party of the Soviet Union by Nikita S. Khrushchev*, annotated by Boris I. Nicolaevsky (New York: *The New Leader*, 1962), p. S13.

4. *Ibid.*, p. S7.

5. *Ibid.*, pp. S34, S46.

6. *Ibid.*, pp. S46, S34.

7. *Ibid.*, p. S26.

8. *Ibid.*, pp. S55–S56.

9. *Ibid.*, p. S17.

10. V. Pomerantsev, "Ob iskrennosti v literature" (On Sincerity in Literature), *Novy mir* (New World) (December 1953), p. 236.

11. The Constitution of the Union of Writers, adopted at the First All-Union Congress of Soviet Writers in 1934, defined socialist realism as follows: "Socialist Realism, the basic method of Soviet literature and literary criticism, demands from the author a truthful and historically concrete depiction of reality in its revolutionary development. Moreover, this truthful and historically concrete artistic depiction of reality must be combined with the task of ideological remolding and education of the workers in the spirit of socialism." *Pervyi vsesoiuznyi sezd sovetskikh pisatelei, 1934. Stenograficheskii otchet* (The First All-Union Congress of Soviet Writers, 1934. A Stenographic Account) (Moscow: Gosudarstvennoe izdatelstvo "Khudozhestvennaia Literatura", 1934), p. 716.

In practical terms, the literary method of nineteenth-century realism is to be used to advance the aims and policies of the Communist Party. The statement concisely summarizes the aesthetic, ideological, and political constraints on Soviet literature.

12. "Ob oshibkakh zhurnala 'Novyi mir'. Rezoliutsiia prezidiuma pravleniia Soiuza sovetskikh pisatelei" (On the Mistakes of the Magazine *Novy mir*. Resolution of the Presidium of the Board of the Union of Soviet Writers), *Novy mir* (September 1954), p. 3.

13. Hugh McLean and Walter N. Vickery, trans. and eds., *The Year of Protest, 1956: An Anthology of Soviet Literary Materials* (New York: Random House, Vintage Books, 1961), p. 205.

14. *Ibid.*, p. 208.

15. *Ibid.*, p. 119.

16. *Ibid.*, p. 157. Paustovsky's speech was not published in the Soviet Union, but a transcript of it found its way to the West.

17. Boris Pasternak, *Doctor Zhivago,* translated by Max Hayward et al. (New York: Pantheon Books, 1958), p. 454.

18. *Ibid.*, p. 338.

19. *Ibid.*, p. 404.

20. "This unity with the whole was the breath of life to them. And the elevation of man above the rest of nature, the modern coddling and worshiping of man, never appealed to them. A social system based on such a false premise, as well as its political application, struck them as pathetically amateurish and made no sense to them." *Ibid.*, pp. 501–2. In contrast to Trotsky's vision, and to the Marxist outlook in general, man here is seen as a subject of nature, not as master or molder of it.

21. *Ibid.*, p. 375.

22. Vissarion Grigorevich Belinskii, "Letter to N. V. Gogol," translated by Valentine Snow, in Marc Raeff, ed., *Russian Intellectual History: An Anthology* (New York: Harcourt Brace Jovanovich, 1966), p. 258.

23. Nadezhda Mandelstam, *Hope against Hope: A Memoir,* translated by Max Hayward (New York: Atheneum, 1970), p. 159.

24. Abraham Brumberg, ed., *In Quest of Justice: Protest and Dissent in the Soviet Union Today* (New York: Praeger, 1970), p. 247.

25. Alexander Solzhenitsyn, *Nobel Prize Lecture/Nobelevskaia lektsiia,* translated by Nicholas Bethell (London: Stenvalley Press, 1973), p. 29. Some fifty years ealier, writing in the midst of the Russian Revolution, Maxim Gorky had expressed a very similar view: "The good qualities in our soul are most successfully and forcefully awakened by the power of art. Just as science is the intellect of the world, art is its soul. Politics and religion divide people

into separate groups; art, revealing in man that which is common to all humanity, unites us." Maxim Gorky, *Untimely Thoughts: Essays on Revolution, Culture and the Bolsheviks, 1917–1918,* translated by Herman Ermolaev (New York: Paul S. Eriksson, 1968), p. 8.

Chapter 6. The Siniavsky–Daniel trial and its aftermath

1. *The Grigorenko Papers: Writings by General P. G. Grigorenko and Documents on His Case,* translated by A. Knight et al. (London: Hurst, 1976), p. 132 (translation revised).

2. "The Trial of Iosif Brodsky," translated by Collyer Bowen, *The New Leader* (August 31, 1964), pp. 6–7.

3. *Ibid.,* p. 17. For a first-hand account of the Brodsky trial, see Efim Etkind, *Notes of a Non-Conspirator,* translated by Peter France (Oxford University Press, 1978), pp. 84–104.

4. In late 1966, evidently in response to difficulties that arose at the Siniavsky–Daniel trial, two new articles were added to the Criminal Code, 190/1 and 190/3, to facilitate the prosecution of dissidents. The first is entitled "Circulation of Fabrications Known to Be False Which Defame the Soviet State and Social System," while the second prohibits "group actions which violate public order." For the full text of the RSFSR Criminal Code and Code of Criminal Procedure, see Harold J. Berman and James W. Spindler, trans., *Soviet Criminal Law and Procedure: The RSFSR Codes,* 2nd edition (Cambridge, Mass.: Harvard University Press, 1972). Equivalent articles are contained in the law codes of other republics; in the Soviet federal system, criminal law comes under the jurisdiction of the fifteen Union republics.

5. Leopold Labedz and Max Hayward, eds., *On Trial: The Case of Sinyavsky (Tertz) and Daniel (Arzhak)* (London: Harvill Press, 1967), p. 269. See also pp. 171–2.

6. *Ibid.,* p. 275.

7. *Ibid.,* pp. 195, 200.

8. Both the dissidents themselves and Western commentators have used a variety of terms to characterize Soviet dissent as it has evolved since the Siniavsky-Daniel trial: the Human Rights Movement, the Democratic Movement, the Civil Rights Movement. Of these, the last seems to me the most appropriate. Certainly the dissidents are demanding that people be treated more humanely, but "human rights" is too vague a characterization of their objectives. On the other hand, the dissidents present a wide spectrum of political ideas on how best to guarantee the rights and security they seek, and not all of them advocate "democracy" in a sense that Westerners would recognize. What links them and gives their varied protests and activities some consistency is the desire for the kinds of individual rights that we generally term "civil liberties": freedom of thought and expression, legal security, autonomy in personal matters, due process of law. It should be added, however, that although the term "movement" is probably unavoidable for the sake of convenience, it suggests a degree of organization and cohesion that may not in fact be present.

9. Labedz and Hayward, eds., *On Trial,* p. 295.

10. In the words of one Soviet jurist, "The demand that the work of the judge be subject to the law and the demand that it be subject to the policy of the Communist Party cannot be in contradiction in our country." Quoted in Merle Fainsod, *How Russia Is Ruled,* revised edition (Cambridge, Mass.: Harvard University Press, 1963), p. 375.

11. Labedz and Hayward, eds., *On Trial,* p. 270.

12. *The Trial of the Four: A Collection of Materials on the Case of Galanskov, Ginzburg, Dobrovolsky & Lashkova, 1967–68,* compiled by Pavel Litvinov, translated by Janis Sapiets et al., edited by Peter Reddaway (New York: Viking Press, 1972), p. 200.

13. *Ibid.,* p. 260.

14. Pavel Litvinov, ed., *The Demonstration in Pushkin Square,* translated by Manya Harari

(Boston: Gambit, 1969), p. 127. In his recent memoirs Bukovsky, one of the leading figures in the legal campaign, attributes the tactic of challenging the authorities by means of their own laws to the mathematician Alexander Esenin-Volpin (who, like Bukovsky, is now in emigration). Vladimir Bukovsky, *To Build a Castle – My Life As a Dissenter,* translated by Michael Scammell (New York: Viking Press, 1979), pp. 234–41.

15. *The Trial of the Four,* p. 140.

16. Natalia Gorbanevskaya, ed., *Red Square at Noon,* translated by Alexander Lieven (New York: Holt, Rinehart and Winston, 1972), pp. 213–14.

17. *Ibid.,* p. 221.

18. Among the journals that regularly publish *samizdat* materials are *Posev* (Sowing) and *Grani* (Facets), both issued by Possev; *Vetnik russkogo khristianskogo dvizheniia* (Herald of the Russian Christian Movement, formerly Herald of the Russian Student Christian Movement), published in Paris; *Novy zhurnal* (The New Review), New York; and *Survey* and *Index on Censorship,* both published in London.

19. For a list and brief description of these journals, see F.J.M. Feldbrugge, *Samizdat and Political Dissent in the Soviet Union* (Leyden: A. W. Sijthoff, 1975), pp. 49–54; and Alexander Motley, "USSR's Alternative Press," *Index on Censorship* (March–April 1978), pp. 22–8.

20. Peter Reddaway, trans. and ed., *Uncensored Russia: Protest and Dissent in the Soviet Union* (New York: American Heritage, 1972), p. 54.

21. No. 38 of the *Chronicle,* however, dated December 31, 1975, in an item reporting the emigration of Natalia Gorbanevskaia (one of the participants in the demonstration against the invasion of Czechoslovakia), describes her as "the moving spirit behind the foundation of the *Chronicle of Current Events* in the spring of 1968" (p. 143). For more details on the origins and editorial methods of the *Chronicle,* see Joshua Rubenstein, "The Enduring Voice of the Soviet Dissidents," *Columbia Journalism Review* (September–October 1978), pp. 32–9.

22. *Dokumenty komiteta prav cheloveka/Proceedings of the Moscow Human Rights Committee, November, 1970–December, 1971* (New York: International League for the Rights of Man, 1972), p. 12.

23. There is a brief survey of these groups in Feldbrugge, *Samizdat and Political Dissent in the Soviet Union,* pp. 37–49. For a more extended discussion, see Borys Lewytzkyj, *Politische Opposition in der Sowjetunion, 1960–1972: Analyse und Dokumentation* (Munich: Deutsche Taschenbuch Verlag, 1972), pp. 53–117.

Chapter 7. The Soviet dissidents

1. Nadezhda Mandelstam, *Hope against Hope: A Memoir,* translated by Max Hayward (New York: Atheneum, 1970), p. 39.

2. Andrei Amalrik, *Will the Soviet Union Survive until 1984?* (New York: Harper & Row, 1970), p. 15.

3. According to one recent estimate, by the end of the 1960s over twelve million Soviet citizens, more than one in twenty of the total population, had received postsecondary education, a proportion lower than in the United States but higher than in most European countries. L. G. Churchward, *The Soviet Intelligentsia: An Essay on the Social Structure and Roles of Soviet Intellectuals during the 1960s* (London: Routledge & Kegan Paul, 1973), p. 16.

4. Abraham Brumberg, ed., *In Quest of Justice: Protest and Dissent in the Soviet Union Today* (New York: Praeger, 1970), p. 246. Three years later, in an open letter to *Pravda* and other publications protesting the press campaign against Solzhenitsyn, the cellist Mstislav Rostropovich voiced the same complaint: "But explain to me please, why in our literature and art so often people absolutely incompetent in this field have the final word?" "An Open Letter to *Pravda,*" *New York Times,* November 16, 1970, p. 37.

5. A. A. Voznesensky, "Letter to *Pravda*, June 22, 1967," *Problems of Communism* (September–October 1968), p. 55.

6. Priscilla Johnson and Leopold Labedz, eds., *Khrushchev and the Arts: The Politics of Soviet Culture, 1962–1964* (Cambridge, Mass.: M.I.T. Press, 1965), pp. 103–4.

7. Quoted in Patricia Blake and Max Hayward, eds., *Half-way to the Moon: New Writing from Russia* (Garden City, N.Y.: Doubleday, Anchor Books, 1965), p. xix.

8. Victor Nekrasov, "On Both Sides of the Ocean" (excerpts), *ibid.*, p. 204.

9. Physicists and mathematicians are a particularly notable instance of this paradox. Soviet opinion studies have found physics and mathematics to rank among the topmost professions in the Soviet Union in terms of social prestige. See Murray Yanowitch and Norton T. Dodge, "The Social Evaluation of Occupations in the Soviet Union," *Slavic Review* (December 1969), pp. 619–43. Yet, physicists and mathematicians – Sakharov, Tverdokhlebov, Chalidze, Turchin, Orlov, Litvinov, to mention only those already referred to in this book – have been unusually prominent among the activist dissidents.

10. Zhores A. Medvedev, *The Medvedev Papers,* translated by Vera Rich (London: Macmillan, 1971), p. 18. This incident illustrates another source of irritation between the scientists and the state, one undoubtedly shared by other sections of the educated elite: the disparity between the sophisticated intellectual level of their work and the crude simplicities of the official culture that surrounds them. Scientists are among the most avid private collectors of abstract art in the Soviet Union, for instance, and physics institutes in Moscow have held unofficial exhibits of nonconformist art that could not be displayed publicly. See Irina Kirk, *Profiles in Russian Resistance* (New York: Quadrangle, 1975), p. 103. Andrei Voznesensky told a Western correspondent that the readers of his poetry, which is often very complex, were mainly members of the "technological intelligentsia": "Many of them work on sputniks and other enormously complicated machines and they want poetry to be complicated too. They have no use for rhymed editorials." Quoted in Abraham Rothberg, *The Heirs of Stalin: Dissidence and the Soviet Regime, 1953–1970* (Ithaca, N.Y.: Cornell University Press, 1972), p. 326.

11. Medvedev, *The Medvedev Papers,* p. 19.

12. The journalist Robert Kaiser suggests that the desire for foreign travel by the educated elite may involve more than just professional requirements. He quotes a professor of chemistry: "A few days or weeks abroad give a man a chance to feel like a real man, to do things he could never do at home, to rule his own life, for however brief a time." Robert G. Kaiser, *Russia: The People and the Power* (New York: Atheneum, 1976), p. 401. This statement indicates the impact on Soviet dissidents of the cultural exchanges and other contacts with Western life initiated under Khrushchev, an impact closely parallel to what Radishchev, the Decembrists, and their successors experienced.

13. Andrei D. Sakharov, *Sakharov Speaks,* edited by Harrison E. Salisbury (New York: Random House, Vintage Books, 1974), p. 31.

14. *Ibid.*, p. 33. Khrushchev's own account of this episode confirms Sakharov's characterization of his attitude. According to Khrushchev, he explained his position to Sakharov with the following argument, which could hardly have satisfied the scientist: "I'm sure you know what kind of suffering was inflicted on our people during World War II. We can't risk the lives of our people again by giving our adversary a free hand to develop new means of destruction." *Khrushchev Remembers: The Last Testament,* translated and edited by Strobe Talbott (Boston: Little, Brown, 1974), p. 70.

15. Sakharov, *Sakharov Speaks,* p. 34.

16. In 1970, the mathematician Revolt Pimenov, whose apartment had just been searched for *samizdat* literature, told a Party official: "For some time now we scientists have lost our sense of personal security. Roughly since the end of 1966. Until then somehow we

weren't afraid . . . It is the threat to personal security that makes us concern ourselves with politics. And it all began with those trials." *Chronicle of Current Events,* No. 15 (August 31, 1970), in *Posev,* Sixth Special Issue (February 1971), p. 15.

17. *Russia's Underground Poets,* translated by Keith Bosley et al. (New York: Praeger, 1969), pp. 31, 33–4.

18. Anatole Shub, *The New Russian Tragedy* (New York: Norton, 1969), p. 53.

19. Sakharov, *Sakharov Speaks,* p. 173.

20. Natalia Gorbanevskaya, ed., *Red Square at Noon,* translated by Alexander Lieven (New York: Holt, Rinehart and Winston, 1972), p. 282.

21. Yevgeny Yevtushenko [Evgeny Evtushenko], *A Precocious Autobiography,* translated by Andrew R. MacAndrew (New York: Dutton, 1964), p. 84.

22. *Ibid.,* p. 97.

23. There are indications, however, that in the national and perhaps also in the religious protest movements family dramas reminiscent of the past are being played out. A particularly poignant example is the three generations of the Slepak family in Moscow. Vladimir Slepak, a "refusenik" (a Jew who has been refused permission to emigrate to Israel), has been renounced by his father, a dedicated communist official, while his young sons have an even stronger sense of Jewish identity than he does. To anyone familiar with the emergence of revolutionaries in tsarist Russia, especially those from pious Jewish families – and Vladimir Slepak's Bolshevik father is the son of a rabbi – such a story eerily suggests a historical film being run backwards. See David K. Shipler, "Vladimir Slepak, Like His Father and Sons a Russian Dissident, Now Isolated from Both," *New York Times,* November 26, 1977, p. 7. In June 1978, Slepak was prosecuted and sentenced to five years in exile.

24. Sakharov, *Sakharov Speaks,* p. 32.

25. Jay Axelbank, "A Talk with a Dissident Who Built Russia's Bomb," *Newsweek* (November 13, 1972), p. 55.

26. *A Chronicle of Human Rights in the USSR,* No. 25 (January–March 1977), p. 87.

27. Zhores A. Medvedev, "Rasskaz o roditeliakh" (The Story of My Parents), *Novy zhurnal* (The New Review), No. 112 (1973), pp. 190–207.

28. *The Trial of the Four: A Collection of Materials on the Case of Galanskov, Ginzburg, Dobrovolsky & Lashkova, 1967–68,* compiled by Pavel Litvinov, translated by Janis Sapiets et al., edited by Peter Reddaway (New York: Viking Press, 1972), pp. 230, 241.

29. Leopold Labedz and Max Hayward, eds., *On Trial: The Case of Sinyavsky (Tertz) and Daniel (Arzhak)* (London: Harvill Press, 1967), p. 55.

30. *Ibid.,* p. 191.

Chapter 8. Programs and prospects

1. Quoted by Helène Peltier-Zamoyska, in Max Hayward, ed. and trans., *On Trial: The Soviet State versus "Abram Tertz" and "Nikolai Arzhak",* revised and enlarged edition (New York: Harper & Row, 1967), p. 4.

2. Nadezhda Mandelstam, *Hope Abandoned,* translated by Max Hayward (New York: Atheneum, 1974), p. 178.

3. Andrei D. Sakharov, *My Country and the World,* translated by Guy V. Daniels (New York: Random House, Vintage Books, 1975), pp. 102–3.

4. Lev Kopelev, the real-life figure on whom Rubin is modeled, ultimately arrived at a different position from Rubin's: he has become a dissident. In his memoirs, he observes: "I came to understand that my fate, which had seemed so senselessly, so undeservedly cruel,

was actually fortunate and just. It was just because I did deserve to be punished – for the many years I had zealously participated in plundering the peasants, worshiping Stalin, lying and deceiving myself in the name of 'historical necessity,' and teaching others to believe in lies and to bow before scoundrels . . . Gradually I was able to free myself of the sticky web of dialectical sophistry and syllogism which can transform the best of men into villains and executioners." Leb Kopelev, *To Be Preserved Forever*, translated and edited by Anthony Austin (Philadelphia: Lippincott, 1977), p. 261.

5. Aleksandr I. Solzhenitsyn, *The First Circle*, translated by Thomas P. Whitney (New York: Harper & Row, 1968), p. 515.

6. Roy A. Medvedev, *Let History Judge: The Origins and Consequences of Stalinism*, translated by Colleen Taylor, edited by David Joravsky and Georges Haupt (New York: Knopf, 1971), p. 564.

7. *Ibid.*, p. 398.

8. *Ibid.*, p. 384.

9. *Ibid.* In the revised edition, published (in Russian only) in 1974, this sentence is omitted. R. A. Medvedev, *K sudu istorii: Genezis i posledstviia Stalinizma* (New York: Knopf, 1974), p. 748.

10. Roy A. Medvedev, *On Socialist Democracy*, translated and edited by Ellen de Kadt (New York: Knopf, 1975), p. xv.

11. *Ibid.*, p. 101.

12. *Ibid.*, pp. 106–7.

13. *Ibid.*, p. 56.

14. Roy Medvedev, "On Solzhenitsyn's 'Gulag Archipelago'," translated by Hilary Sternberg, *Index on Censorship* (Summer 1974), p. 69. In *On Stalin and Stalinism*, a book which supplements the earlier *Let History Judge*, Medvedev writes: "Of course many features of authoritarian rule developed by Stalin first appeared under Lenin and in some cases he played a direct role in introducing them. The one-party system, restrictions on democracy at large and, later, the restrictions on democratic practices and discussion within the Party are all obvious examples. But these are by no means inherent features of Leninism" (p. 197). See also his *The October Revolution*, translated by George Saunders (New York: Columbia University Press, 1979).

15. Medvedev, *On Socialist Democracy*, p. 325; Roy Medvedev, "Chto nas zhdet vperedi? O pisme A. I. Solzhenitsyna" (What Does the Future Hold in Store for Us? On A. I. Solzhenitsyn's "Letter"), dated May 20, 1974, *Arkhiv samizdata (Samizdat Archive)*, No. 1874, p. 14.

16. Vadim Borisov, "Personality and National Awareness," *From under the Rubble*, translated by A. M. Brock et al. (Boston: Little, Brown, 1975), p. 200. As this volume indicates, there is no clear correlation between the occupation or professional training of a dissident and the views he may espouse. The coeditor of *From under the Rubble* and author of three of its essays is the mathematician Igor Shafarevich, while among its other contributors is a cyberneticist, Mikhail Agursky.

17. Aleksandr I. Solzhenitsyn, *The Gulag Archipelago, 1918–1956: An Experiment in Literary Investigation*, 3 vols., translated by Thomas P. Whitney (Vols. I and II) and Harry Willetts (Vol. III) (New York: Harper & Row, 1974–8), II, 606.

18. *Ibid.*, p. 273. Similarly, one of the contributors to *From under the Rubble*, asking why there has been a revival of Christian consciousness in Russia, remarks: "In glorious destitution, in utter defenselessness in the face of suffering, our hearts have been kindled by an inner spiritual warmth and have opened to new unexpected impulses." A. B., "The Direction of Change," *From under the Rubble*, p. 146.

19. Solzhenitsyn, *Gulag Archipelago*, II, 239.

20. *Ibid.*, p. 249.

21. Alexander Solzhenitsyn, "As Breathing and Consciousness Return," *From under the Rubble*, pp. 22, 25.

22. *Ibid.*, p. 24.

23. Solzhenitsyn, *Gulag Archipelago*, I, 168.

24. Andrei D. Sakharov, *Sakharov Speaks*, edited by Harrison E. Salisbury (New York: Random House, Vintage Books, 1974), pp. 99, 110.

25. Sakharov, *My Country and the World*, p. 92.

26. *Ibid.*, pp. 100–2. Sakharov referred to a multiparty system in his *Thoughts on Progress*, but in a more muted and ambiguous form.

27. Quoted in Jay Axelbank, "A Talk with a Dissident Who Built Russia's Bomb," *Newsweek* (November 13, 1972), p. 55.

28. Andrei Sakharov, "On Alexander Solzhenitsyn's 'A Letter to the Soviet Leaders'," *Kontinent*, edited by Vladimir Maximov (Garden City, N.Y.: Doubleday, Anchor Books, 1976), pp. 6–7, 10. Sakharov expressed similar sentiments in his Nobel Peace Prize Lecture of 1975. See Andrei D. Sakharov, *Alarm and Hope*, edited by Efrem Yankelevich and Alfred Friendly, Jr. (New York: Random House, Vintage Books, 1978), pp. 3–18.

29. [Evgeny Evtushenko], *The Poetry of Yevgeny Yevtushenko, 1953 to 1965*, translated by George Reavey (New York: October House, 1965), pp. 144–9.

30. [Anna Akhmatova], *Poems of Akhmatova/ Izbrannye stikhi*, translated by Stanley Kunitz and Max Hayward (Boston: Little, Brown, 1973), p. 99.

31. Glazov quoted in Irina Kirk, *Profiles in Russian Resistance* (New York: Quadrangle, 1975), p. 51; Peter Reddaway, trans. and ed., *Uncensored Russia: Protest and Dissent in the Soviet Union* (New York: American Heritage, 1972), p. 23; L. G. Churchward, *The Soviet Intelligentsia: An Essay on the Social Structure and Roles of Soviet Intellectuals during the 1960s* (London: Routledge & Kegan Paul, 1973), p. 138.

32. Mandelstam, *Hope Abandoned*, p. 92.

33. One Western scholar has described their attitude in the following terms: "[Soviet] political culture links the bureaucratic elite and the masses more closely than it links the dissidents to either... The masses do not demand legality, representative institutions, freedom; these are unfamiliar and exotic concepts. Their economic demands are modest – housing, consumer goods, food – and they are being satisfied, albeit with interruptions." Walter D. Connor, "Differentiation, Integration, and Political Dissent in the USSR," in Rudolf L. Tökés, ed., *Dissent in the USSR: Politics, Ideology, and People* (Baltimore: Johns Hopkins University Press, 1975), p. 155. On the other hand, there have been efforts recently by some workers to organize trade unions independent of the state. Those involved have been subjected to arrest and, in some cases, to psychiatric confinement. See Craig R. Whitney, "Dissident Unionists in Moscow Pledge Continuing Struggle," *New York Times*, February 28, 1978, p. 7; and *AIUSA Matchbox* (November 1979), p. 10.

34. The national and religious protest movements are sometimes treated as an integral part of Soviet dissent. Certainly the grievances of these groups are an important aspect of unofficial criticism of the existing Soviet system. For reasons indicated below, however, I feel that these elements of protest must be distinguished from the civil liberties dissidents, even while recognizing that their objectives often overlap and intertwine.

35. Reddaway, ed., *Uncensored Russia*, p. 325. Levitin-Krasnov has since emigrated to the West.

36. Abraham Brumberg, ed., *In Quest of Justice: Protest and Dissent in the Soviet Union Today* (New York: Praeger, 1970), pp. 200–4.

37. The five men released from prison in April 1979 – but expelled to the United States –

in exchange for two convicted Soviet spies, formed virtually a living catalogue of the various protest currents plaguing the Soviet authorities: Alexander Ginzburg, a long-time dissident and member of the Moscow Helsinki Watch Group; Edward Kuznetsov and Mark Dymshits, convicted in 1970 of conspiring to hijack a plane as part of a plan to reach Israel; Georgy Vins, a leader of the Baptist *Initsiativniki;* and Valentin Moroz, a leading spokesman of Ukrainian nationalism.

38. The text of their letter may be found in Sakharov, *Sakharov Speaks,* pp. 116–34.

Select bibliography

The following bibliography, with only a few exceptions, is restricted to books in English. It is intended for the English-speaking reader who wishes to pursue the subject of this book further. Complete references to other works cited in the text but not listed below may be found in the notes. The bibliography is divided into two sections: books on topics up to the death of Stalin in 1953, and books on the period since 1953. Given the two very unequal time spans, the first part is considerably more selective than the second. The first section is limited to works on themes touched on in the text, while the second provides a comprehensive, though not exhaustive, list of books on post-Stalin dissent. Where a title is not self-explanatory, or some additional commentary seemed necessary, I have supplied a brief annotation.

I

Aksakov, Sergei T. *A Family Chronicle.* Translated by M. C. Beverley. New York: Dutton, 1961. A charming description, on the borderline between memoir and fiction, of provincial gentry life in the reign of Catherine the Great.

Anderson, Thornton, ed. *Masters of Russian Marxism.* New York: Prentice-Hall, 1963. An anthology of Russian Marxist writings.

Avrich, Paul. *Russian Rebels, 1600–1800.* New York: Schocken Books, 1972. An account of the peasant rebellions of the seventeenth and eighteenth centuries.

Bailes, Kendall E. *Technology and Society under Lenin and Stalin: Origins of the Soviet Technical Intelligentsia, 1917–1941.* Princeton University Press, 1978.

Barratt, G.R.V., trans. and ed. *Voices in Exile: The Decembrist Memoirs.* Montreal: McGill-Queen's University Press, 1974. An anthology.

Berdyaev, Nicolas [Berdiaev, Nicholas]. *The Russian Idea.* Translated by R. M. French. Boston: Beacon Press, 1962. First published 1947. An interpretation of nineteenth-century Russian thought by the outstanding religious philosopher.

Billington, James H. *The Icon and the Axe: An Interpretive History of Russian Culture.* New York: Knopf, 1966. A comprehensive treatment of Russian intellectual history.

Blum, Jerome. *Lord and Peasant in Russia from the Ninth to the Nineteenth Century.* Princeton University Press, 1961. Russian agricultural history, and the development and practice of serfdom.

Brower, Daniel P. *Training the Nihilists: Education and Radicalism in Tsarist Russia.* Ithaca, N.Y.: Cornell University Press, 1975.

Carr, E. H. *Bakunin*. London: Macmillan, 1937. Badly outdated, but the only full-length biography in English.

[Catherine the Great]. *Documents of Catherine the Great*. Edited by W. F. Reddaway. Cambridge University Press, 1931. Includes her *Instruction* of 1767.

The Memoirs of Catherine the Great. Translated by Moura Budberg. Edited by Dominique Maroger. New York: Macmillan, 1955.

Chernyshevsky, N. G. *What Is to Be Done? Tales about New People*. Translated by Benjamin R. Tucker. Revised and abridged by Ludmilla B. Turkevich. New York: Vintage Books, 1961. An abridgement of the Tucker translation, which was first published in 1886 and is itself incomplete.

Chukovskaya [Chukovskaia], Lydia. *The Deserted House*. Translated by Aline B. Werth. New York: Dutton, 1967. A fictionalized account of life during the Great Purge.

Clements, Barbara Evans. *Bolshevik Feminist: The Life of Alexandra Kollontai*. Bloomington: Indiana University Press, 1979.

Conquest, Robert. *The Great Terror: Stalin's Purge of the Thirties*. Revised edition. New York: Collier Books, 1973. The most thorough history of the Great Purge to date.

Crummey, Robert O. *The Old Believers & the World of Antichrist: The Vyg Community & the Russian State, 1694–1855*. Madison, Wis.: University of Wisconsin Press, 1970.

Deutscher, Isaac. *The Prophet Armed. Trotsky: 1879–1921*. London: Oxford University Press, 1954. With the two following volumes, a very sympathetic biography of Trotsky.

The Prophet Unarmed. Trotsky: 1922–1929. London: Oxford University Press, 1959.

The Prophet Outcast. Trotsky: 1929–1940. London: Oxford University Press, 1963.

Stalin: A Political Biography. Second edition. New York: Oxford University Press, 1967.

Dukes, Paul. *Catherine the Great and the Russian Nobility. A Study Based on the Materials of the Legislative Commission of 1767*. Cambridge University Press, 1967.

Erikson, Erik H. *Childhood and Society*. Second edition, revised and enlarged. New York: Norton, 1963. Contains a "psychohistorical" essay on Gorky.

Fennell, J.L.I., trans. and ed. *The Correspondence between Prince A. M. Kurbsky and Tsar Ivan IV of Russia, 1564–1579*. Cambridge University Press, 1963. For an argument against the authenticity of the correspondence, see Edward L. Keenan, *The Kurbskii–Groznyi Apocrypha: The Seventeenth-Century Genesis of the "Correspondence" Attributed to Prince A. M. Kurbskii and Tsar Ivan IV*. Cambridge, Mass.: Harvard University Press, 1971.

Field, Daniel. *The End of Serfdom: Nobility and Bureaucracy in Russia, 1855–1861*. Cambridge, Mass.: Harvard University Press, 1976. The process by which Russia's serfs were emancipated.

Fitzpatrick, Sheila. *Education and Social Mobility in the Soviet Union, 1921–1934*. Cambridge University Press, 1979.

Ginzburg, Eugenia Semyonovna. *Journey into the Whirlwind*. Translated by Paul Stevenson and Max Hayward. New York: Harcourt Brace Jovanovich, 1967. A memoir of prisons and labor camps during the Great Purge, still unpublished in the Soviet Union.

[Gorbatov, A. V.]. *Years off My Life: The Memoirs of General of the Soviet Army A. V. Gorbatov*. Translated by Gordon Clough and Anthony Cash. London: Constable, 1964. The prison and labor-camp experiences of a high-ranking military officer who was arrested during the Great Purge, then released and restored to command. The English translation was made from the version published in *Novy mir* in 1964. When published in book form in the Soviet Union in 1965, under the title *Gody i voiny* (Years and Wars), Gorbatov's criticism of Stalinist practices had been noticeably toned down.

Gorky, Maxim. *The Autobiography of Maxim Gorky*. New York: Collier Books, 1962.

Untimely Thoughts: Essays on Revolution, Culture and the Bolsheviks, 1917–1918. Translated by Herman Ermolaev. New York: Paul S. Eriksson, 1968.

Grossman, Vasily. *Forever Flowing*. Translated by Thomas P. Whitney. New York: Harper & Row, 1972. A "de-Stalinizing" novel.

Hellie, Richard. *Enserfment and Military Change in Muscovy*. University of Chicago Press, 1971. Traces the connection between serfdom and the state's military needs.

Herzen, Alexander. *My Past and Thoughts: The Memoirs of Alexander Herzen*. Translated by Constance Garnett. Revised by Humphrey Higgins. 4 vols. New York: Knopf, 1968.

[Ivanov-Razumnik, R. V.]. *The Memoirs of Ivanov-Razumnik*. Translated by P. S. Squire. London: Oxford University Press, 1965. Memoirs of the Great Purge.

Jones, Robert E. *The Emancipation of the Russian Nobility, 1762–1785*. Princeton University Press, 1973.

Klyuchevsky, Vasili [Kliuchevsky, Vasily]. *Peter the Great*. Translated by Liliana Archibald. London: Macmillan, 1961. The classic work on Peter.

Koestler, Arthur. *Darkness at Noon*. Translated by Daphne Hardy. New York: Macmillan, 1941.

Kollontai, Alexandra. *The Autobiography of a Sexually Emancipated Communist Woman*. Translated by Salvator Attanasio. Edited by Irving Fetscher. New York: Herder and Herder, 1971.

Kropotkin, P. *Memoirs of a Revolutionist*. Boston: Houghton Mifflin, 1899. Kropotkin first wrote his memoirs for *The Atlantic Monthly* magazine, then expanded them for the book edition. He wrote in English, while composing a parallel, and slightly different, version in Russian.

Lenin, V. I. *What Is to Be Done? Burning Questions of Our Movement*. New York: International Publishers, 1943. Lenin's work of 1902 on Party organization.

McConnell, Allen. *A Russian Philosophe: Alexander Radishchev, 1749–1802*. The Hague: Martinus Nijhoff, 1964.

Tsar Alexander I: Paternalistic Reformer. New York: Crowell, 1970.

Malia, Martin. *Alexander Herzen and the Birth of Russian Socialism, 1812–1855*. Cambridge, Mass.: Harvard University Press, 1961.

Mandelstam, Nadezhda. *Hope against Hope: A Memoir*. Translated by Max Hayward. New York: Atheneum, 1970.

Hope Abandoned. Translated by Max Hayward. New York: Atheneum, 1974. The sequel to *Hope against Hope*. Memoirs of Osip Mandelstam's widow.

Mayakovsky [Maiakovsky], Vladimir. *The Bedbug and Selected Poetry*. Translated by Max Hayward and George Reavey. Edited by Patricia Blake. New York: Meridian Books, 1960.

Mazour, Anatole. *The First Russian Revolution, 1825. The Decembrist Movement: Its Origins, Development, and Significance*. Stanford University Press, 1961.

Miller, Martin A. *Kropotkin*. University of Chicago Press, 1976. A recent biography.

Mosse, W. E. *Alexander II and the Modernization of Russia*. Revised edition. New York: Collier Books, 1962. A concise account of the reign of Alexander II and his reforms.

Nedava, Joseph. *Trotsky and the Jews*. Philadelphia: Jewish Publication Society of America, 1972. Argues that Trotsky had a "complex" about his Jewishness, which affected his life and career.

Papmehl, K. A. *Freedom of Expression in Eighteenth Century Russia*. The Hague: Martinus Nijhoff, 1971.

Pethybridge, Roger. *The Social Prelude to Stalinism*. London: Macmillan, 1974. A study of Russian social conditions that contributed to the rise of Stalinism.

Pipes, Richard. *Russia under the Old Regime*. New York: Scribner, 1974. The political evolution of Russia to 1881.

Pipes, Richard, ed. *The Russian Intelligentsia*. New York: Columbia University Press, 1961. A collection of articles, dealing with both the prerevolutionary and Soviet periods.

Radishchev, Aleksandr Nikolaevich. *A Journey from St. Petersburg to Moscow*. Translated by Leo Wiener. Edited by Roderick Page Thaler. Cambridge, Mass.: Harvard University Press, 1958.

Raeff, Marc. *The Decembrist Movement*. Englewood Cliffs, N.J.: Prentice-Hall, 1966. A documentary collection.

   Origins of the Russian Intelligentsia: The Eighteenth-Century Nobility. New York: Harcourt Brace Jovanovich, 1966. A study of the nobility's life-experiences and their relevance to the formation of the intelligentsia. For two other recent works on the eighteenth-century nobility, see the books listed above by Paul Dukes and Robert E. Jones.

Raeff, Marc, ed. *Russian Intellectual History: An Anthology*. New York: Harcourt Brace Jovanovich, 1966.

Reeve, F. D., ed. *An Anthology of Russian Plays*. 2 vols. New York: Random House, Vintage Books, 1961.

Riasanovsky, Nicholas V. *A Parting of Ways: Government and the Educated Public in Russia, 1801–1855*. Oxford: Clarendon Press, 1976.

Rogger, Hans. *National Consciousness in Eighteenth-Century Russia*. Cambridge, Mass.: Harvard University Press, 1960.

Schapiro, Leonard. *Rationalism and Nationalism in Russian Nineteenth-Century Political Thought*. New Haven: Yale University Press, 1967.

Segel, Harold B., trans. and ed. *The Literature of Eighteenth-Century Russia*. 2 vols. New York: Dutton, 1967. An anthology containing, among other items, Kniazhnin's comic opera *Misfortune from a Coach* and a journalistic exchange between Catherine and Novikov.

[*Signposts*]. *Vekhi (Signposts): A Collection of Articles on the Russian Intelligentsia*. Translated and edited by Marshall S. Shatz and Judith Zimmerman. Serialized in *Canadian Slavic Studies*, Summer 1968 to Fall 1971. Originally published Moscow, 1909. Another translation, available in book form, is *Landmarks: A Collection of Essays on the Russian Intelligentsia*. Translated by Marian Schwartz. Edited by Boris Shragin and Albert Todd. New York: Karz Howard, 1977.

Sinel, Allen. *The Classroom and the Chancellery: State Educational Reform in Russia under Count Dmitry Tolstoi*. Cambridge, Mass.: Harvard University Press, 1973. Education policy in the reign of Alexander II.

Stavrou, Theofanis George, ed. *Russia under the Last Tsar*. Minneapolis: University of Minnesota Press, 1969. A collection of articles on Russian conditions in the reign of Nicholas II.

Timasheff, Nicholas S. *The Great Retreat: The Growth and Decline of Communism in Russia*. New York: Dutton, 1946. The trend toward cultural and social discipline in the thirties.

Trotsky, Leon. *Literature and Revolution*. Translated by Rose Strunsky. Ann Arbor: University of Michigan Press, 1960.

   My Life: An Attempt at an Autobiography. New York: Scribner, 1930.

   The Young Lenin. Translated by Max Eastman. Edited by Maurice Friedberg. Garden City, N.Y.: Doubleday, 1972.

Turgenev, Ivan. *Fathers and Sons*. Translated by Bernard Isaacs. New York: Washington Square Press, 1962.

Ulam, Adam B. *The Bolsheviks*. New York: Macmillan, 1965. A biography of Lenin.

   Stalin: The Man and His Era. New York: Viking Press, 1973. A biography, more up-to-date and balanced than Deutscher's classic work listed above.

Valentinov, Nikolay [N. V. Volsky]. *Encounters with Lenin*. Translated by Paul Rosta and Brian Pearce. London: Oxford University Press, 1968.

Venturi, Franco. *Roots of Revolution: A History of the Populist and Socialist Movements in*

Nineteenth Century Russia. Translated by Francis Haskell. New York: Knopf, 1960. An extensive treatment of the Russian revolutionary movement from the 1830s to 1881.

Walicki, Andrzej. *The Slavophile Controversy: History of a Conservative Utopia in Nineteenth-Century Russian Thought.* Translated by Hilda Andrews-Rusiecka. Oxford University Press, 1975. A substantial discussion of Slavophilism and its intellectual progeny.

Woehrlin, William F. *Chernyshevskii: The Man and the Journalist.* Cambridge, Mass.: Harvard University Press, 1971.

Wolfe, Bertram D. *Three Who Made a Revolution.* Fourth revised edition. New York: Dell, 1964. A highly readable biographical study of Lenin, Trotsky, and Stalin.

Wolfenstein, E. Victor. *The Revolutionary Personality: Lenin, Trotsky, Gandhi.* Princeton University Press, 1967. A highly speculative psychoanalytic study.

Zamiatin, Yevgeny [Evgeny]. *We.* Translated by Mirra Ginsburg. New York: Viking Press, 1972.

Zetkin, Klara. *Reminiscences of Lenin.* London: Modern Books, 1929.

II

[Akhmatova, Anna]. *Poems of Akhmatova/Izbrannye stikhi.* Translated by Stanley Kunitz and Max Hayward. Boston: Little Brown, 1973.

Amalrik, Andrei. *Involuntary Journey to Siberia.* Translated by Manya Harari and Max Hayward. New York: Harcourt Brace Jovanovich, 1970.

Will the Soviet Union Survive until 1984? New York: Harper & Row, 1970. One of the most penetrating analyses of Soviet dissent.

The Anti-Stalin Campaign and International Communism: A Selection of Documents. New York: Columbia University Press, 1956. The text of Khrushchev's "secret speech" and international communist reactions to it.

Arkhiv samizdata (The *Samizdat* Archive). A serially numbered collection maintained by the Research Department of Radio Liberty, Munich. The collection has been organized into a series of volumes under the title *Sobranie dokumentov samizdata* (A Collection of *Samizdat* Documents), reproduced by the Center for Slavic and East European Studies, The Ohio State University, Columbus, Ohio. There is an index to these volumes in English as well as Russian. The collection represents the most comprehensive file of *samizdat* material available in the West.

Barghoorn, Frederick C. *Détente and the Democratic Movement in the USSR.* New York: Free Press, 1976. The impact of dissent, and the Soviet government's treatment of it, on East–West relations.

Berman, Harold J., and Spindler, James W., trans. *Soviet Criminal Law and Procedure: The RSFSR Codes.* Second edition. Cambridge, Mass.: Harvard University Press, 1972.

Blake, Patricia, and Hayward, Max, eds. *Half-way to the Moon: New Writing from Russia.* Garden City, N.Y.: Doubleday (Anchor Books), 1965. An anthology of poetry and prose.

Bloch, Sidney, and Reddaway, Peter. *Russia's Political Hospitals: The Abuse of Psychiatry in the Soviet Union.* London: Victor Gollancz, 1977. The use of psychiatric hospitals as an instrument against dissidents.

Bonavia, David. *Fat Sasha and the Urban Guerilla.* New York: Atheneum, 1973. A British correspondent's encounters with dissidents.

Bosley, Keith, trans. and ed. *Russia's Underground Poets.* New York: Praeger, 1969.

Bourdeaux, Michael. *Patriarch and Prophets: Persecution of the Russian Orthodox Church Today.* London: Macmillan, 1969.

Religious Ferment in Russia: Protestant Opposition to Soviet Religious Policy. London: Macmillan, 1968. On the Baptist *Initsiativniki.*

Brown, Deming. *Soviet Russian Literature since Stalin.* Cambridge University Press, 1978. Contains a survey of the "village writers."

Browne, Michael, ed. Ferment in the Ukraine. New York: Praeger 1971. A documentary collection on the national movement in the Ukraine.

Brumberg, Abraham, ed. *In Quest of Justice: Protest and Dissent in the Soviet Union Today.* New York: Praeger, 1970. A collection of articles and documents; the contents, with some deletions, of the July-August and September-October 1968, issues of *Problems of Communism.*

Bukovsky, Vladimir. *To Build a Castle—My Life As a Dissenter.* Translated by Michael Scammell. New York: Viking Press, 1979. Memoirs of one of the central figures in the legal campaign of the late sixties and early seventies.

The Case of Leonid Plyushch. Translated by Marite Sapiets et al. Edited by Tatyana Khodorovich. London: C. Hurst & Co., 1976. Documents on the psychiatric confinement of a dissident. For his memoirs, see below, Plyushch, *History's Carnival.*

Churchward, L. G. *The Soviet Intelligentsia: An Essay on the Social Structure and Roles of Soviet Intellectuals during the 1960s.* London: Routledge & Kegan Paul, 1973.

Conquest, Robert. *The Pasternak Affair: Courage of Genius.* Philadelphia: Lippincott, 1962. Background to the publication of *Doctor Zhivago* and a documentary account of the campaign against its author.

The Crimes of the Stalin Era. Special Report to the 20th Congress of the Soviet Union by Nikita S. Khrushchev. Annotated by Boris I. Nicolaevsky. New York: *The New Leader,* 1962. A helpfully annotated edition of Khrushchev's speech.

Dudintsev, Vladimir. *Not by Bread Alone.* Translated by Edith Bone. New York: Dutton, 1957.

Dunlop, John B. *The New Russian Revolutionaries.* Belmont, Mass.: Nordland, 1976. A study of the All-Russian Social-Christian Union for the Liberation of the People.

Dzyuba [Dziuba], Ivan. *Internationalism or Russification? A Study in the Soviet Nationalities Problem.* Third edition. New York: Monad Press, distributed by Pathfinder Press, 1974. A detailed defense (written in 1965) of Ukrainian national culture.

Ehrenburg, Ilya [Ilia]. *The Thaw.* London: Harvill Press, 1955.

Etkind, Efim. *Notes of a Non-Conspirator.* Translated by Peter France. Oxford University Press, 1978. A personal account of the hounding of an independent-minded literary and linguistic scholar.

[Evtushenko, Evgeny]. *The Poetry of Yevgeny Yevtushenko, 1953 to 1965.* Translated by George Reavey. New York: October House, 1965. A bilingual edition.

Yevtushenko, Yevgeny. *A Precocious Autobiography.* Translated by Andrew R. MacAndrew. New York: Dutton, 1964.

Fainsod, Merle. *How Russia Is Ruled.* Revised edition. Cambridge, Mass.: Harvard University Press, 1963. The classic exposition of the Soviet political system.

Feldbrugge, F. J. M. *Samizdat and Political Dissent in the Soviet Union.* Leyden: A. W. Sijthoff, 1975.

Gerstenmaier, Cornelia. *The Voices of the Silent.* Translated by Susan Hecker. New York: Hart, 1972. An account of the development of Soviet dissent, with documents. Poorly translated from the German.

Golomshtok, Igor, and Glezer, Alexander. *Soviet Art in Exile.* New York: Random House, 1977. A well-illustrated study of "unofficial" art and its practitioners. See also the book by Sjeklocha and Mead below.

Gorbanevskaya [Gorbanevskaia], Natalia, ed. *Red Square at Noon.* Translated by Alexander Lieven. New York: Holt, Rinehart and Winston, 1972. The trial of the seven who demonstrated against the invasion of Czechoslovakia.

[Grigorenko, Peter]. *The Grigorenko Papers: Writings by General P. G. Grigorenko and Documents on His Case.* Translated by A. Knight et al. London: Hurst, 1976.

James, C. Vaughan. *Soviet Socialist Realism: Origins and Theory.* London: Macmillan, 1973.

Johnson, Priscilla, and Labedz, Leopold, eds. *Khrushchev and the Arts: The Politics of Soviet Culture, 1962–1964.* Cambridge, Mass.: M.I.T. Press, 1965.

Kaiser, Robert G. *Russia: The People and the Power.* New York: Atheneum, 1976.

Katz, Zev. *Soviet Dissenters and Social Structure in the USSR.* Cambridge, Mass.: Center for International Studies, M.I.T., 1971. *Samizdat* views on the structure of Soviet society and its shortcomings.

[Khrushchev, Nikita]. *Khrushchev Remembers.* Translated and edited by Strobe Talbott. Boston: Little, Brown, 1970. With the following volume, Khrushchev's memoirs.

   Khrushchev Remembers: The Last Testament. Translated and edited by Strobe Talbott. Boston: Little, Brown, 1974.

Kirk, Irina. *Profiles in Russian Resistance.* New York: Quadrangle, 1975. Interviews with a variety of dissidents, nonconformists, and free spirits now living in emigration.

Kochan, Lionel, ed. *The Jews in Soviet Russia since 1917.* Third edition. London: Oxford University Press, 1978. A collection of articles.

Kopelev, Lev. *To Be Preserved Forever.* Translated and edited by Anthony Austin. Philadelphia: Lippincott, 1977. Memoirs of the war and postwar period by a Moscow dissident.

Labedz, Leopold, ed. *Solzhenitsyn: A Documentary Record.* Enlarged edition. Bloomington: Indiana University Press, 1973.

Labedz, Leopold, and Hayward, Max, eds. *On Trial: The Case of Sinyavsky (Tertz) and Daniel (Arzhak).* London: Harvill Press, 1967. American edition: Max Hayward, trans. and ed., *On Trial: The Soviet State versus "Abram Tertz" and "Nikolai Arzhak."* Revised and enlarged edition. New York: Harper & Row, 1967. The two editions differ slightly, and the London edition contains some background material omitted in the New York edition.

Lane, Christel. *Christian Religion in the Soviet Union: A Sociological Study.* London: Allen & Unwin, 1978. A detailed survey of the current status of the various Christian groups.

Langland, Joseph, et al., trans. and eds. *Poetry from the Russian Underground: A Bilingual Anthology.* New York: Harper & Row, 1973.

Litvinov, Pavel, ed. *The Demonstration in Pushkin Square.* Translated by Manya Harari. Boston: Gambit, 1969.

McLean, Hugh, and Vickery, Walter N., trans. and eds. *The Year of Protest, 1956. An Anthology of Soviet Literary Materials.* New York: Random House, Vintage Books, 1961.

Marchenko, Anatoly. *My Testimony.* Translated by Michael Scammell. New York: Dutton, 1969. A first-hand account of labor camps in the 1960s.

Medvedev, Roy A. *Let History Judge: The Origins and Consequences of Stalinism.* Translated by Colleen Taylor. Edited by David Joravsky and Georges Haupt. New York: Knopf, 1971. Revised Russian edition: New York: Knopf, 1974.

   On Socialist Democracy. Translated by Ellen de Kadt. New York: Knopf, 1974.

   The October Revolution. Translated by George Saunders. New York: Columbia University Press, 1979.

   On Stalin and Stalinism. Translated by Ellen de Kadt. Oxford University Press, 1979.

Medvedev, Roy A., ed. *The Samizdat Register.* New York: Norton, 1977. A collection of articles on varied themes from *XX Century,* a *samizdat* journal edited by Medvedev.

Medvedev, Roy A., and Medvedev, Zhores A. *Khrushchev: The Years in Power.* Translated by Andrew R. Durkin. New York: Columbia University Press, 1976.

Medvedev, Zhores A. *The Medvedev Papers.* Translated by Vera Rich. London: Macmillan, 1971. A scientist's battles with the Soviet bureaucracy.

   The Rise and Fall of T. D. Lysenko. Translated by I. Michael Lerner. New York: Columbia University Press, 1969.

Soviet Science. New York: Norton, 1978. The evolution of Soviet science and of the political controls on it, concentrating on the post-Stalin period.

10 Years after Ivan Denisovich. Translated by Hilary Sternberg. London: Macmillan, 1973. The treatment of Solzhenitsyn and his writings in the decade after the publication of his first novel, as told by a fellow dissident. Solzhenitsyn's own account of these years is contained in his *Bodalsia telenok s dubom* (The Calf Butted the Oak), published by YMCA-Press in Paris, 1975.

Medvedev, Zhores A., and Medvedev, Roy A. *A Question of Madness.* Translated by Ellen de Kadt. New York: Knopf, 1971. Zhores Medvedev's confinement in a mental hospital, and the struggle to release him.

Meerson-Aksenov, Michael, and Shragin, Boris, eds. *The Political, Social and Religious Thought of Russian "Samizdat": An Anthology.* Translated by Nickolas Lupinin. Belmont, Mass.: Nordland, 1977.

Pasternak, Boris. *Doctor Zhivago.* Translated by Max Hayward et al. New York: Pantheon Books, 1958.

Plyushch, Leonid. *History's Carnival: A Dissident's Autobiography.* Translated and edited by Marco Carynnyk. New York: Harcourt Brace Jovanovich, 1979. Memoirs of a Ukrainian mathematician who was confined in a psychiatric hospital.

Potichnyi, Peter J., ed. *Dissent in the Soviet Union.* Papers and Proceedings of the Fifth Annual Conference organized by the Interdepartmental Committee on Communist and East European Affairs, McMaster University, held at Hamilton, Ontario, on October 22 and 23, 1971. Hamilton, Ont.: McMaster University, 1972.

Reddaway, Peter, trans. and ed. *Uncensored Russia: Protest and Dissent in the Soviet Union.* New York: American Heritage, 1972. A translation of Nos. 1–11 (1968–9) of the *Chronicle of Current Events,* with references to Nos. 12–21 (1970–1). Items are grouped topically. No. 16 and subsequent issues of the *Chronicle* have been published in English translation by Amnesty International, London. Russian texts have been appearing in special issues of the journal *Posev,* published in Frankfurt/Main. *A Chronicle of Human Rights in the USSR,* published by Khronika Press in New York, is an émigré journal closely modeled on the *Chronicle of Current Events.* Issued in both English and Russian editions, it incorporates much of the latter's material.

Rothberg, Abraham. *The Heirs of Stalin: Dissidence and the Soviet Regime, 1953–1970.* Ithaca, N. Y.: Cornell University Press, 1972. The best narrative account of the rise of post-Stalin dissent.

Saikowski, Charlotte, and Gruliow, Leo. *Current Soviet Policies IV: The Documentary Record of the 22nd Congress of the Communist Party of the Soviet Union.* New York: Columbia University Press, 1962.

Sakharov, Andrei D. *Alarm and Hope.* Edited by Efrem Yankelevich and Alfred Friendly, Jr. New York: Random House, Vintage Books, 1978. Statements by Sakharov on a variety of issues, along with his Nobel Peace Prize lecture of 1975.

My Country and the World. Translated by Guy V. Daniels. New York: Random House, Vintage Books, 1975. Sakharov's view of the relationship between Soviet dissent and détente.

Sakharov Speaks. Edited by Harrison E. Salisbury. New York: Random House, Vintage Books, 1974. Includes the text of *Progress, Coexistence, and Intellectual Freedom,* as well as other statements and interviews.

Saunders, George, ed. *Samizdat: Voices of the Soviet Opposition.* New York: Monad Press, distributed by Pathfinder Press, 1974. An anthology of *samizdat* writings, concentrating on dissident Marxists and implying a link with the Trotskyite opposition of the twenties.

Scammel, Michael, ed. *Russia's Other Writers: Selections from Samizdat Literature*. New York: Praeger, 1971.

Shub, Anatole. *The New Russian Tragedy*. New York: Norton, 1969. Reports by an American correspondent who was stationed in Moscow in the late 1960s.

Simon, Gerhard. *Church, State and Opposition in the USSR*. Translated by Kathleen Matchett. Berkeley and Los Angeles: University of California Press, 1974. Essays and documents on relations between the Christian churches and the Soviet state.

Sjeklocha, Paul, and Mead, Igor. *Unofficial Art in the Soviet Union*. Berkeley and Los Angeles: University of California Press, 1967. Nonconformist Soviet art and artists. See also the more recent book by Golomshtok and Glezer, listed above.

Smith, Hedrick. *The Russians*. New York: Quadrangle/The New York Times Book Co., 1976. Along with Kaiser's *Russia*, the best journalistic description of contemporary life in the Soviet Union.

Solzhenitsyn, Alexander. *Cancer Ward*. Translated by Nicholas Bethell and David Burg. New York: Farrar, Straus & Giroux, 1969.

   The First Circle. Translated by Thomas P. Whitney. New York: Harper & Row, 1968.

Solzhenitsyn, Alexander, ed. *From under the Rubble*. Translated by A. M. Brock et al. Boston: Little, Brown, 1975.

   The Gulag Archipelago, 1918–1956. 3 vols. Volumes I and II translated by Thomas P. Whitney. Volume III translated by Harry Willetts. New York: Harper & Row, 1974–8. Solzhenitsyn's massive investigation of the Soviet prison-camp system.

   Letter to Soviet Leaders. Translated by Hilary Sternberg. London: Collins/Harvill, 1974.

   Nobel Prize Lecture/Nobelevskaia lektsiia. Translated by Nicholas Bethell. London: Stenvalley Press, 1973. Russian and English texts.

   One Day in the Life of Ivan Denisovich. Translated by Max Hayward and Ronald Hingley. New York: Praeger, 1963.

   Stories and Prose Poems. Translated by Michael Glenny. New York: Farrar, Straus & Giroux, 1971. Includes *Matryona's House*.

Svirsky, Grigory. *Hostages: The Personal Testimony of a Soviet Jew*. Translated by Gordon Clough. New York: Knopf, 1976. A first-hand account of Soviet anti-Semitism since the Second World War.

Swayze, Harold. *Political Control of Literature in the USSR, 1946–1959*. Cambridge, Mass.: Harvard University Press, 1962. Soviet literary politics.

Tatu, Michel. *Power in the Kremlin: From Khrushchev to Kosygin*. Translated by Helen Katel. New York: Viking Press, 1969. A detailed account of high Soviet politics in the 1960s.

Tertz, Abram [Andrei Siniavsky]. *Fantastic Stories*. Translated by R. Hingley. New York: Pantheon Books, 1963.

   The Trial Begins and On Socialist Realism. Translated by Max Hayward and George Dennis. New York: Random House, Vintage Books, 1960. A novel and a literary essay.

Tökés, Rudolf L., ed. *Dissent in the USSR: Politics, Ideology, and People*. Baltimore: Johns Hopkins University Press, 1975. A set of original articles on various aspects of Soviet dissent.

The Trial of the Four. Compiled by Pavel Litvinov. Translated by Janis Sapiets et al. Edited by Peter Reddaway. New York: Viking Press, 1972. The trial of Galanskov, Ginzburg, Dobrovolsky, and Lashkova.

Wolfe, Bertram D. *Khrushchev and Stalin's Ghost*. New York: Praeger, 1957. Some background on the Twentieth Congress, with the text of Khrushchev's speech and other documents.

Yanov, Alexander. *The Russian New Right: Right-Wing Ideologies in the Contemporary USSR*. Translated by Stephen P. Dunn. Berkeley: Institute of International Studies, University of California, 1978.

Index